MILLER'S

COLLECTING
BOOKS

Miller's Collecting Books
by Catherine Porter
Special photography by Ken Adlard

First published in Great Britain in 1995 by Miller's,
a division of Mitchell Beazley,
imprints of Octopus Publishing Group Ltd,
2-4 Heron Quays, London E14 4JP

Executive Editor Alison Starling
Project Editor Katie Piper
Editor Kirsty Seymour-Ure
Executive Art Editor Vivienne Brar
Art Editor Rozelle Bentheim
Designer Steve Byrne
Index Hilary Bird
Production Heather O'Connell

A CIP catalogue record for this book is available from the British Library

ISBN 1 85732 543 5

Set in Granjon and Helvetica Neue
Produced by Toppan Printing Co., (HK) Ltd
Printed and bound in China

MILLER'S

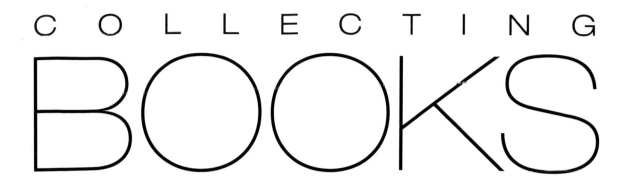

COLLECTING BOOKS

Catherine Porter

The Contributors

Alan Grant is the owner of Grant and Shaw Ltd., 62 West Port, Edinburgh. Grant and Shaw, established in 1989, deal with a fairly wide range of books, the majority published before 1850, with special emphasis on literature and travel.

Eric Korn trained as a biologist but abandoned practical science in 1969. An early player on the bookfair circuit, he tries to maintain a base (in London) and a specialism (in Charles Darwin) but continually risks succumbing to the temptations of full-time nomadism.

William Reese is a leading dealer in Americana. His firm, based in New Haven, Connecticut, also deals in English and American literature. He is the Advisor to the Western Americana Collection at the Beinecke Library, Yale University, and has served on the Councils of the Grolier Club in New York and the American Antiquarian Society. He has published widely in the field of American bibliography.

Christopher Edwards was educated at Oxford University and took an MA in Bibliography and Textual Criticism at Leeds University. He worked for four years at Christie's in the Book Department and then for nine years at the London antiquarian booksellers Pickering and Chatto. In 1992 he established his own antiquarian book business specializing in English literature and early printed books.

Anthony Rota is head of Bertram Rota Limited, a firm specializing in first editions of modern English literature. He has spoken, written and broadcast on both sides of the Atlantic on various aspects of bookselling and bibliography. In 1984 he gave the Englehard Lecture at the Library of Congress. In 1988 he was a Distinguished Visiting Fellow at the University of Tulsa. He regularly served on the faculty of the Rare Book School at Columbia University. He is the immediate past President of the International League of Antiquarian Booksellers.

David Chambers is a book collector specializing in eighteenth and nineteenth century privately printed books. A retired Lloyd's underwriter, he is the owner of the Cuckoo Hill Press, and author of Cock-a-Hoop (with Christopher Sandford), 1976, *Joan Hassall*, 1984, and *Gogmagog* (with Colin Franklin and Alan Tucker), 1991, also editor of *Private Press Books*, 1961–79. He is the Hon. Publications Secretary of the Private Libraries Association.

Edward Bayntun-Coward read history at University College, Oxford, then spent five years at Maggs Bros. specializing in early English literature and fine bindings. While continuing to work as a part-time consultant at Maggs, he is now also an active partner in the family firm of George Bayntun. Bayntun's were established in Bath in 1894 (today also incorporating the bindery of Robert Rivière) and the shop and bindery continue to flourish, with catalogues issued regularly.

Rupert Neelands started working in books when he took a part-time job with Ken Trotman, a military bookshop in Hampstead, whilst he was a postgraduate student. He joined Christie's in 1982, and is now head of the Book Department at Christie's South Kensington. Although his great grandfather was captain of Burnley football team, his own favourite sports are skiing, swimming, motoring and chess.

Roger Gaskell was born in the year the *Book Collector* was founded: his father was the first editor. He took a degree in biochemistry at Bristol University and then went to work for Bernard Quaritch Ltd., where, after an apprenticeship in art, topography and natural history, he became manager of the science and medicine department. When Lord Rees-Mogg's Pickering and Chatto Ltd took over Dawsons of Pall Mall in 1981 he moved there, first as manager of science and medicine, then managing director. He was also responsible for setting up Pickering and Chatto (Publishers) Ltd. In 1989 he started his own business and has issued a series of highly regarded catalogues.

Contents

Introduction

Book-collecting is often associated with academics or dark, musty shops; a secret, inaccessible world for the initiated only – and maybe this was once so. But today these are myths, and this guide seeks to dispel them. It is surprising how many people buy one or two books, and slowly, without necessarily meaning to, begin to build up a collection and become hooked.

Any guide to the collecting of books taken as a whole can only be a general one because of the vast quantity of material: the British Library in London alone has over 18 million books in stock, and each one is potentially of interest to a collector somewhere. *Miller's Collecting Books* is an introductory guide to a fascinating and rewarding area. The major areas of interest are looked at in the following chapters with the aim of providing a brief outline of each area. Each topic has a short introduction written by an acknowledged expert in that particular field, followed by the main body of the chapter in which the topic is further explored, usually chronologically.

It is useful to have a general knowledge of the subject, at whatever level you start to collect; and whether your interest lies with literature or science, in spending £50, £500 or £5,000, it will be important to know something about the likely prices of, say, Shakespeare and Jane Austen, or Copernicus and Newton. Thus the major names in each collecting area are mentioned, even where these are expensive, or almost impossible to acquire in the original for most new collectors.

Collecting books: why and who

Why collect "old" books at all, why not simply buy the modern reprint, the paperback or new hardback edition with an attractive dust-jacket? Perhaps it is the historical link with the author: the first edition would have been the one pored over eagerly and regarded with pride, subsequent editions being far removed from that initial sense of excitement. In some areas (science and medical books for example) the preferred version may be a later revised text: the author's final word. Earlier editions are often more beautifully presented, with a more elegant typeface and superior illustrations. An 18th-century binding is far more desirable than a modern cloth one, even if protected by an attractive dust-jacket. However, many authors are unattainable in the first edition, through scarcity or cost; in such cases, seek as early an edition as possible or the one that is the most attractive; use whatever criteria are the basis for your own collection.

Who collects books? In the 18th century most houses of a reasonable size would have contained a library, added to by subsequent generations. Many were broken up and dispersed in the 19th and early 20th centuries and it is now quite an event when an old "country house" library comes onto the market, usually via auction. There have been obsessive collectors for whom the love of the book overshadowed everything else, their houses becoming so full there was hardly any living space. Sir Thomas Phillips is possibly the best known, having formed a collection of over 100,000 volumes in the 19th century. Many famous names of the past have collected books: the diarist Samuel Pepys, Earl Spencer, the banker J. Pierpont Morgan, the songwriter Jerome Kern and the horticulturist Robert de Belder being but a few. But by far the majority of book-collectors are simply people with modest means and one thing in common: first and foremost they buy through the love of books, and not principally for investment.

Buying and selling

The principal ways of buying and selling books are through auctions, booksellers (operating from a shop or from home by appointment) and book fairs. (Names and addresses of a number of booksellers can be found in Useful Addresses on p.186–7; dates of auctions and book fairs will be listed in the periodicals suggested in Further Reading on p.185–6.)

Auction houses exist in many forms. The major ones have specialist departments devoted to books, staffed by experts; they may issue a dozen or more auction catalogues a year. Smaller provincial auction houses will have small book sales when they acquire enough books to do so. Finally, there are small specialist book auctioneers. Auction houses act purely as brokers or middle-men between the vendor and the purchaser. A commission is taken from the vendor, usually between 10 and 15 per cent (although this figure will be reduced on occasions if a particularly large library or important book is offered for sale), and also from the purchaser. The latter is known as a premium and in most instances is 15 per cent, although some smaller auction houses charge 10 per cent. VAT is also payable on this premium, and both these sums should be taken into account when bidding at auction: the price at which the hammer falls is not the final price the purchaser has to pay. Auctions provide an element of competition that booksellers do not; two determined parties can push a price way above people's expectations. Buying at auction can appear to be rather daunting, but it need not be so. There will be a catalogue available with descriptions of the books on offer, and also public viewing days at which the books can be inspected. There is also a short period after the sale when the books can be returned if they prove to be imperfect, or not as described. Read the small print in the catalogues so that you understand your rights when purchasing at auction. Auction houses usually request personal and bank details at registration before a sale. Bid by clearly raising your hand or numbered paddle, if provided, and cease doing so or shake your head when you wish to stop. Contrary to popular belief, you will not find yourself the owner of a £1,000 item simply by sneezing! Private collectors often choose to instruct a dealer to bid on their behalf at the sale, for a 10 per cent commission. If you bid in person it is always wise to set a limit in your own mind; always be prepared to walk away and bid for a copy on another day if the price goes too high – although if a book is really scarce you may have to be flexible with regard to this limit.

Most collectors find their books through booksellers. Booksellers during the 18th and 19th centuries would have sold old and new books, published some titles themselves, and sold prints, games or stationery. Specialization occurred this century as the number of books published escalated. Although there are still a few large general second-hand or antiquarian bookshops, more and more dealers have come to specialize, or work from home with viewing of their stock by appointment only. Most booksellers issue catalogues, some sporadically, others regularly, and will happily send you a few upon enquiry. Build up a rapport with a dealer and you will have a friend, confidant and teacher – and someone who might offer you books prior to their appearance in a catalogue. Should you choose to bid through a dealer at auction you can then benefit from their far greater knowledge. They will have the relevant reference books with which they can collate a book and the responsibility for completeness ultimately lies with them. Most dealers are quite happy imparting their knowledge and love of books to someone eager to learn.

The number of book fairs has grown rapidly in the past decade and every week somewhere in the country such a fair will take place. They are used particularly by dealers who work from private premises as an opportunity to show their books to the public. For the collector, there will be more choice of books than can ever be found in one bookshop or indeed at one auction. There are two main organizations that arrange fairs in Britain, the Antiquarian Booksellers' Association (A.B.A.) and the Provincial Booksellers' Fairs Association (P.B.F.A.), both will advertise the dates of fairs well in advance.

What to collect

The following chapters provide a few guides as to the more popular and traditional areas of collecting, mentioning some of the more important names or topics within each field. However, as these will often be the most expensive, the new collector may wish to follow alternative paths. In reality a collection can be formed upon anything, or around any interest. If no one has been there before you, this can prove to be exciting ground. But be aware that not everyone will share your enthusiasm and that if you re-sell (as most collectors do at some point, if only to fund subsequent purchases) you may not see substantial gains. Books have, however, steadily climbed in value over the 20th century, outstripping the rate of inflation and property prices. There have been times when prices have been spectacularly high in certain areas – notably colour-plate books; these then become the focus for investors, and it often takes some time before a profit can be seen. Fashion dictates much: authors fashionable in the 1930s and commanding high prices then may not do so today. Buying wisely and carefully will nearly always reap rewards.

Collecting should be fun: read the books and enjoy them for what they are. If you wish to collect books on chimney sweeps, then do so. American pulp fiction offers an exciting alternative to books by the classic literary names – but beware if you are collecting for investment purposes: this is popular now in America, but will such a trend last? Will anyone know who the authors are in ten years' time, and will they care? If this does not bother you, then carry on and collect them. You may wish to collect children's annuals, but whilst certainly attractive and indicative of trends and fashions in the lucrative world of children's books, these have always been printed in large quantities. There is no rarity value: they will always be available: hence prices will not rise as steeply as similarly dated books printed in smaller numbers.

Fortunately, not everyone is interested in the same things: buy what interests and excites you. Buy for the thrill of it, for the adventure and for what you will learn along the way. It is more fun and far more rewarding to build up a collection of Wisden's *Cricketer's Almanac* volume by volume, as opposed to buying an already complete set: think of the feeling of satisfaction as you complete each decade.

Price: condition and binding

Prices for books vary considerably and there will never be a fixed price for one particular book.

Condition is one of the main determining factors. For some rare books it is possible that the only copy to be had will be in poor condition or imperfect, in which case this will be better than nothing. Generally, however, the rule is always to buy the best copy you can find, and upgrade if you find a better one. Always make sure the book is complete ("imperfect" is the term used if it is not). Previous owners may have discarded half-titles and advertisements as being unnecessary, but these features are now demanded by purists. Avoid stained or dirty books (the brown marks are caused by chemicals in the paper), and books that have been heavily repaired.

It is preferable to seek a book in the original binding wherever possible, that is, in the state in which it emerged from the printer. A higher price will always be demanded for a fine copy in the original binding, as opposed to one that has been rebound. The earliest books would have been issued unbound or sewn into boards, initially of oak, later of pasteboard. These would often have been covered in vellum or a type of leather, and would have been inserted into a more elaborate binding at a later stage by a future owner. Few early books survive in the original binding and, prior to the 18th century, one should be content to look for the presence of a contemporary binding. During the 18th century these temporary bindings were of paper-covered boards, the books to be rebound as the purchaser wished. Inevitably some were never rebound and this has now become the most desirable way of acquiring such books: that is, in "original boards". In the 1820s the publisher William Pickering began to issue books with cloth covering the boards as standard, providing the purchaser with a more durable covering. The most sought-after editions of the great 19th-century novelists will therefore be those in the original cloth or boards. Association copies, with inscriptions from an author, illustrator or previous owner of importance or interest, or known to have come from an important library, will also command a higher price than an ordinary copy.

There can be discrepancies between prices paid for books at auction and those acquired through a bookseller. A bookseller often purchases at auction and has to make a profit, will often not sell a book immediately, and has higher overheads. You are also paying for their expertise. With great rarities, though, there is often little or no difference; the auction price may be the top price, possibly being paid by a dealer bidding on behalf of a private client.

Providing a guide to book prices is notoriously difficult: it can be inaccurate and misleading as there are so many variables. It is important for the new collector, however, to have some idea as to whether a particular book is likely to cost £100 or £1,000. The prices provided beside each book illustrated are therefore to be taken as a **general guide only for the particular copy described**, and it is to be assumed that the book is in good condition. The price band gives an upper and a lower limit for the price that may be asked for a particular item; with rarer books this band can be quite wide.

Care of books

Books are remarkably hardy, simply disliking extremes: of temperature, humidity or light. Keep them away from radiators and especially open fires. Prevent sunlight pouring onto them, or you will find the spines fade rapidly. Do not keep them in damp cellars or attics, where the pages will brown unevenly and smell musty. Otherwise books like being handled, as long as you do not treat them like a telephone directory or paperback. Leather bindings, in particular, need handling in order for the leather to absorb moisture from our skin. They also benefit from being treated with one of the various creams available from binders and some bookshops. If pages start to come loose, joints and hinges to crack and spines to disintegrate, take the book to a good binder and ask them to make some sympathetic repairs. The life of the book will be considerably prolonged.

Acquiring knowledge

There are many ways of increasing your knowledge of books, such as reading reference books and catalogues from auction houses and booksellers; browsing through bookshops and auctions; and studying collections that have been bequeathed to a library and are open to the public. Talk to dealers and experts at the auction houses, and to other private collectors. Do not be afraid to show a lack of knowledge: everyone has to start somewhere. At the end of this book is a list of useful reference books, some aimed at the more general reader, others more specialized studies such as bibliographies; public libraries will have many of the books listed.

Subscribe to auction catalogues and request booksellers' catalogues: some will be scholarly works in their own right with comprehensive notes; others will offer more simple descriptions. On pp.182–4 there is a glossary of terms used regularly in describing books. Every dealer will have a different catalogue style, which will again differ from that used by the auction houses. Once the basics have been understood the descriptions will be easy to follow.

Finally, the book world is a friendly one. Make yourself known and express your interest and you will reap rewards. Books are a wonderful world in their own right, once you step past what is often perceived as a rather forbidding exterior: a world in which it is easy to become absorbed.

Understanding Catalogue Entries

A typical auction catalogue entry:

202 B[USBY] (T[HOMAS] L[ORD]) Costume of the Lower Orders in Paris, *etched pictorial title-page and 28 plates, coloured by hand, one folding, captioned in French and English, half-morocco, [Colas 493], 12mo, [London, watermarked 1821]*

£500–600

- AUTHOR'S (or ARTIST'S) SURNAME is listed first with the first name(s) in round brackets. Here the author's full name is further enclosed in square brackets, indicating that the name is only present in the book as initials. Square brackets are used to indicate information that has been supplied from elsewhere, that is, not actually printed in the book.

- ILLUSTRATIONS are described and counted, with further comment where required, such as captions, folding.

- BINDING is described as "half-morocco", the lack of "original" indicating it has been rebound at a later stage with leather spine and corners.

- BIBLIOGRAPHICAL REFERENCE: "Colas" in square brackets is a bibliographical reference to aid identification. Reference books are usually identified by the author's surname, followed by a reference to a page or item number.

- SIZE OF THE BOOK is 12mo (see Sizes in the glossary on p.182).

- PLACE OF PUBLICATION: English books are assumed to have been printed in London; if elsewhere, the place is given. London and the date are in square brackets in this example because they are not printed in the book, but have been deduced from the bibliography (for the place), and from watermarks on the paper (for the date).

- THE PRICE: Auction houses will suggest a price band, based on previous copies sold at auction. This is only a guide and may be exceeded or not even reached. The majority of items sold at auction will have a reserve price agreed and known only to the vendor and auction house: below this figure the item will not be sold.

A bookseller's catalogue entry:

62 NEWTON, Sir Isaac (1642–1727) Opticks: or a treatise on the reflection, refractions, inflections and colours of light. The fourth edition, corrected, *London, for William Innys*, 1730.

Octavo (198 x 120mm) A4 B-2B8, pp. viii 382 [2] advertisements, 12 folding engraved plates numbered 1–5 1=2 1=4 1, numerous attractive wood- (or brass-) cut headpieces and initials. Some foxing throughout and water stains in the inner margins at the beginning and end of the volume. *Binding:* contemporary sprinkled polished calf with double gilt ruled sides and spine, raised bands, new label, joints cracked but sound.

Fourth edition, Wallis 178; Babson 136; ESTC to 69138

£650

The final text of the *Opticks*, incorporating Newton's last corrections and the complete set of 31 Queries. The Queries contain some of Newton's most influential and speculative writing.

This is a particularly comprehensive entry – providing a collation of the book, a more detailed description of the binding and an informative footnote as to the book's importance. Unfortunately not all booksellers take the time and trouble to expand as fully as this and the auction houses do not have the time to go into such depth for every book they describe.

Captions

The general style of the captions in this book is to feature the name of the author in bold type, followed by the title, a description of the type of illustrations (where relevant), the publisher, year of publication, and the edition. In Illustrated Books (pp.82–99), the name of the artist or illustrator appears on the first line, followed (where relevant) by the name of the author and the title of the book. Where there is no one author, or where a book is more popularly known by its title, the title will appear in bold type.

The first price range given in each caption appears in bold type, and refers to the item illustrated. Information on different editions of the same title, or other titles by the same author may also be given, with price ranges in non-bold type.

The Book

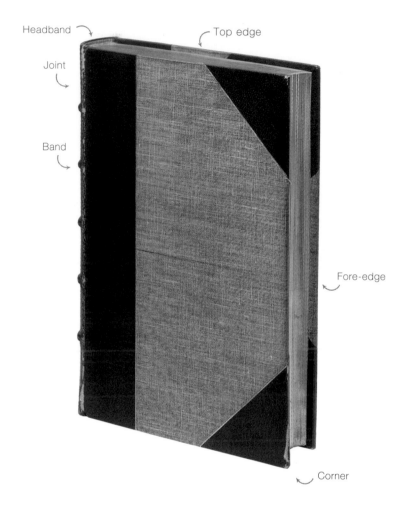

Headband

Joint

Band

Top edge

Fore-edge

Corner

This book is bound in half-morocco, that is, the boards are covered with cloth, the spine and corners with morocco.

Spine

Head of spine

LA CHAN SON D'EVE

Lower cover

Foot of spine

Upper cover

This book is bound in full morocco decorated with gilt tooling and coloured morocco onlays.

Original cloth covering
used as an endpaper

Front free endpaper:
this one is marbled

Bookplate

Inner edges

Front free endpaper

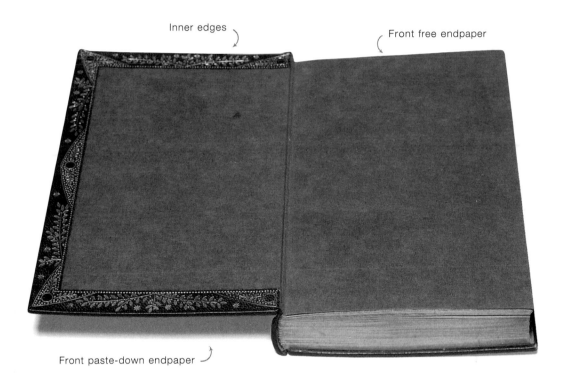

Front paste-down endpaper

Preliminary blank

Half-title

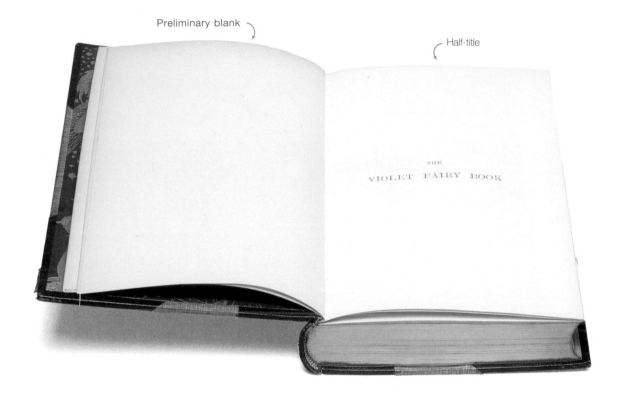

THE

VIOLET FAIRY BOOK

Frontispiece

Title-page

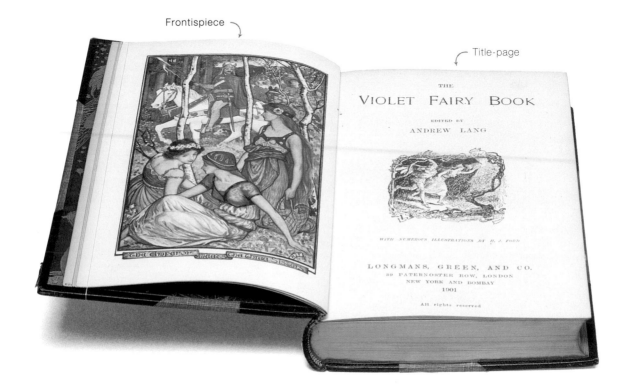

Binding a Book

1. A book is collated, unpicked and cleaned.

2. After the pages are pasted the book is resewn.

3. New endpapers are made and fixed, and the books are passed for forwarding, the main construction work before the book moves on for gilding. The stages are known as squaring, rounding and backing. The boards are laced in, pressed and the edges trimmed.

4, 5 A number of volumes are placed in a large laying press, and the edges are scraped and prepared (chalked and pasted with egg albumen) before gold leaf is laid on and burnished.

6. The book then has new headbands of coloured silks sewn in around strips of vellum or cane.

7 The books are now ready to have the new spines added: they are lined up with mull (strong muslin) and kraft paper and bands are put on. This completes the process before the outer covering is selected. Leather is chosen and cut to size, either for the full covering, or simply for the spine and corners if the boards are to be covered in cloth or marbled paper.

8, 9 The leather is pared (outer edges shaved) before covering. It is pasted so that it becomes pliable and can be moulded over the boards, spine and bands.

10, 11 All books then go to the finishers for completion. This comprises lettering the title and author's name on the spine, and additional decoration where required.

12 The books are finally polished and pressed.

13 A selection of marbled papers used for the endpapers, and for the boards if the book is to be half-bound in leather.

14 Leather of many different colours and of varying quality is used.

15 A selection of the rolls used to tool the borders and inside edges.

16 A selection of pallets and fillets used for decoration.

17 In addition to completely rebinding books, restoration work is carried out: replacing the endpapers and spine, known as rebacking; general repairs to corners, joints, and hinges; pages washed and reinserted.

18 A selection of individual tools used for decoration of the outer covers and spines. Larger binderies may own thousands of these tools.

Illustration Processes

Today the majority of books are illustrated through photo-mechanical methods of reproduction, with original processes being used in small print-runs only. The earliest form of illustration in the printed book was the simple woodcut. Over the centuries, engraving on wood matured and developed into a highly effective form of illustration. Engraving on metal was first used in the 16th century, but the technique was not utilized fully until the 17th century. Lithography was invented at the end of the 18th century. Colour was initially added to illustrations by hand, with great advances being made in the printing of colour by the end of the 19th century. Colour can also be added through the application of stencils, a process brought from France, where it is known as *pochoir*, to Britain in the 1920s.

This section will explain and demonstrate some of the different techniques used in the illustration of books. There are three principal types of process: relief, intaglio and planographic.

Relief

Relief processes include those techniques in which the area to be inked is raised above that which is to remain white.

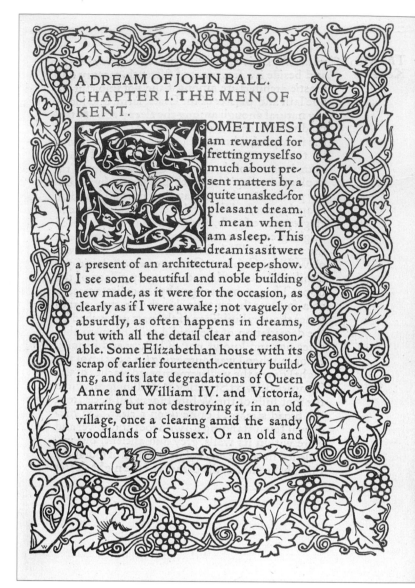

▲ Ornamental woodcut border and initial for a page of William Morris's *A Dream of John Ball*, Kelmscott Press, 1892.

Woodcut

Initially a drawing is made on a smooth block of soft wood, such as pear, sycamore, cherry or beech, which is cut lengthwise along the grain. The lines of the design are untouched and the wood is cut away on either side with a knife, the larger areas with a chisel, leaving a raised image which will retain the ink when it is applied. The block is then inked, the paper laid over the design and pressure asserted by hand or using a printing press.

Involving a simple process easily adapted to the primitive printing presses, woodcuts were the earliest form of illustration to be used in Europe, appearing at the end of the 14th century. The technique had become less popular by the end of the 16th century, as other methods evolved that produced more subtle effects, but was revived at the end of the 19th century by artists such as Paul Gauguin, Edvard Munch and the German Expressionists.

▲ Enlarged detail showing the difference between the woodcut border and the finer lines of the wood-engraved illustration.

▶ Wood-engraved illustration by Sir Edward Burne-Jones for *A Dream of John Ball*, Kelmscott Press, 1892.

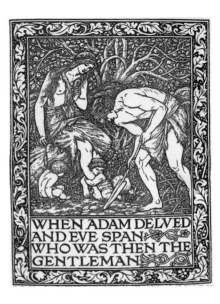

Wood-engraving

Similar to a woodcut, but the drawing is made on a block of wood (usually a hard wood such as box) cut across the grain. Cut in this fashion, the wood is less likely to splinter. The design is cut with a burin (a steel rod with a sharpened tip) rather than a knife, and a greater degree of delicacy in outline and shading can be achieved. The fine lines are lower than the surface that carries the ink and they print white, whereas on a woodcut the design prints black. As the engraver works white chalk will often be rubbed into the lines to clarify the outline of the design.

The first artist to exploit this technique fully was Thomas Bewick in the late 18th century, and it has been used continually ever since. Wood-engravings were printed in colour by using separate blocks for each colour or by adding one colour at a time, the lightest first. Edmund Evans perfected this process with his books for children in the late 19th century.

Intaglio

Intaglio processes are where the surface to be inked is lower than the areas remaining blank. The surface is usually of metal, copper or steel, although linoleum, celluloid and wood can be used. Copper came into general use around 1520, but does not wear well; in the 1820s, with larger print-runs, steel was used as a more durable printing surface. But steel is very hard to engrave upon, and today copper is used, being faced with steel after the engraving has been carried out. The ink is applied with a roller and forced into the grooves. The surface of the plate is then wiped clean before the plate and paper are pressed together, forcing the paper into the grooves to receive the ink.

▲ Engraved illustration for John Goodman's *American Natural History*, Philadelphia, 1831.

▶ Enlarged detail showing the fine lines typical of an engraving.

Engraving

A burin is used to cut a design on the metal plate, rough edges being removed with a scraper. The technique was first used for printing on paper in the second quarter of the 15th century in Germany and Italy, remaining predominantly a method of reproducing original work until the 20th century. With the advent of photographic reproduction, artists turned to the medium afresh. Illustrators such as Stephen Gooden and Eric Gill produced original engravings for books in the 20th century.

▲ Enlarged detail showing the striking tones of black and grey.

◀ Mezzotint after John Martin, John Milton's *Paradise Lost*, 1827.

Mezzotint

This is a form of engraving with tone rather than line, and the design is worked from dark to light. The plate is prepared so as to print an even black, being pitted with a rocker (a tool like a chisel). This uneven surface can be smoothed so different areas will hold varying quantities of ink and print in tones of grey. To achieve white areas, the plate is burnished smooth so when wiped no ink remains. Invented in the Netherlands in the 17th century, it was used most in England, particularly for the reproduction of paintings.

◄ Enlarged detail showing the softer finish caused by the acid.

◄◄ Etched illustration by Tsougouharu Foujita in Michel Vaucaire's *Barres parallèles*, 1927.

Etching

Grooves and hollows are formed by the corrosive action (biting) of acid, rather than by cutting with a tool. The plate is coated with a waxy substance (the ground) impervious to acid, and the design is made through this with a needle, laying bare the metal. Then, the back and edges of the plate are protected with varnish and the plate is dipped in acid. This corrodes the bare metal, and is done in stages according to the light and dark required; each completed area is coated in varnish. Finally the ground and varnish are removed and the plate is inked. The result is softer than an engraving, due to the uneven effect of acid on the metal.

Aquatint

This is a method of etching in tone. The ground is composed of fine particles and the acid seeps through irregularly. Degrees of tone are achieved by immersing the plate for varying lengths of time. Popular for reproducing watercolours and wash drawings, it was fully developed in the mid-18th century.

▲ Aquatint illustration for Wallis's *Juvenile Diorama*, c.1825. These cards are coloured by hand.

► Enlarged detail showing the tones, seen most clearly by looking at the trees and the foreground. It can also be seen where the colour, applied by hand, has gone beyond the outline of the aquatint.

Planographic

Planographic processes are those in which the printing surface is at the same level as that to remain blank. This is achieved by using the simple phenomenon that grease and water do not mix. The area to be printed is impregnated with grease and the blank areas are moistened. When the greasy ink is applied it adheres to the greased area and not that which is wet.

Lithograph

The image is drawn onto the surface, traditionally stone but now usually a metal plate, which will absorb grease and water equally. Lithographic chalk (a mixture of wax or soap, lamp-black and shellac) or ink (the chalk dissolved in water) is used to draw the image. The design is protected with a solution of gum arabic and acid, before the remaining areas are moistened. A heavy ink is rolled over the surface. The paper and the plate are then placed in a press. Lithography was invented in 1798 by Aloys Senefelder and was often used to reproduce scenic views. Both text and illustrations in Edward Lear's *Book of Nonsense* were lithographed.

▲ Lithographed illustration by Kathleen Hale for her story *"Henrietta" the Faithful Hen*, 1943.

◄ Enlarged detail showing the printed colours.

Schwytz.   *Unterwalden.*

▲ Lithographed illustration for the miniature panorama *Costumes Suisses*, c.1850.

► Enlarged detail showing the outline printed by lithography and with colouring added by hand.

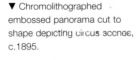

▼ Chromolithographed embossed panorama cut to shape depicting circus scenes, c.1895.

► Enlarged detail showing the strong glossy colours indicative of chromolithography.

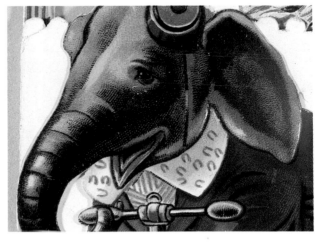

Chromolithograph

Colour lithography was in use from about 1820; its heyday came in the 1880s. A separate printing surface is required to apply each colour. It was especially suitable for the reproduction of natural history illustrations and the illustrations in children's books, where strong colours were needed. It was also used for the reproduction of illuminated manuscripts by Henry Noel Humphreys and by Owen Jones in his pattern and ornament books.

Early Printed Books

The birth of printing: from the exceptionally rare Gutenberg Bible printed in 1455 to a wealth of 16th- and 17th-century imprints

The first printer in Western Europe was Johann Gutenberg, a German craftsman who, in an astonishing burst of creativity in about 1450, not only invented but also perfected the art of printing from moveable types – that is, printing from individually cast letters which could then be assembled to compose complete texts. This infinitely flexible system was the basis of all printing in the West until the late 18th century; it revolutionized the dissemination of news as well as learning, and it made possible the modern world.

The Gutenberg Bible, printed in the early 1450s, was produced in an edition of fewer than 200 copies: about a quarter of them still survive today. All the complete copies, and most of the incomplete ones, are now in institutional libraries. Substantial fragments are prohibitively expensive, when they become available, but some individual leaves do appear on the market, and can be bought for comparatively modest amounts. Gutenberg's early associates, Johann Fust and Peter Schoeffer, later took over his press and produced their own books: their best and earliest works are also expensive but it is not impossible to buy their less significant books, or early fragments from their press, and thus to possess a piece of printing by one who personally knew the founder of the art.

Many collectors of *incunabula* – literally, something "from the cradle", and, by extension, books printed in the 15th century –

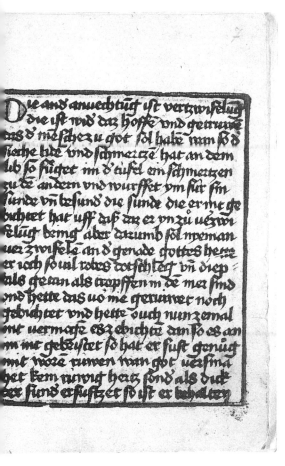

▲ Ars moriendi
South Germany, c.1475. This blockbook was printed from 26 single-page woodcuts, 11 pictorial, 15 textual. The illustrations were then coloured by hand. This blockbook relates the battle between devils and angels for the soul of a dying man. £180,000–220,000

▼ Biblia Latina
Initials illuminated by a contemporary hand, Mainz, Johann Gutenberg and Johann Fust, 1455. First edition of Vulgate (Gutenberg) Bible. 12 copies on vellum and 35 on paper exist, only two in private hands. This sold in 1987 for **£3,267,418**

base their collections on the spread of printing throughout Europe. From Mainz, Gutenberg's adopted town, the technique spread slowly throughout Germany and then more rapidly to Italy, France, the Low Countries, England and Spain. The great trading cities such as Venice, Nuremberg, and Paris naturally became the most important printing centres, and *incunabula* from such places are comparatively easy to find. The "first book" from any town will always be expensive, however, and the smaller and more obscure the town, paradoxically, the rarer and more costly the book is likely to be.

William Caxton began printing in England, at Westminster, in about 1476: he had learnt the art in Belgium and as an ambitious merchant he grasped the commercial opportunity to introduce printing to his native country. Since the 18th century, when English collectors first began to compete for his books, Caxtons have always been a high-priced commodity. Complete copies seldom appear for sale, and even imperfect ones are sought-after. However, single leaves, and sometimes even sections of a book, still appear for sale.

English printing was slow to develop, partly because of government restrictions, and there is little until the late 16th century that can be called fine; but Caxton was unique among prototypographers in that his first books were classics in his native language – Chaucer, Malory and Higden, rather than

▲ Marcus Tullius Cicero
Tusculanae quaestiones, illuminated with historiated chapter initials and an armorial frontispiece by the "Putti Master", Venice, Nicolaus Jenson, 1472. £60,000–90,000

▼ Giovanni Boccaccio
De claris mulieribus, historiated woodcut initials, 81 woodcut illustrations, Ulm, Johann Zainer, 1473. The first illustrated book printed in Ulm and one of the greatest of early German illustrated books. £150,000–200,000

▲ Publius Ovidius Naso
Opera, third edition, illuminated frontispiece, rubricated and historiated initials, Venice, Jacobus Rubeus, 1474. £20,000–30,000

◀ Saint Thomas Aquinas
Postilla in Job, woodcut and rubricated initials, Esslingen, Conrad Fyner, 1474. First edition of this work printed by the only 15th-century printer working in Esslingen. Much of his material would have come from Strasbourg. £5,000–7,000

▶ Geoffrey Chaucer
Canterbury Tales, Westminster, William Caxton, 1477. A fragment of 65 leaves of the first edition of Chaucer's great work and one of the earliest books printed in England. £35,000–45,000
A single leaf, £2,000–3,000

biblical commentaries or classical philosophers – and this attachment to the native literature influenced many of his successors in London such as the Dutchman Wynkyn de Worde, and Richard Pynson.

In Europe, Caxton's contemporaries had many texts waiting to be printed: the first appearance of classical and medieval texts makes a natural alternative theme for a collection of *incunabula*. Again, the most significant authors are usually expensive – Horace, Aristotle, Boccaccio, Aquinas – even

though printed long after the lifetimes of the writers. Early in the 16th century, however, and even before, printers were actively seeking out new texts to feed the ever-growing appetite of readers.

New formats, such as pocket-size octavos (popularized by Aldus Manutius of Venice), and more legible typefaces (roman rather than gothic), followed such developments. The academic and the reading public became more fond of fine printing, and printers such as Josse Bade (known as Badius Ascensius) in

▼ **Johannes Noder**
De vierundzwanzig goldenen Harfen,
woodcut initials and 2 full-page
illustrations with contemporary
colouring, Augsburg, Johannes
Bamler, 1478. The fourth edition,
but the second with illustrations, and
exceedingly rare. **£40,000–80,000**

▲ **Hartmann Schedel**
Liber chronicarum, 1809 woodcut
illustrations, double-page map,
Nuremberg, Anton Koberger, 12 July
1493. The Nuremberg Chronicle was
published in German and Latin.
Complete copy. **£15,000–20,000**
Single-leaf woodcuts, £200–600

▶ **Aesop**
*Appologi sive mythologi cum quibusdam carminum et
fabularum additionibus* Sebastiana Brant, 2 volumes,
woodcut portraits of Aesop and Brant, 335 illustrations
and initials, Basel, Jacob Wolff, 1501. First edition of
this edition of Aesop. **£30,000–50,000**
Late 16th- and early 17th-century editions are more
common: *Aesopi Phrygis Etaliorum Fabulae*, Venice,
1618, £200–400

▲ **Marcus Valerius Martialis**
Epigrammata, woodcut device on
title and final leaf, Venice, Aldus
Manutius, 1517. One of Aldus
Manutius's popular octavo printings.
£200–400

Paris, and the Estienne family in Paris and
Geneva, following in the great tradition of
Aldus at Venice, competed to satisfy a demand
for the fine as well as the useful. Minor works
by these great printers are still easy to find on
the market and because they printed in large
editions even their major works frequently
appear for sale.

Printing had become a major industry by
the later 16th century, with workshops such as
Christopher Plantin's at Antwerp employing
as many as 20 presses at a time. There is thus a
vast diversity to collect from the first 150 years
of printing – not only in quality of production,
but also in style, language, illustration and
subject-matter. From Gutenberg's original
invention, the technique had spread into every
corner of Europe, from Scotland to Sicily.
New inventions such as stereotyping and
lithography were to follow, but not for almost
two centuries: printing as an art had already
achieved heights which succeeding craftsmen
were to strive after in vain.

CHRISTOPHER EDWARDS

▼ Desiderius Erasmus

Opus epistolarum, woodcut initials, Basel, Hieronymous Froben, Johannes Hervagius and Nicolaus Episcopius, 1529. Second, expanded edition of this collection of letters first published in 1521. **£250–500**

Marcus Annaeus Lucanus ▲

De bello civili libri decem, woodcut device on title, Paris, Robert Estienne, 1545. **£200–300**

▲ Giles Corrozet

Icones historiarum veteris testamenti, 94 woodcuts by Hans Lützelberger after Hans Holbein, 4 medallion woodcuts of the Evangelists, Lyons, Jean Frellon, 1547. This series of woodcuts first published in 1538 was the first of its kind, hugely popular and widely imitated. **£3,000–4,000**

The Early Printers

At the turn of the 19th century the great book-collectors turned their attention and vast wealth to the earliest printed books, Earl Spencer, the Marquess of Blandford and the Duke of Devonshire vying for the greatest works. The Roxburghe Club, an aristocratic society for bibliophiles, was founded by these three on the occasion of the first four-figure price being paid for a book: the "Valdarfer Boccaccio", the first dated edition of the *Decameron*, printed by Valdarfer in Venice in 1471. Earl Spencer was outbid by the Marquess of Blandford at £2,200, but eventually acquired the book for only £918, after Blandford's death.

The past two decades have witnessed the sale at auction of several remarkable libraries devoted to or containing fine early printed books. The sale of the Broxbourne Library in 1977 and 1978 was marked by a two-volume auction catalogue arranged according to the towns where the books were printed. This is now an invaluable reference work. More recently the sales of the Estelle Doheny collection, duplicate volumes from the John Rylands University Library,

the George Abrams collection, books from Beriah Botfield's Library at Longleat, from the Schoyen collection, the Court Library at Donaueschingen, and most recently from one of the greatest private collections formed this century, that of Otto Schäfer, have all provided, in addition to the opportunity of seeing and even handling some of the greatest books ever printed, magnificent catalogues that are also useful for reference. Few people will be able to afford to purchase at these grand sales, most having to be content to look, appreciate and expand their knowledge. With these catalogues, you will have at your fingertips descriptions of superb examples of many of the finest early printed books.

Not all *incunabula* are expensive; age is no guarantee of value, and one can acquire 15th-century books for smaller sums than some of the fine 20th-century private-press books. Books from the 16th century can often be found for very reasonable sums and for those interested in early printing this can be a good area to start. It is important to learn who the best printers are, to understand and appreciate the

▼ Camillo Agrippa
Trattato di scientia d'arme, engraved portrait, 2 full-page illustrations and 54 illustrations, woodcut initials, Rome, Antonio Blado, 1553. The illustrations depict fencing and duelling positions. **£2,000–3,000**

◄ Pietro Francesco Zini
De philosophiae laudibus, Venice, Giovanni Griffio, c.1547. A speech delivered on the occasion of Zini's inauguration as Professor of Economics at the University of Padua. **£500–800**

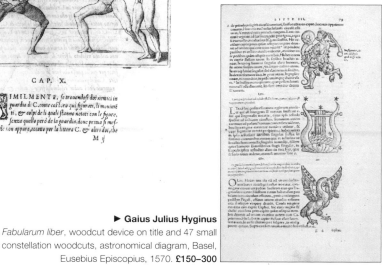

▲ Hadrianus Junius
Emblemata, 58 woodcut emblems by Gerard Janssen van Kampen and Arnold Nicolai after Geoffroy Ballain and Peter Huys, decorative typographical borders to titles, Antwerp, Christopher Plantin, 1565. First edition of important Dutch emblem book. **£1,200–1,500**

► Gaius Julius Hyginus
Fabularum liber, woodcut device on title and 47 small constellation woodcuts, astronomical diagram, Basel, Eusebius Episcopius, 1570. **£150–300**

printed page, the typography and layout. Look for the works of the Estienne family, and of Nicolas Jensen, and for the many fine books printed by Aldus Manutius. His editions of the great classic authors will be sought after and expensive, especially the first collected editions of Aristotle and Plato, but one can find minor works and later octavo editions that will still be good examples of his skilful work.

These early printers popularized the smaller octavo size, which meant that books could be carried around and discussed, whereas the larger folio editions had to remain *in situ*; these can be an affordable way of collecting early printed books. Most of the good early printing came from Italy and France; Caxton has immense appeal for British and American collectors, but his work is not as fine artistically as his contemporaries', reflecting the insular nature of English culture at that time. Most of his books are in institutional libraries, but again, individual leaves are sometimes available on the market for quite modest prices. There is a wide range of material for the collector to choose, from Bibles and religious tracts to verse and fables, classic literary texts from the days before printing, letters and academic treatises. However, the combination of an important text with fine typography and layout, accompanied by illustrations, particularly if by an artist of the calibre of Holbein or Dürer, or with fine illumination added by hand, will always ensure the highest prices.

A work popular at the time and reprinted often will be more widely available: Philippus Beroaldus's verse work *De felicitate*, first printed in Bologna on 1 April 1495, is known to have survived in more than 40 different editions dated prior to 1501. The works of Desiderius Erasmus were influential and widely read and can be found in numerous editions, and whilst his major works such as *Moriae encomium* or *Adagiorum chiliades tres* will be extremely expensive in first or even early editions, his later or more minor works can be acquired with less expense. A 15th-century edition of Plutarch printed in Venice by the great Nicolas Jenson will command thousands of pounds, but a late 16th-century edition printed in Basel may be a few hundred pounds only.

English Literature

Literature in English from the 16th to 19th centuries: a brief introduction to the great names of literature from Chaucer to Dickens

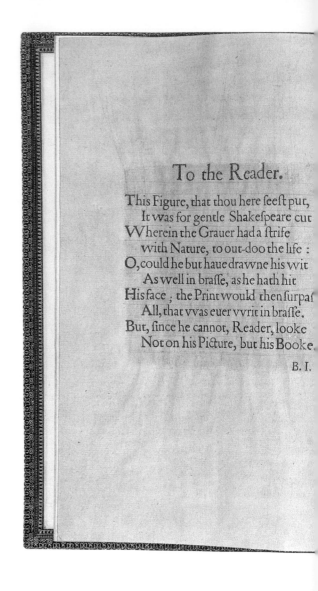

To the Reader.

This Figure, that thou here feeft put,
It was for gentle Shakefpeare cut
Wherein the Grauer had a ftrife
with Nature, to out-doo the life :
O, could he but haue drawne his wit
As well in braffe, as he hath hit
His face ; the Print would then furpaf
All, that vvas euer vvrit in braffe.
But, fince he cannot, Reader, looke
Not on his Picture, but his Booke.

B. I.

Literature in English is such a wide field for the new collector that even the most generous outline will appear to exclude something worth collecting. Every writer worth reading could be classed as literary: Francis Bacon and Charles Darwin were, after all, stylists as well as scientists. However, before the English Civil War, printed secular literature in the sense that modern readers understand it – poetry, fiction, drama – is scarce, not merely because there was comparatively little being written, but also because most such books were haphazardly printed and casually preserved. It was not until the middle of the 18th century that collectors and librarians began to prize the poetry and drama of the 16th and 17th centuries; since then, such

books have never gone out of fashion, and it is now a time-consuming and expensive hobby to collect Shakespeare and Chaucer in the early editions.

Printing in Britain begins with Caxton at Westminster in the mid-1470s, and – uniquely among those who brought printing to new countries – it was with the secular literature that Caxton began his output. Nearly all the best copies (sometimes the only ones surviving) of his great editions of poets such as Chaucer and Gower, and of the English chroniclers such as Ranulph Higden, have long since disappeared into the great libraries of the world, and even incomplete Caxtons are expensive and seldom seen. However, it is not difficult to find single leaves from books printed by Caxton, or his successor Wynkyn

▼ **Jane Austen**
Emma, a Novel, 3 volumes, John Murray, 1816.
A first edition in the original boards with the half-titles.
£5,000–10,000
Rebound, lacking half-titles, £1,500–2,500

◄ **William Shakespeare**
Comedies, Histories, & Tragedies, engraved portrait, William and Isaac Jaggard for Edward Blount, John Smethwick and William Aspley, 1623. This is known as the First Folio edition of Shakespeare and contains 20 plays not printed before. **£100,000+**

de Worde, on the market. Throughout the 16th century original English literature tended to be a pursuit for the vulgar, and "serious" literature was written in Latin. Courtiers or scholars who did write in English seldom committed their work to print. Shakespeare himself made little attempt to collect his own plays, although half of them were printed in his lifetime, all in small quarto editions; but it was not until 1623, seven years after his death, that his fellow actors Heminges and Condell published the famous "First Folio".

Early printing in Britain, even up to the beginning of the 18th century, is not remarkable for its beauty, although there are a few exceptions such as Joseph Barnes at Oxford (printing between 1585 and 1617). Barnes was not a "fine printer" in the same

sense as his contemporaries and predecessors in Paris or Venice, but his books are always well produced and attractively designed: he represents the best to be found in Britain before the 18th century. It was at that time that increasing wealth and education led British book-buyers to indulge a taste for works that were both finely produced and beautifully bound.

So, the goal for most collectors of early English books is the text itself, in its original condition (so far as possible) and in first edition. In this respect, collecting English literature differs very much from collecting, say, fine colour-plate books, or even French literature, where a subsequent edition may be held to be an improvement, and so more desirable. For English books up to the

▲ **Edmund Spenser**
The Shepheardes Calender, Hugh
Singleton, 1559. One of only 7 copies
recorded. **£30,000–40,000**
One of 350 copies published by the
Cresset Press in 1930, £200–300

▼ **John Keats**
Poems, C. & J. Ollier, 1817. First
edition of Keats's first book in the
original boards. **£8,000–15,000**
Rebound in contemporary calf,
£4,000–6,000

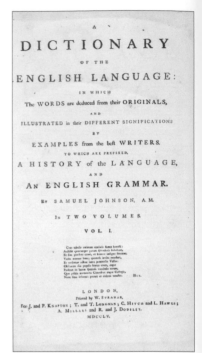

▲ **Samuel Johnson**
A Dictionary of the English Language,
2 volumes, by W Strahan for J. and
P. Knapton; T. and T. Longman et al,
1755. This was the first dictionary of
its kind in English, with definitions of
over 40,000 words illustrated by over
114,000 quotations. First edition in
original boards. **£10,000–15,000**
Rebound, £4,000–8,000; five editions
were published in his lifetime and all
are affordable: fourth edition, revised
by the author, £1,000–2,000

mid-18th century, "original condition" means
in a contemporary binding; thereafter many
books can be found in "original boards" – a
basic binding of pasteboard with a paper
spine – but the survival rate of most books
in this condition is low, and the price
consequently higher.

From the Restoration in 1660, when civil
peace and aristocratic patronage brought the
polite arts once more into fashion, English
literature becomes far more accessible to the
modern collector. Books were printed in
greater quantities, and were better preserved;
by the early 18th century, collecting contemporary literature was no longer an eccentricity.
The age of Dryden is not only more modern to

most of us than that of Spenser, it is also far
easier to find the literature in early editions.
Consequently, the 18th- and 19th-century
writers, particularly the poets and novelists,
are more widely and eagerly collected than
any others, sometimes to the point where
prices for later and more common books
exceed those for the scarce, early literature,
because collectors were discouraged long ago
from seeking what could only be found with
difficulty.

Of course, taste and relative merit are an
important part of any collector's judgment:
no one would dispute that Dickens is a better
novelist than Fanny Burney, so it is right that
an average novel of his is at least as expensive

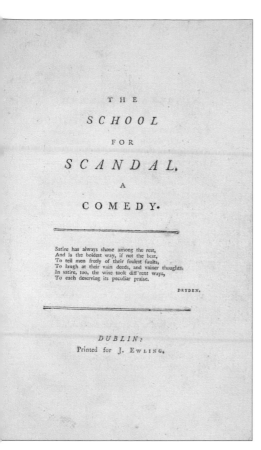

▲ Richard Brinsley Sheridan
The School for Scandal, a Comedy, Dublin, J. Ewling,
[after 1780]. This was long thought to be the first edition,
but bibliographers now claim that it could have been
printed after 1795 and not in Dublin.
£400–800
The first printing, also an unauthorized piracy as is this
edition, Dublin, 1780, £8,000–10,000

▼ George Eliot
Middlemarch: a Study of Provincial Life, 4 volumes,
Edinburgh and London, William Blackwood and Sons,
1871. First edition in book form in original cloth.
£1,500–3,000
Rebound, £300–600. First edition in original 8 parts,
£600–1,200

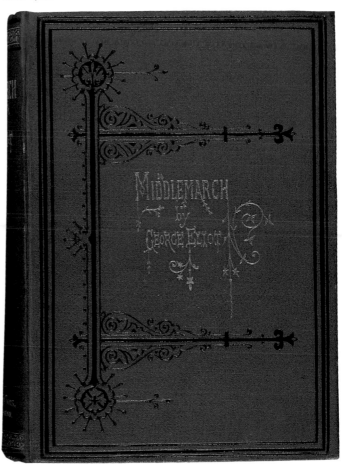

as one of hers, even if Dickens is far more common. In the 19th century, mass production went hand in hand with literacy: a new market for literature demanded ever more books for increasing numbers of readers. Most critics would agree, however, that the quality of literature did not fail to keep pace with this demand – English fiction and poetry from the Romantics to the death of Queen Victoria are among the principal achievements of our literature. They are also the touchstone by which most of us judge common literacy: to be familiar with Wordsworth or George Eliot is to be an educated member of society, whereas a detailed knowledge of Chaucer or Marlowe is for the specialist only.

English 19th-century literature, therefore, is the most widely collected of all periods. First editions of many important writers are readily available – the commoner books by Scott or Tennyson can still be bought for very modest sums – and the most popular literature was reprinted again and again, so that early editions may still be within the reach of anyone with a few pounds to spare. But scarcity is still the force that drives most collectors – where is the joy in having what anyone else can possess? – and if you begin with an easy quarry, you will certainly be lured into seeking more difficult, more expensive, and ultimately more satisfying prey.

Christopher Edwards

▼ **Geoffrey Chaucer**
The Workes, black letter, woodcut architectural borders, illustrations and initials, Richard Grafton, for William Bonham, 1542. Second edition, a reprint of the 1532 *Works*, adding "The Ploughman's Tale". **£3,000–4,000**

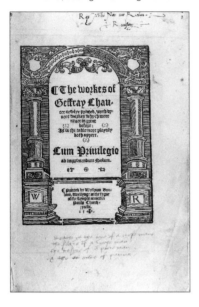

▶ **Walter Ralegh**
The History of the World, third edition, engraved title-page, 8 double-page maps and plans, William Jaggard for Walter Burre, 1621. The first edition was published in 1614. **£600–1,200**

Early English Writers

It is generally accepted that to collect literature means to look for an author in the first edition, and whilst this is always desirable, the great names of literature have become expensive in their first printing, as more and more wealthy collectors attempt to build a library on this basis, pushing up prices beyond the reach of most people. So although this chapter will look at literature from a chronological viewpoint, identifying many of the greatest names of each age, with the aim of providing a working knowledge, it may be that in order to form a collection of literature with a more modest outlay, one has to turn to areas that have been hitherto neglected or unfashionable. Later editions may have to be sought with the aim of concentrating on an author's texts rather than the edition.

Two of the earliest and most enduring authors to write in English, whose work is no longer available to the private collector in the first edition as almost all copies are in public libraries, are Sir Thomas Malory and Geoffrey Chaucer, whose works were made available to a wide audience by William Caxton. Malory's *Le Morte D'Arthur*, printed in 1485, and Chaucer's *Canterbury Tales*, although very different, are each concerned in their own way with behaviour and morals. Malory's work, chronicling the Arthurian legends, had a profound influence over generations of writers from Spenser to Tennyson. Both authors have been reprinted numerous times with a wealth of editions to choose from, many illustrated by fine artists.

Later chroniclers such as Raphael Holinshed and Sir Thomas North, translating Plutarch from the Greek, followed the example of Malory and gathered together the exploits of earlier times, proving to be rich source material for Shakespeare. These chronicles were reprinted frequently, making it easier for the new collector to obtain copies. North's edition of Plutarch, for example, was reissued by the Nonesuch Press in 1929–30. It was not until the mid-16th century when Henry VIII broke from the Church of Rome, that English became the common language, and English poetry came to be viewed with pride – French and Latin having previously been used at court and for serious literature. William Thynne issued a complete edition of Chaucer's works in 1532. A new generation of poets such as Henry Howard, Earl of Surrey and Sir Thomas Wyatt, wrote poetry in plain English, and although it may not be possible to collect their works in first edition, these poems of courtly love have been reprinted in editions worth collecting. The Nonesuch Press once again is particularly good for obtaining such early texts.

▼ Caius Plinius Secundus
The Historie of the World, translated by Philemon Holland, 2 volumes, woodcut head- and tail-pieces, Adam Islip, 1601. The first English edition of this work, used by Shakespeare as a source-book. **£1,200–1,800**

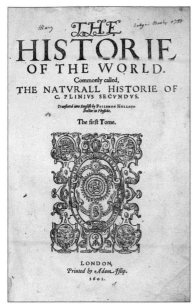

Collecting
The Bible

▼ The Bible translated according to the Ebrew & Greeke
Titles within woodcut borders, Deputies of Christopher Barker, 1594. This edition known as the "Breeches" Bible due to the translation in Genesis, 3:7. **£150–300**

▲ The Holy Bible
Cambridge, John Baskerville, 1763. There are various issues of this edition according to the length of the list of subscribers, and the price varies greatly according to the quality of the binding. **£400–1,200**

Politics & religion

A great deal of 16th- and 17th-century literature reflected the political and religious upheavals taking place in British society at the time, and a collection formed around these two themes can make fascinating reading from an historical viewpoint.

Many religious works from this period can be picked up for relatively modest sums, although anyone attempting to collect the two great humanist intellectuals of this period in first edition will find it more difficult. The great Dutch humanist Desiderius Erasmus wrote in Latin, although his work was soon translated into English, and can be found relatively easily in 17th- and 18th-century editions. Sir Thomas More's *Utopia*, first published in Latin in 1516, was not published in English until 1551. Whilst first editions in Latin and English are scarce and costly, 17th-century editions can be acquired without too much expense.

Another influential book of this period, published posthumously in 1570, was Roger Ascham's *The Scholemaster*, in which the author sets forth the virtues of a classical education. This work had been reprinted numerous times by the middle of the following century, and so where once again a first edition will be prohibitively expensive, it is perfectly possible to obtain one of the early editions.

The New Testament was first translated into English from the Greek by William Tyndale, and published in 1525–26 at Cologne and Worms. Early copies brought into England were denounced by bishops and destroyed. The only known complete copy was purchased by the British Museum in 1994 for £1million. The English Bible in its entirety was translated by Miles Coverdale in 1535. Numerous versions of the Bible were printed during the 16th and 17th centuries, the emphasis dependent on the translator and the prevailing beliefs of the monarch. During Queen Mary's reign the reformers had to take refuge abroad, many fleeing to Geneva, where the "Breeches" Bible was issued in 1560. This Calvinistic translation proved so popular that the "Bishop's" Bible was prepared to counteract its impact. King James I's "Authorized Version" of 1611, upon which the Bible used today is based, came mainly from Tyndale's translation and the Bishop's Bible. The variety of revisions and finely printed or bound editions of the Bible up to the end of the 19th century make a rewarding area of collecting; prices are generally not high for editions printed after 1680. Victorian family Bibles can be obtained for a few pounds, often with family trees, annotations or ornate bindings. The Bible has been issued in miniature format, often illustrated with engravings, quite regularly from the 18th century – another inexpensive field.

▼ Richard Brathwaite
The English Gentleman, engraved frontispiece, woodcut initials, John Haviland for Robert Bostock, 1630. First edition of important English courtesy book. **£400–800**

► John Donne
Poems, by J.D. with Elegies on the Authors Death, engraved portrait frontispiece, Miles Flesher for John Marriot, 1635. This second edition differs from the first edition of 1633, containing 17 additional poems. **£1,000–2,500**
First edition, **£2,500–4,000**

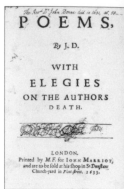

◄ James Sibbald
The Manner of the Beheading of Duke Hambleton, woodcut on title-page, for Robert Ibbotson, 9 March 1648/9. One of only 4 recorded copies. **£800–1,200**

16th- & 17th-Century Literature

The Elizabethan Age witnessed an expansion of literacy and a greater awareness of Society. Baldassare Castiglione's *Il Cortegiano* (Venice, 1528), translated by Sir Thomas Hoby in 1561, which contained a definition of the ideal gentleman, rules of conduct for the lady and a discussion of platonic love, was the prototype of the "courtesy" book published in numerous formats during the 17th century. This work had more influence in Britain than elsewhere in Europe, resulting in two extremely popular works, Henry Peacham's *The Compleat Gentleman* (1622) and Richard Brathwaite's *The English Gentleman* (1630). The conversational style of these two books had an important influence on the poetry and drama of the age. Similar books were issued throughout the 17th and 18th centuries, often in pocket-size format, and could form a fascinating means of assessing society's ideal codes of behaviour.

Sir Philip Sidney was regarded by his contemporaries as the "perfect Renaissance man": patron, soldier, lover, courtier and poet. None of his works, however, were published during his lifetime; they were probably passed around in manuscript form, preserved by friends and patrons. His major works are a prose romance, *Arcadia* (1590), and *A Defence of Poetry* (1590). It was to Sidney that Edmund Spenser dedicated *The Shepheardes Calender* (1579), of which only seven copies are known in the first edition. Spenser's most successful work was *The Faerie Queene* (1590–96), which greatly influenced generations of poets. Fine copies in first edition will command high prices and the collector will probably have to resort to later editions.

Drama in the 17th century

The theatre had established itself as part of popular culture in London by the end of the 16th century. The first permanent theatre was opened in 1576 at Shoreditch, with the Swan and the Globe opening in 1595 and 1599 respectively. Francis Beaumont and John Fletcher were typical in writing tragi-comedies, providing an escapism not found in earlier drama. Shakespeare's great and popular contemporaries, the dramatists Thomas Kyd and Christopher Marlowe are virtually impossible for the new collector to find in the original, but the many dramatists of the 17th century can make rewarding collecting, and less well-known or later names such as John Dryden and Thomas Shadwell, whose works were published after 1640, are easier to find. Many writers, such as Ben Jonson, issued their works in a collected edition, and these can be found for modest sums.

Metaphysical poets

From the body of 17th-century theological writing, John Donne stands out. He was forced to seek a living in the Church after displeasing his patron by marrying his niece. Much of his work – sermons, essays, poetry – was published posthumously, but he is regarded as a founder of the school of "metaphysical poets", which was mostly spiritual in tone. Lesser-known poets, such as George Herbert and Henry Vaughan, were not held in high esteem during the 18th and 19th centuries, but were re-evaluated this century. First editions are rare, but 17th-century second editions are more affordable, as are 20th-century private press editions.

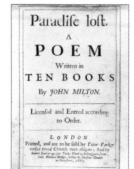

The effects of the Civil War

With the outbreak of the English Civil War in 1642, the theatres were closed and the whole nature of literature changed. Royal censorship of the printing presses had controlled output, but now a wealth of publications appeared. It had never before been possible to print on such a scale, and with such immediacy, all shades of political opinion. Pamphlets reported on Acts of Parliament, battles and intrigues almost as soon as they had taken place. The enormous variety of such material makes for a rich field to collect.

Much of the material was anonymous, but John Milton spent years producing controversial and political works defending religious, civil and domestic liberties. *Areopagitica; a Speech for the Liberty of Unlicenc'd Printing, to the Parliament of England* (1644), was a plea for freedom of speech and printing, its forerunner being the *Doctrine and Discipline of Divorce* (1643), which shocked many at the time. Milton's greatest works, however, *Paradise Lost* (1667), and the sequel *Paradise Regained* (1671), were written in his years of semi-retirement and seclusion from Royalist retribution. These and his early pieces are rare and expensive in first edition.

Unlike Milton, John Locke was initially opposed to religious freedom, but later defended such rights on moral and economic grounds. His early work *The Two Treatises of Government* (1690) explored democracy; his greatest philosophical work – now sought after and expensive – is *An Essay concerning Humane Understanding*, from the same year, an examination of the mind and its powers of perception.

Collecting *William Shakespeare*

William Shakespeare was a leading member of London's leading company of actors, the Lord Chamberlain's Men. The Globe Theatre became their permanent home in 1599, and upon the accession of King James I in 1603, they became known as the King's Men. Shakespeare probably began writing for the stage in the 1580s, but, as was customary, his plays were not officially published. His scripts would often have been written down as heard on stage, and subsequently printed. These early editions are known as "bad quartos", and are extremely difficult to date. After his death, his fellow actors, Heminges and Condell, prepared *Mr William Shakespeare's Comedies, Histories and Tragedies* – the First Folio; this was published in 1623, with about half the plays appearing in print for the first time. This edition is the most sought after of all. It is not as rare as some books, but the great demand ensures the price remains beyond most people's reach. The earlier editions of individual plays are also very rare, but late 17th and 18th-century editions can be picked up. With the 19th century comes a wealth of illustrated and annotated editions, often arranged by famous actors such as Sir Henry Irving or publishers like Charles Knight. There is a vast array of critical material on Shakespeare which could also make fascinating collecting, many of the authors important in their own right, including Dryden, Johnson and Coleridge.

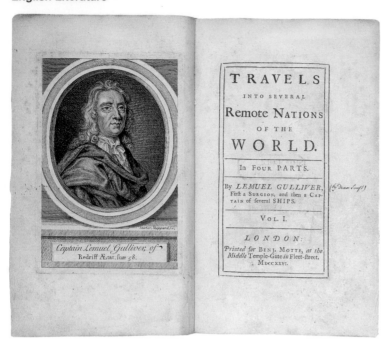

▼ **Alexander Pope**
The Rape of the Lock, engraved frontispiece and 5 plates, for Bernard Lintott, 1714. Original wrappers.
£2,000–4,000
Rebound, £500–800

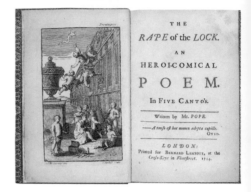

▲ **Jonathan Swift**
Travels into Several Remote Nations of the World. By Lemuel Gulliver, 2 volumes, engraved portrait, 4 maps and 2 plans, for Benjamin Motte, 1726. There are various issue points to the first edition, resulting in a wide range of prices. **£1,500–6,000**

Literature in the 18th Century

The 18th century was a period of political intrigue and battle. The two great Jacobite Rebellions of 1715 and 1745, and riots in Edinburgh and London, heralded a period of urban violence and popular opposition to the ruling parties. This was a period of reflection on the ideas of law and order, and saw the birth of the penal colonies in Australia. There was a continuing interest in education and the first English encyclopedia was published in 1704 by John Harris. The first *Encyclopaedia Britannica* did not appear until 1771. Literature and the arts portrayed a society liable to disruption from the lower classes. Two of the greatest writers of this period, Daniel Defoe and Jonathan Swift, whose major works have lasted perhaps partly due to their appeal to children, spent many years composing anonymous political and controversial pamphlets, before each composing a tale that would swiftly bring them popularity. Defoe's novel *Robinson Crusoe* (1719) shows man pitted against nature, while Swift's *Travels into Several Remote Nations of the World. By Lemuel Gulliver, First a Surgeon, and then a Captain of several Ships* (1726), is a brilliant fantasy and satire on society, court and government. Much of the Dublin-born Swift's early

work, including *A Tale of a Tub* (1704), was religious and political in content, and his later work was often concerned with Irish affairs. Defoe's topographical work *A Tour through the Whole Island of Great Britain* (1724–27), and his historical, almost fictional, narratives *A Journal of the Plague Year* (1722) and *Memoirs of a Cavalier* (1724), provide a rich insight into life in Britain. Being classic texts, the fictional tales of both authors are highly sought after in first edition, but they are easily found in later editions, and much of their other writing can be obtained quite easily in first edition. Swift's use of satire was taken further by his friend Alexander Pope, whose *Rape of the Lock* appeared in 1712, but was not published separately until 1714. Between 1715 and 1720 Pope translated Homer's *Iliad* into verse, followed by *The Odyssey* (1725–26).

18th-century poetry

Much scholarly work has been done recently on this period, particularly on the poets who have not in the past been avidly collected, and although prices may have risen as a result, there is still a wealth of material available for those who wish to spend a little time on research. James Thomson's *The Seasons* is an

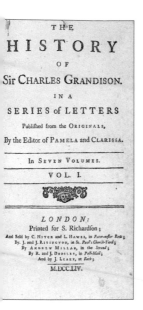

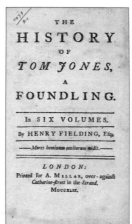

▲ **Samuel Richardson**
*The History of Sir Charles Grandison
in a series of Letters,* 7 volumes, for
S. Richardson, 1754. **£250–500**

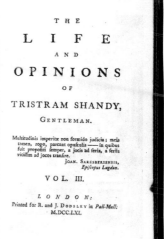

▲ **Laurence Sterne**
The Life and Opinions of Tristram Shandy, 9 volumes,
engraved plate, volumes 5,7,9 signed by the author,
R. and J. Dodsley; T. Beckett and P.A. Dehondt,
1760–67. **£2,000–4,000**
A mixed set with the early volume present as later
editions, £300–600

interesting poem to look at, for as with much 18th-century verse, it grew in size and changed over the years as the author revised it. Three parts, *Winter* (1726), *Summer* (1727) and *Spring* (1728), each revised and augmented, were published with *Autumn*, in a collected edition in 1730. The last edition published in Thomson's lifetime, in 1746, was hugely popular and has been reprinted many times. Although it provides an invaluable picture of social history, *The Seasons* is not as popular now as it has been, and is therefore relatively inexpensive.

18th-century novels

As prose fiction developed and matured, its potential as both instructor and entertainer to the growing numbers of the middle classes was recognized. Women were becoming better educated and many of the novels were written specifically for them. Morally serious, realistic literature with heroes and heroines undertaking adventures of a personal nature, proved especially appealing. The phenomenal popularity of such works is evident when one realizes that Samuel Richardson's *Pamela* (1740) appeared in six London editions in its first year. Both this and Richardson's *Clarissa* (1747–49) were imme-

diately translated into French and became as widely read in France. So whilst a first edition may be scarce, later ones from the same year are more easily found. It is with this period that the presence of an original binding and its condition become determining factors in price for the collector.

The first circulating libraries had been set up in Edinburgh in 1726, with London's first in 1740, all promoting the popularity of the novel. Many were published anonymously, especially those written by women. The scarcity of these lesser-known authors from this period of the founding of the English modern novel has now meant a revival of interest and hence an increase in value. Nonetheless, with hard work one can still find and identify reasonable examples of work by such authors as Colley Cibber, Nicholas Rowe and Susannah Centlivre amongst many others. Henry Fielding was initially a dramatist, but with the government's censorship of his plays, he turned to prose fiction, and *The History of Tom Jones* was published in 1749. Unlike Richardson's novels, which took the form of a series of letters, Fielding worked in straight prose, much of it comic, in a style that was the forerunner of the great 19th-century novelists. Tobias Smollett and

▼ Edward Gibbon
The History of the Decline and Fall of the Roman Empire,
6 volumes, W. and A. Strahan and T. Cadell, 1776–88.
Second edition of volume 1, the remainder as first
edition. **£2,000–3,000**
Another edition, 12 volumes, 1797, £100–200

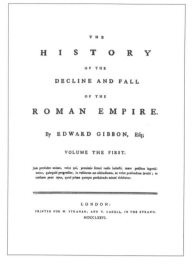

► James Boswell
The Life of Samuel Johnson, 2 volumes, engraved
portrait frontispiece and 2 plates, by Henry Baldwin for
Charles Dilly, 1791. Contemporary calf. **£2,000–6,000**
Modern calf, £800–1,500

Laurence Sterne continued this tradition, the latter's highly popular *The Life and Opinions of Tristram Shandy* (1759–67), being a forerunner of modern stream-of-consciousness novels. The latter part of the 18th century saw publication of Edward Gibbon's *The History of the Decline and Fall of the Roman Empire* (1776–88), a classic work of history still reprinted and occasionally even read, and indicative of the Age of Enlightenment, with its freedom from superstition and interest in the scientific.

Samuel Johnson

The dominant figure of this period is Samuel Johnson; journalist and biographer, poet, editor and critic. His early work was published anonymously; the first work to carry his name was *The Vanity of Human Wishes* (1749). After nine years' intensive labour Johnson's masterpiece, the Dictionary, was published in 1755, bringing him fame and fortune. It was when he met his future biographer James Boswell, that his reputation was assured, for it is Boswell's *Life* that has probably ensured Johnson's lasting fame, with its depiction of his eccentricities and outbursts, his personality larger than life. On one occasion the pair travelled to Scotland, each

writing an account of the trip: Johnson, *A Journey to the Western Islands of Scotland* (1775) and Boswell, *Journal of a Tour to the Hebrides* (1785). Nineteenth- and 20th-century editions of Johnson's works are readily obtainable, and, in addition, many have useful scholarly notes.

18th-century theatre

The 18th century was a prolific time for the London stage, making for a wealth of collectable material: comedies, tragedies, pastorals, modern and classical poured from the dramatists' pens. Much of the output of this time, however, has been overshadowed by the earlier Restoration comedies and, later, by the plays of Oliver Goldsmith and Richard Brinsley Sheridan. Goldsmith's major poems *The Traveller* (1765) and *The Deserted Village* (1770) emphasize social problems such as poverty in town and country. His novel *The Vicar of Wakefield* (1766), and play *She Stoops to Conquer* (1773), are probably the best known of his works today. The plays of both Goldsmith and Sheridan delight in the comic, in amatory intrigues, in confusion and verbal wit, with a clever exploitation of theatrical devices, such as the hidden eavesdroppers in *A School for Scandal*. This

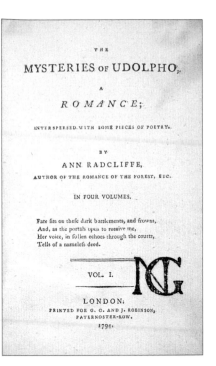

▲ Ann Radcliffe
The Mysteries of Udolpho, 4 volumes, G. and G. Robinson, 1794. A classic Gothic novel. This copy has the ownership monogram of the Swedish Count Nils Gyldenstolpe on each title-page. **£500–1,000**

◄ John Thomas Smith
Vagubondiana; or the Anecdotes of Mendicant Wanderers through the Streets of London, large-paper copy, hand-coloured etched additional title, 48 plates, 1817. **£200–400**

▼ Alexander Smith and Daniel Defoe
A General History of the Lives and Adventures of the Most Famous Highwaymen, Murderers, Street-Robbers, &c, engraved frontispiece and 26 plates, J. Janeway, 1734. **£600–1,200**

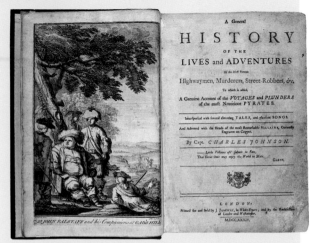

play by Sheridan was first performed in 1777, but was not published until a pirated edition appeared in Dublin in 1780. *A School for Scandal* and *The Rivals* (1775) were highly popular on stage. Official editions of his plays did not appear for some years after they were performed, due mainly to Sheridan's inability to decide which version to publish and a desire to retain the acting rights himself.

Horace Walpole – politician, letter-writer, owner of the Strawberry Hill printing press, and instrumental in the revival of Gothic architecture – was also the author of the first "Gothic" novel, *The Castle of Otranto* (1765). The term "Gothic" in this instance meant "medieval" and a return to fiction based on the ancient romances of chivalry. The term altered in meaning in the early 19th century to include the macabre, fantastic and supernatural; a genre that went on to encompass the work of Edgar Allan Poe and Bram Stoker's *Dracula*, together with modern mystery stories and the horror film. Many of the 19th-century novels had more than a strain of the Gothic running through them. As a genre it is fascinating to collect; the early examples may be hard to find in original state, but they have been reprinted in numerous forms.

John Gay's play *The Beggar's Opera* (1728) and Samuel Johnson's poem *London* (1738) both explored the darker side of life in London, a world of poverty and crime. The late 18th century witnessed a fascination with life amongst the lower classes, and, with the development of graphic satire as a means of comment and depiction of character, a series of studies and parodies appeared, many illustrated by William Hogarth, Thomas Rowlandson or George Cruikshank.

By far the majority of such works concentrated on the characters of London, with Napoleon and the French a close second. The illustrated works will always be more expensive, but all are easily obtainable whether in first edition or later printings, and form a fascinating social picture of the period. A series of books worth collecting are the trades or "Cries" of London from the late 17th to 19th centuries, some for adults, others aimed at children, all with fascinating illustrations of the itinerant dealers and variety of characters found on the streets.

▼ George Gordon, Lord Byron
Hours of Idleness, a Series of Poems, Newark, S. and J. Ridge, 1807. Many of the poems had previously appeared in *Fugitive Pieces*, 1806, which was immediately suppressed by Byron. **£400–900**

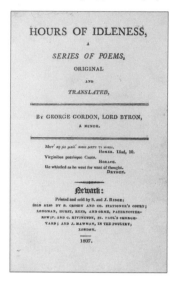

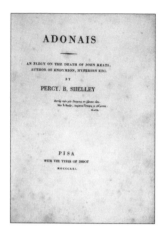

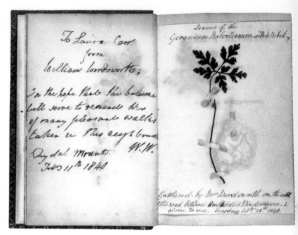

▲ William Wordsworth
Yarrow Revisited and other poems, presentation copy inscribed by author, Edward Moxon, 1839. **£1,200–1,800** Author's collaboration with S.T. Coleridge, *Lyrical Ballads*, 1798, first edition, second issue in original boards, £2,500–5,000; *The White Doe of Rylstone*, 1815, rebound, £350–700

▲ Percy Bysshe Shelley
Adonais. An Elegy on the Death of John Keats, Pisa, 1821. This elegy on the death of Keats was issued in wrappers. **£15,000–20,000**

The Romantics

Boswell's *Life of Johnson* (1791) provided a portrait of a man both public and private, prone to self-examination and doubt, and in the 19th century Johnson came to be seen as a Romantic hero. The Romantic movement was concerned with the self and the value of individual experience, proclaiming the superiority of the emotions over reason. William Wordsworth first defined the Romantic movement in literature, in the preface of the second edition of his *Lyrical Ballads*. The first edition was published anonymously in 1798, appearing in two issues with different title-pages, the earliest and most scarce having a Bristol imprint. The publishers, Longmans, returned the copyright to Wordsworth, who decided to issue a further edition with an additional preface, in which he set forth his theory of poetry and in so doing created a manifesto for the Romantic poets. This is a good instance of a second edition being just as important as the first. These are his most sought-after works, with prices that reflect their importance, but many of his other books are easily affordable, being not uncommon.

Wordsworth's contemporaries Samuel Taylor Coleridge and Robert Southey were political radicals. Coleridge collaborated with Wordsworth on *Lyrical Ballads*, in which perhaps his most famous poem, "The Rime of the Ancient Mariner" appeared. "Christabel" and "Kubla Khan" were first published in 1816, both unfinished fragments only. Copies of the latter work are rare in original boards, but still not as prohibitive in price as the great novelists when found in original cloth in fine condition.

Perhaps the greatest proponents of the Romantic movement were George Gordon, Lord Byron, Percy Bysshe Shelley and John Keats. Many of this second generation travelled widely in Greece, Switzerland and Italy, and used landscapes such as the Alps, the lakes and the bays of Italy as backdrops for their verse and writings. Many of them died young or tragically, and their letters and critical works can be as important and interesting as their poetry. Themes of remembered childhood, unrequited love and the heroic, and their use and exploration of dreams and fantasy, are still appealing to today's reader.

The Romantics also include an emerging field of women writers, notably Dorothy Wordsworth (Wordsworth's sister), who kept many journals of her life and travels with her brother, and Mary Shelley (Shelley's second wife), best remembered for the novel *Frankenstein* (1818).

Collecting
19th-century poetry

▼ Alfred, Lord Tennyson

The Charge of the Light Brigade, 4 pages, 8 August 1855. This famous poem was originally published in *The Examiner*, 9 December 1854, and was to be revised for publication in his next collection of poems, *Maud*, 1855. Upon learning that the Society for the Propagation of the Gospel was about to print a separate edition he issued his own. **£1,000–2,000**

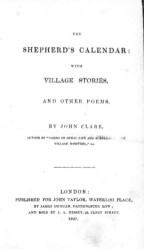

▲ John Clare

Poems descriptive of a Rural Life and Scenery, John Taylor, 1820. Original cloth-backed boards. **£200–400**

► Algernon Charles Swinburne

Rosamund Queen of the Lombards, Chatto and Windus, 1899. Original cloth. **£80–150**

► Elizabeth Barrett Browning

Poems, 2 volumes, Edward Moxon, 1844. Original cloth. **£200–400**

The early pieces by Shelley and Keats are rare; however, Byron's work goes in and out of fashion and is certainly more affordable and less difficult to find. The entire print run of 500 copies of *Childe Harold's Pilgrimage* was sold in a few days in 1812, leading the publishers John Murray to issue future works in runs of 10,000. Byron's works were quickly reprinted, completely overshadowing his contemporaries – who have now become more popular and able to command higher prices than he.

Much of Keats's greatest work, including "The Eve of St. Agnes", "Ode to a Nightingale", and "Lamia", was written shortly before his death from tuberculosis at the age of 25 in Rome. Shelley's great elegiac poem *Adonais* was written upon the death of Keats and published in Pisa in 1821. The works of both Keats and Shelley tend to be expensive in first edition, the result partly of their rarity and partly of their elevation to the role of principal figures of the Romantic movement. The new collector will have to concentrate on later editions of their work, perhaps those issued by the private presses of the 20th century. There are also a number of poets of the mid-19th century, such as Robert Browning, Algernon Charles Swinburne and Alfred, Lord Tennyson, who can be picked up in first edition for relatively little.

A major collection of literature put together during the latter part of the 20th century, that of the American H. Bradley Martin, whose library was sold at Sotheby's during the late 1980s, contained the work of 85 poets from the 19th century. The English and American literature catalogues from the sale are worth hunting out as reference works. The scope for a collector who chooses to concentrate on the poetry of the 19th century is therefore broad, many of the works being found easily for less than £100.

▶ **Charles Dickens**
The Personal History of David Copperfield, etched plates by Phiz, Bradbury and Evans, 1849–50. First edition in the original 20 parts bound as 19, original pictorial wrappers. **£1,000–3,000** First edition in book form, original cloth, £500–800; rebound, £150–300

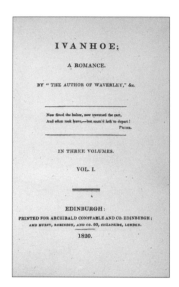

▲ **Sir Walter Scott**
Ivanhoe, a Romance, 3 volumes, Edinburgh, 1820. Rebound. **£250–500**

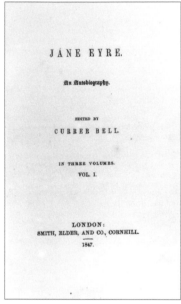

◀ **Charlotte Brontë**
Jane Eyre, an Autobiography, edited by Currer Bell, 3 volumes, Smith, Elder & Co., 1847. Original cloth. **£4,000–7,000**
Rebound, £800–2,500
The Brontë sisters issued their books under the pseudonyms of Currer, Ellis and Acton Bell.

19th-Century Novels

The major area, apart from poetry, for collectors of 19th-century literature, is the novel. Probably the more accessible from a literary point of view, this is perhaps the hardest area when it comes to acquiring some of the great names in original state. While expensive in the original binding, these authors are more affordable when their work is rebound. Fashion also dictates price, and authors sought after during their lifetime may not be so now. There are, however, many good starting points for a new collector, including Sir Walter Scott, Charles Dickens, Anthony Trollope, and Wilkie Collins.

Most of Dickens's works were initially published "in parts": that is, the stories were serialized and issued in paper wrappers on a monthly basis, to be bound up by the buyer at a later date. Once completed, the story was then also issued in a bound form. These features will be indicated in catalogues by "first edition bound from the parts" or "first edition in book form". The works of Dickens are harder to find in fine condition in the original cloth, than in the original parts in comparable condition.

Trollope, Collins and many of the major 19th-century novelists, such as George Eliot (whose real name was Marian Evans), Jane Austen, Charlotte Brontë and her sisters Emily and Anne, had their works issued as "three-deckers": three volumes bound in boards or cloth, the latter often with decorative gilt tooling.

Many collectors choose to concentrate on the vast array of minor names, popularized at the time by circulating libraries, but now obscure to the average reader. Condition and binding are paramount with these 19th-century novelists, and it is also important to check that bibliographically the book is complete; for instance, the half-title may not be present, having been removed when being rebound. Books were often rebound by contemporary owners, the original

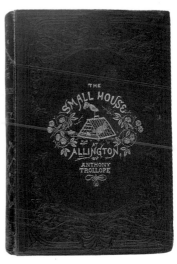

► **Anthony Trollope**
The Small House at Allington,
2 volumes, wood-engraved plates
after J. Millais, Smith, Elder and Co.,
1864. Original cloth. **£400–800**

◄ **Wilkie Collins**
The Woman in White, wood-
engraved illustrations, New York,
Harper & Brothers, 1860. The
American edition was published
in August, the English not until
September. First edition in book form
in original cloth. **£1,000–2,000**
First English edition in original cloth,
£400–800

boards generally being unattractive, or at a later
stage once the original binding of cloth or boards
grew worn. Today, the presence of these original
bindings in fine condition results in high prices for
the work of Eliot, Austen, the Brontës and the early
works of Trollope. But works by the same authors, if
rebound, lacking half-titles or in poor condition, can
still be found for a few hundred rather than thousands of pounds, as can the later and more common
works of Trollope. The works of Dickens, Eliot,
Austen and the Brontës can all be found in later
"Collected" editions; prices for these sets will also
depend on the quality of the printing and the binding: a full leather and gilt binding will be more
sought after than cheaper cloth.

Sir Walter Scott, hugely popular and influential
in his time, has – as with his contemporary Byron –
gone out of fashion, with resultant low prices. The
novels in his "Waverley" series can be seen as the
foundation of the modern historical novel, a genre
which flourished at the end of the century and gave
rise to the numerous adventure stories written for
boys as well as adults. Such novels, by H. Rider
Haggard and R.M. Ballantyne among others, were
set against a factual background of battles and heroism, and can today be picked up very reasonably,
being rather out of fashion with modern readers.

Of the major American authors, Herman
Melville and Edgar Allan Poe are both exceptionally
difficult for a new collector to acquire in first edition
and original bindings. Washington Irving and
Henry Wadsworth Longfellow are more easily
available. Henry James was born in New York,
though he settled in Europe in 1875 and lived in
London for over 20 years; many of his novels
contrast the American and European characters. His
major works in first edition are scarce; less well-
known titles are more readily found.

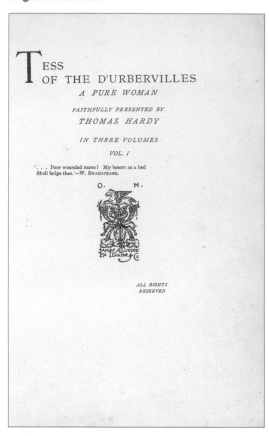

▲ **Thomas Hardy**
Tess of the D'Urbervilles, a Pure Woman Presented Faithfully, 3 volumes, James R. Osgood, McIlvaine & Co, 1891. One of 1,000 copies of the first issue, original cloth. **£800–1,600**
One of 325 copies with illustrations by Vivien Gribble, 1926, £300–500

▼ **Robert Louis Stevenson and Lloyd Osbourne**
The Ebb Tide, William Heinemann, 1894. Original pictorial cloth. **£20–30**

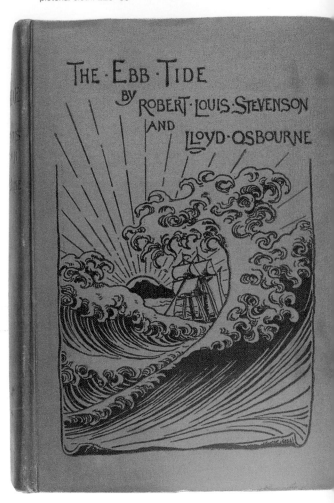

The End of the 19th Century

The strict moral values of Victorian society that were reflected in much 19th-century fiction, began to feel restrictive at the end of the century. Authors such as Rudyard Kipling, Joseph Conrad, Thomas Hardy and Robert Louis Stevenson bridge this period of change and growth towards the literature of the modern movement. Much of the literature of the closing years of the 19th century was questioning the accepted values of Victorian society and several authors attempted to explore the disciplines of science and psychology.

Robert Louis Stevenson achieved fame for his children's books, as well as for his study of human nature, *The Strange Case of Dr Jekyll and Mr Hyde* (1886); this was published in America before the English edition of the same year, both editions being equally valued by collectors. Each was issued in paper wrappers and, although fragile, neither is as

prohibitive in price as the great novels of the mid-19th century. With the exception of his children's classic *Treasure Island* (1883), Stevenson's many other novels can be picked up very reasonably.

There are numerous minor authors to choose from who are rarely read today: Mrs Humphry Ward, Samuel Butler and William Hale White (known as Mark Rutherford) were all widely available in their day, their work issued in long print runs. Many of these writers were concerned with the spiritual disintegration of society and can provide a useful insight into the dilemmas of their age.

Two of Thomas Hardy's major works, *Tess of the D'Urbervilles* (1891) and *The Return of the Native*, (1878), were each published in an edition of only 1,000, and remain sought after and expensive in their original decorative cloth. Hardy's works were reissued quickly and frequently in good reprints.

K I M

BY

RUDYARD KIPLING

ILLUSTRATED BY J. LOCKWOOD KIPLING

LONDON
MACMILLAN AND CO., Ltd.
1901

▲ Rudyard Kipling

Kim, Illustrations by J. Lockwood Kipling, Macmillan,
1901. Original cloth. **£50–100**

The decorative binding for *The Trumpet Major*
(1880) was designed by the author himself.

Rudyard Kipling's first book, *Schoolboy Lyrics*
(1881) was issued by his parents whilst he was still at
school and is exceedingly rare. It is bound in wrappers of which two variant states exist.

Kipling's later works are far easier for the new
collector to find. Many of his works were first published in India, bound in paper wrappers, and care
should be taken over the priority of these. His publishers, Macmillan, quickly reissued his works in less
expensive editions and these are easy to pick up for a
few pounds.

These final years of the 19th century witnessed
the birth of the Modern movement, and the 1890s is
a fascinating period to collect with its mixture of the
old and the new; names known well today and those
whose popularity was short-lived.

Collecting
Thomas J. Wise
and forgery

▼ Wilfred Partington
Thomas J. Wise in the Original Cloth, Robert Hale Ltd.,
1946. First edition. **£30–60**

John Carter and Graham Pollard ▲
*An Enquiry into the Nature of Certain Nineteenth Century
Pamphlets*, Constable & Co. Ltd., 1934. First edition. **£60–120**

Forgery in literature is not as commonplace as
might be thought. With early books one has
to be careful that leaves, especially title-pages,
from another edition have not been inserted;
books composed of leaves from different copies
are known as "made-up copies".

It was not until the early 20th century that
forgery hit the headlines. The great bibliophile
and collector Thomas J. Wise had painstakingly
built up the Ashley Library, composed of literary
first editions from Samuel Johnson onwards,
which was acquired by the British Library in
1937. In 1934 John Carter and Graham Pollard
published *An Enquiry into the Nature of Certain
19th-Century Pamphlets*, proving that many of the
pamphlets in Wise's library, purporting to be
rare, privately printed editions by Tennyson,
Swinburne, Shelley and other major Victorian
authors, were in fact later editions disguised as
contemporary publications. He was finally found
to have stolen leaves from over 40 17th-century
plays from the British Library. He had sold his
forgeries for substantial sums to gain the income
needed to expand his own library. Later in the
20th century, Frederick Prokosch was proved to
be issuing forgeries of purportedly unknown and
rare poems by T.S. Eliot and other major names.

Like the work of the infamous forger of
paintings, Tom Keating, such works often begin
to be collected in their own right.

Modern First Editions

English and American literature in the 20th century: the importance of edition and condition

▲ **Ernest Hemingway**
In Our Time, boards, Paris, Three Mountains Press, 1924.
Limited to 170 copies. **£3,000–6,000**
A Farewell to Arms, New York, 1929, first issue without legal
disclaimer, £700–1,500; first English edition, £100–200.
The Old Man and the Sea, New York, 1952, £150–300

"Modern first editions" is the short-hand description of an area of book collecting that covers first printings of English and American literature of roughly the last hundred years – from, say, the 1890s, the age of Oscar Wilde and the beginnings of the Modern movement, up to the present day. In strict bibliographical parlance an "edition" comprises all the copies of a book printed at any time from one setting of type. The correct term for the copies printed from that setting at any one time is "impression". The earliest form of a given text is really the "first impression" or "first printing", but the term first edition is commonly (if mistakenly) used.

Since first edition collecting is about having the earliest form of the text, it follows that where two or more issues or states exist, the first is clearly the more desirable, and the price will reflect this fact. The reason for the existence of variants can range from dissatisfaction with the illustrations, to the correction of particularly gross errors, and even to the revision of the text because of allegations of libel. Apart from the books themselves, dust-wrappers are not infrequently found in differing forms, perhaps as quotations from reviews and other aids to marketing are added. Collectors need to be aware of the bibliographical points which distinguish one variant from another. Nowadays the modern first edition field is well covered by bibliographies which make these things plain, but reputable and knowledgeable booksellers and auctioneers

▲ William Boyd
A Good Man in Africa, Hamish
Hamilton, 1981. **£100–250**
First American edition, £20–30

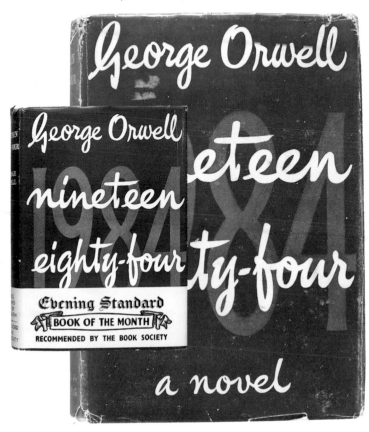

ought always to make clear precisely what
they are selling.

Because the earliest text is what the
collector strives for, it follows that proof copies
have a great attraction. Over the last two or
three decades, it has become common practice
for publishers to produce so-called advance
proof copies, not so much for authors to
correct, as for the publicity and sales
departments to use to promote the book.
Copies are sent to eminent writers who might
be persuaded to come up with a quotable
comment, and to booksellers who might be
expected to place a large order. The possibility
– even probability – that careful study will
reveal differences in text between these proof
copies and the regular first editions make the
former attractive to the collector.

Condition has always been an important
factor in the pricing of modern books, and
this is especially true today. A fine copy will
command more than one that is merely in
what booksellers call "reasonable second-hand
condition" – meaning a copy which has all too
obviously been well read – and the premium
is well worth paying: the superior copy will
always prove the better bargain in the end.

Dust-jackets, scorned by earlier
generations of collectors because they were
not an integral part of the book, are now *de
rigueur*. They were not in common use in
Britain or America until around 1910, and
even then they were by no means universal.
They were originally no more than a way of
keeping books clean until the time of their
sale, and were often discarded thereafter.

▼ **John Steinbeck**
Of Mice and Men, New York, Covici Friede, 1937, first
issue with bullet between the 8s on page 88. **£150–300**
Second issue, £50–100

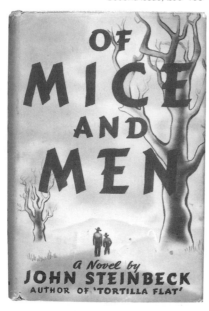

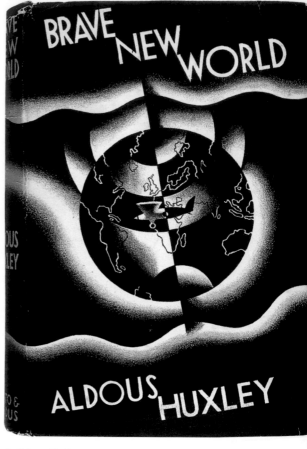

▲ **Aldous Huxley**
Brave New World, Chatto and Windus, 1932.
£300–450
The Doors of Perception, 1954, £25–45

◄ **James Joyce**
Ulysses, wrappers, Paris, Shakespeare and Company,
1922. Limited to 1,000 copies, one of 100 on hand-
made paper signed by the artist. **£10,000–20,000**
First edition printed in England, 1936, one of 900,
£400–800; *Dubliners*, 1914, £500–900; *Finnegan's
Wake*, 1939 £300–700; *Pomes Penyeach*, boards,
Paris, 1927, £100–200

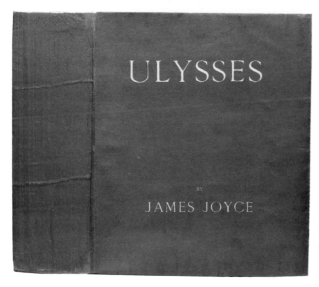

The first jackets were completely plain, some
having a panel cut in them to allow the author
and title to be read from the spine of the book.
Later it became the practice to print this
information, plus the name of the publisher,
on the jacket itself. Soon the potential of the
jacket as an aid to sales was realized and jacket
illustrations and promotional material began
to appear.

Among the reasons that jackets are sought
after today are that they may be illustrated by
distinguished artists; that they may contain
a précis or autobiographical material by the
author; they give bibliographical information
(such as details about price and edition); and,
most of all, that today's collectors think books
incomplete without them. As a rule of thumb
it is wise to insist on jackets for books from the
1950s onwards but to be more tolerant in the
case of earlier publications, lest the gaps on
your shelves are never filled.

Which first editions should one collect?

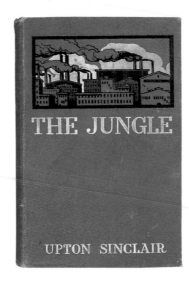

◄ **Ted Hughes**
Lupercal, Faber, 1960. **£40–80**
First book, *The Hawk in the Rain*, 1957, £150–300;
Remains of Elmete, 1979, with photographs by
Rumer Godden, £30–40

◄ **Upton Sinclair**
The Jungle, pictorial cloth,
New York, Doubleday, Page &
Company, 1906, second issue.
£60–120

▼ **J.R.R. Tolkien**
The Hobbit, George Allen & Unwin, 1937.
£2,000–3,000
The Lord of the Rings, 3 volumes, 1954–55,
£3,000–4,000. *The Silmarillion*, 1977, £30–50

► **V.S. Naipaul**
The Mystic Masseur, New York,
Vanguard Press, 1959, first
American edition of the author's first
book. **£40–60**
First English edition, 1957, £120–
250; without dust-jacket, £30–50

► **Sylvia Plath**
Ariel, Faber, 1965. **£70–125**
Her only novel, *The Bell Jar*, published under the
pseudonym of Victoria Lucas, 1963, £300–600

It is sound advice to ignore what is merely
fashionable and back your own judgment
instead. Pick authors you think are
undervalued or just plain neglected. It makes
sense to collect associated books, such as the
works of West Country novelists or other
regional writers, political novels, novels by
poets, the works of the Angry Young Men,
and so on. Alternatively, collecting all the
publications of a minor but worthy publisher
can be rewarding. So can building a collection
based on a particular year of publication –
perhaps the year of one's birth or a significant
year in history, such as the mid-point of the
century or the beginning or end of one of the
world wars. Modern first editions probably
represent the easiest and most accessible area
of book-collecting for the newcomer.

Anthony Rota

► **H.G. Wells**
The Open Conspiracy, Victor Gollancz, 1928, dust-jacket designed by E. McKnight Kauffer. **£25–50**
The Time Machine, 1895, without dust-jacket, £150–300

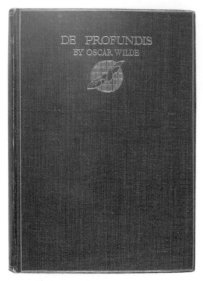

▲ **Oscar Wilde**
De Profundis, Methuen and Co., 1905, without dust-jacket. **£40–90**
The Picture of Dorian Gray, 1891, first edition in book form, first issue, boards, £800–1,200; *Salomé*, Paris, 1893, £400–600, first edition in English, limited to 500 copies, boards, £500–800

The Seeds of Modernism

The closing decades of the 19th century brought with them change. New beliefs were being expounded; Darwin's theories on the evolution of man and Freud's theories of psychoanalysis had a profoundly disturbing effect on society. With the break-up of Victorian Liberalism, there was a reassessment of Britain's place in the world. The fight for women's rights was beginning; and a greater awareness and questioning of sexuality was emerging.

H.G. Wells, W.B. Yeats and Oscar Wilde were three writers who bridged the old and the new, growing up with Victorian values but breaking free to form the start of the Modern movement. The immensely prolific Wells was well read in modern science and his visions of a futuristic world, *The*

Time Machine (1895) and *The War of the Worlds* (1898), anticipate later science fiction works. The works of Wilde epitomized the decadent society of the 1890s; *The Picture of Dorian Gray* (1890) scandalized society; the play *Salomé* (written in French 1893, translated 1894) was refused a licence in London. Wilde served a prison sentence for homosexuality, an experience he later recalled in *The Ballad of Reading Goal* (1898). Quite different in emphasis are his comic plays, such as *The Importance of Being Earnest* (1895), in which he mixes dazzling wit with shrewd social comment. The great poet and playwright Yeats presided over one of the finest periods of literary activity in Ireland. A fervent nationalist, he created an Irish national theatre, and explored

STORIES OF RED HANRAHAN BY
WILLIAM BUTLER YEATS

Rewritten with the help of Lady Gregory
WBYeats 1917

THE DUN EMER PRESS
DUNDRUM MCMIV

◄ **W.B. Yeats**
Stories of Red Hanrahan, boards, Dundrum, The
Dun Emer Press, 1904. Limited to 500 copies.
Inscribed by the author, "Rewritten with the help of
Lady Gregory. W.B. Yeats 1917". **£800–1,600**
The first version of most of these stories appeared
in *The Secret Rose*. Yeats initially wrote the stories
in literary English but "could not get any sense of
the village life with the words". With Lady Gregory's
help the stories have a more folkloric feel: "They are
but half mine now, & often her beautiful idiom is the
better half". Uninscribed copy, £150–300

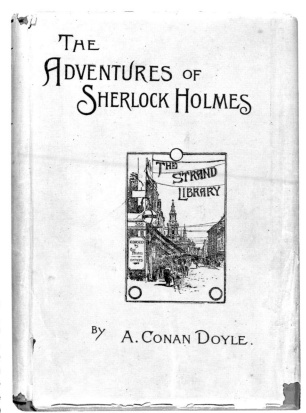

► **Arthur Conan Doyle**
The Adventures of Sherlock Holmes, George Newnes,
1892. With the rare dust-jacket. **£10,000–15,000**
Without the dust-jacket, £500–800; *A Study in Scarlet*,
1888, first edition in book form, £5,000–8,000; *The
Return of Sherlock Holmes*, 1905, more common
without dust-jacket, £200–400; *The Hound of the
Baskervilles*, 1802, common in rather worn state
without dust-jacket, £150–300; fine, £500–800

innovatory stage technique using symbolic and ritu-
alistic drama. Influenced by Irish tradition, he later
evolved a complex spiritualist symbolism and imagery, underlying many of the poems in such works
as *The Tower* (1928) and *The Winding Stair* (1929).

Interest in the underworld, seen in the 18th century depictions of "low-life" and Victorian novels
portraying the seedier side of life in the city, had not
abated, and contributed to the success of Sherlock
Holmes, Arthur Conan Doyle's great creation, who
first appeared in *A Study in Scarlet* (1887); the stories
were then serialized in *Strand Magazine* from 1890,
and the adventures retain their appeal to the present
day. There was great interest in the darker side of
man, his evolution from the ape, his possible return

to this state, and the power of environment or hered-
ity; themes explored in Bram Stoker's *Dracula* (1897),
R.L. Stevenson's *The Strange Case of Dr. Jekyll and
Mr. Hyde* (1886), and Edgar Rice Burroughs's
Tarzan of the Apes (1914). In fine condition, all three
will be beyond the pockets of most collectors.

These authors can be regarded amongst the
founding fathers of modern literature and any collection attempting to cover the development of modern literature should contain some of their work.
Not all these early works were issued in dust-jackets,
making bibliographies essential, and where present,
the jacket will make the price of the book beyond the
reach of the average collector. The emphasis should
be on finding copies in the best condition possible.

▲ W. Somerset Maugham
The Making of a Saint, pictorial cloth, Boston, 1898, this American edition preceded the English edition by one month. **£100–200**
Cakes and Ale, 1930, £40–80

► Robert Graves
Over the Brazier, wrappers with cover design by Claud Lovat Fraser, Poetry Bookshop, 1916. **£800–1,200** The author's first book. *Goodbye to All That*, 1929, first issue with the Siegfried Sassoon poem, £250–400; *Claudius the God*, 1934, £40–80

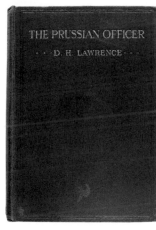

◄ D.H. Lawrence
The Prussian Officer and other Stories, Duckworth & Co., 1914. Without dust-jacket, in first state of binding of dark blue cloth gilt, the second being in light blue cloth with dark blue lettering. **£100–200**
Later issue in third state of binding with dust-jacket, £400–600; *Women in Love*, New York, 1920, one of 50 copies for publication in England and signed by the author, without dust-jacket, £1,000–1,500

The Early 20th Century

If one's aim is to form a representative collection of literature of the 20th century, then the names discussed on the following pages should be sought after and titles chosen according to budget; the contemporary writers can be approached more subjectively, very much according to one's personal tastes.

The First World War

The First World War brings a whole range of novelists and poets for the collector to concentrate on, many of whom did not survive its duration, whose work provides a full picture of the development of the war and changing attitudes towards it. The early poetry was nostalgic, full of the traditional concepts of honour and valour, epitomized by Rupert Brooke's "The Soldier", with the immortal lines

beginning, "If I should die, think only this of me …". The poetry developed to tackle the horrors of a war that involved human slaughter on a scale almost impossible to comprehend, depicted most forcefully by Wilfred Owen. It was with poems such as "Dulce et Decorum Est", on the use of mustard gas in the trenches, that poetry as a vehicle for protest was born. Only four of Owen's poems were published in his lifetime. His finest poems, written over an intense 11-month period prior to his death a week before the Armistice, were published in 1920 by Siegfried Sassoon, whom Owen had met during a spell in hospital and who had encouraged him.

Sassoon himself wrote poetry dealing with the futility of war, as seen in *The Old Huntsman* (1917). He found popular acclaim with the publication of

▶ **G.K. Chesterton**
The Coloured Lands, New York, Sheed and Ward,1938. First American edition. **£40–80**
The Secret of Father Brown, 1927, without dust-jacket, £30–50

▼ **Siegfried Sassoon**
Memoirs of a Fox-hunting Man, illustrations by William Nicholson, Faber, 1929. First illustrated edition. **£100–150**
First edition limited to 260 copies, without dust-jacket, 1928, £60–100; *Sherston's Progress*, 1936, £15–20

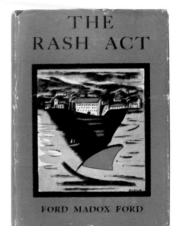

▶ **Ford Madox Ford**
The Rash Act, New York, Ray Long & Richard R. Smith, Inc., 1933, precedes first English edition by six months **£100–200**
First English edition, £60–90

his semi-autobiographical trilogy, *Memoirs of a Fox-Hunting Man* (1928), *Memoirs of an Infantry Officer* (1930) and *Sherston's Progress* (1936). The middle book is concerned with his war experiences. Sassoon's later poetry reflected his growing interest in spirituality and Catholicism.

Robert Graves's *Over the Brazier* (1916) appeared whilst he was fighting, but it is in his autobiography, *Goodbye to All That* (1929), that he describes the full horror of life in the trenches. The first issue of this book contains an unpublished and rejected poem by Sassoon, which was taken out of later editions due to Sassoon's displeasure at this breach of copyright and of his friendship. Graves's later works include historical novels, *I, Claudius* and *Claudius the God* (both 1934), love poetry and books of mythology.

D.H. Lawrence

Lawrence's first major novel, *Sons and Lovers* (1913), was autobiographical, an account of his youth amongst the miners in Nottinghamshire, coloured by a strong love for his mother. His next novel, *The Rainbow* (1915), was confiscated on the grounds of obscenity, a problem which was to hound him all his life. It culminated in the case against *Lady Chatterley's Lover*, which he had privately printed in Florence in 1928; the complete text was not published in Britain until 1960. It is exceptionally rare to find Lawrence's early books in the dust-jacket. Several works were issued privately from Florence in limited editions. His major novels are more sought after than later critical or psychoanalytical works or short stories, and this is reflected in their respective values.

Ring for Jeeves, Herbert and Jenkins, 1953. First issued as a play *Come on Jeeves*, in conjunction with Guy Bolton. **£60–125**

Love Among the Chickens, 1906, issued without a dust-jacket, the author's first adult novel, £2,000–3,000; *Big Money*, 1931, first English edition, without dust-jacket, £70-120; *Ice in the Bedroom*, 1961, £15–30

▶ **T.S. Eliot**

Four Quartets, New York, Harcourt, Brace and Co., 1943. First printing with "first American edition" on verso of title-page. Rare, of the 4,165 copies all but 788 copies were destroyed owing to bad margins and these were kept only for copyright and review purposes. **£600–1,200**

Prufrock and other Observations, wrappers, The Egoist, 1917, the author's first published work, limited to 500 copies, £1,000–2,500; *Old Possum's Book of Practical Cats*, 1939, £150–300; first illustrated edition by Nicholas Bentley, 1940, £50–75; *The Cocktail Party*, 1950, £25–45

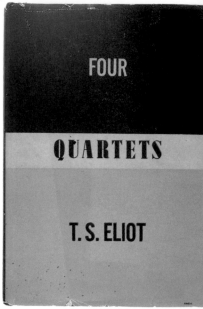

▶ **Evelyn Waugh**

Men at Arms, Chapman and Hall, 1952. Presentation copy inscribed by the author to Lady Dorothy Lygon. **£1,000–2,000**

Uninscribed copy, £40–80; *Scoop*, 1938, first issue with letter "s" dropped from last word page 88, first issue dust-jacket with "Daily Beast" logo, £350–650; without dust-jacket, £30–60

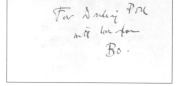

The 1920s & 1930s

The 1920s were filled with exhilaration, with colour and exuberance, as seen in French painting and Russian ballet and stage design, and as heard in the music of the time: jazz. But after the war, things could never be the same again. In the novels of P.G. Wodehouse and Evelyn Waugh, it may have seemed that the aristocracy had never had such a good time, but Waugh's early, satirical novels, such as *Vile Bodies* (1930) and *A Handful of Dust* (1934), captured the brittleness and cynical frivolity of the post-war generation. His most popular novel, *Brideshead Revisited* (1945), explored with more gravity and some nostalgia the fortunes of an aristocratic family, set in a framework of the Second World War. The humorist P.G. Wodehouse wrote over 120 books – a serious challenge for a keen collector – including the hugely popular series featuring the amiable Bertie Wooster and his loyal manservant Jeeves. Wodehouse settled in the United

States after the Second World War. Several of his earliest novels published before the first war were issued without dust-jackets and these titles are now sought after in fine condition, whereas his later novels can be picked up for very reasonable prices.

The Bloomsbury Group

The fragmentation of Europe after the First World War was reflected in much of the experimental literature and art of the 1920s. The Bloomsbury Group was a loose, informal circle of friends – writers, artists and intellectuals, including economist John Maynard Keynes, writer E.M. Forster and artist Vanessa Bell – who later came to be seen as reacting against the strictures of Victorian art and society. Vanessa Bell designed many of the dust-jackets on the books of her sister Virginia Woolf, in whose Bloomsbury house the group used to meet. In Woolf's later novels such as *To the Lighthouse* (1927)

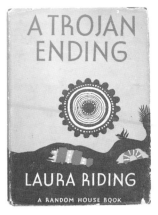

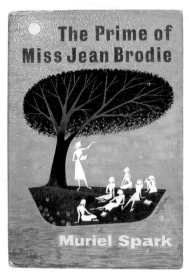

◀ **Laura Riding**
A Trojan Ending, New York, Random House, 1937. **£80–120** Signed copy, £125–175

▲ **Dorothy Richardson**
The Trap, Duckworth, 1925. One in her autobiographical "Pilgrimage" series. **£60–100** Her books are rare in dust-jackets. A signed copy, £100–175

▲ **Muriel Spark**
The Prime of Miss Jean Brodie, Macmillan, 1961. **£40–80**

◀ **Virginia Woolf**
To the Lighthouse, New York, Harcourt, Brace & Co., 1927. First American edition, dust-jacket by Vanessa Bell. **£70–135**
First edition, without dust-jacket, Hogarth Press, £80–200; *Between the Acts*, 1941, £60–110

and *The Waves* (1931), she used a lyrical, stream-of-consciousness style that echoed the fragmentary outlook of contemporary avant-garde painters, all seeking new ways of exploring individual identity.

Eliot and Joyce

Many of the best poets of this period first published their work in magazines such as T.S. Eliot's *The Criterion*. Titles often lasted only a few years, including Wyndham Lewis's *Blast* (1914–15), and these can make a rewarding collection. Eliot published *The Waste Land* in the first issue of *The Criterion* in 1922. This strangely disordered poem, written by an American resident in London, was seen by many as indicative of modern post-war life, bleak, depressing and empty. Eliot, who became a director of the publishers Faber and Faber, was one of the greatest voices and influences of the mid-century, his work ranging from the spiritual concerns of *Four Quartets*

(1939–42), to drama, *The Cocktail Party* (1950), and his classic children's verse, *Old Possum's Book of Practical Cats* (1939). This and his earliest works remain the most highly prized, with his later works and plays still fetching very reasonable sums.

Much of Eliot's work revolved around the relationship of the subjective consciousness with the objective world, themes taken up by James Joyce. His complex novels were set in and influenced by his native Dublin. *Ulysses* was published in Paris in 1922 in a limited edition; subsequent editions were confiscated on grounds of pornography in Britain and America. It was not legally available in America until 1933 and not published in London until 1937. Joyce's books are scarce in first edition, and the texts difficult to read and not to everyone's taste, but he remains an important figure in the development of the modern novel. His works are priced accordingly, putting him beyond the reach of many collectors.

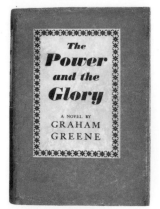

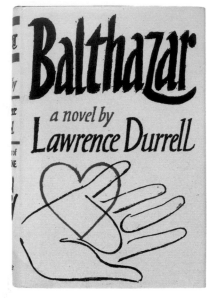

◀ **Graham Greene**
The Power and the Glory, William Heinemann, 1940.
Scarce in the dust-jacket. **£1,500–3,000**
Without dust-jacket £100–250; *Dr. Fischer of Geneva*,
1980, £15–30

▲ **Martin Amis**
The Rachel Papers, Jonathan Cape,
1973. The author's scarce
first book. **£100–200**
Money, 1984, £20–40

▲ **Lawrence Durrell**
Balthazar, Faber, 1958. **£50–100**
The *Alexandria Quartet*, 1962,
one of 500 signed by the author, £150–300

◀ **Tom Sharpe**
Blott on the Landscape, Secker and
Warburg, 1975. **£20–40**

20th-Century Novelists

No collection of 20th-century novelists would be complete without Graham Greene, the best-known and most-respected novelist of his generation. His first novel, *The Man Within* (1929), remains scarce, as does *Brighton Rock*, first published in America in 1938. A prolific writer, Greene focused on a world wounded by colonialism and peopled with rebels and outsiders, and on what he saw as the paradoxes of Catholicism. In *The Power and the Glory* (1940) he coined the phrase "whisky-priest". Much of his best work was written after the Second World War, set in smashed and disoriented countries: *The Third Man* (1950), set in Vienna, and *The Heart of the Matter* (1948), in West Africa.

With the aftermath of the war and a greater stability finally returning to Europe, many writers travelled far afield once again. Lawrence Durrell was born in India, but settled in Greece and later in Egypt; he used these countries as backdrops for his novels, which were full of political and sexual intrigue, notably the *Alexandria Quartet* comprising *Justine* (1957), *Balthazar* and *Mountolive* (both 1958) and *Clea* (1960).

A large number of good post-war writers are more readily available to the new collector on a small budget. Women writers offer many possibilities. From the earlier years, names less well known today include Dorothy Richardson, friend of H.G. Wells and influential on Virginia Woolf and James Joyce, and authors from the 1930s such as the Americans Laura Riding, who lived with Robert Graves for many years, and legendary humorist Dorothy Parker, whose sketches and short stories were published in the *New Yorker*. Christina Stead, an Australian who lived in London during the 1950s and 1960s, was a left-wing writer whose novels manifest her fierce independence and feminism.

There are numerous current authors to choose from, such as Muriel Spark, whose early work was neglected for a long time; popular and critical acclaim came with the publication of *The Prime of Miss Jean Brodie* (1961). Doris Lessing, Iris Murdoch, the late Angela Carter and Margaret Drabble are just a few of those worth adding to a collection that might attempt to trace the path of the development of women in this century.

▲ **William Golding**
Lord of the Flies, Faber, 1954, first impression.
£450–750
Without dust-jacket, £50–80; *The Inheritors*, 1955,
£75–150

It might be that one's tastes lie with mystical and grandiose writers such as John Fowles or Anthony Burgess. Which of the newly collectable novelists such as Martin Amis, V.S. Naipaul, Tom Sharpe or Ian McEwan one decides to include, will depend largely on one's own tastes.

The new breed of literary prizes such as the Booker Prize, first awarded in 1969, could be used as a basis for a collection, the winners ostensibly being those who will endure in years to come. It is also worth looking at the winners of the Nobel Prize for Literature. In 1983 the winner was the late William Golding. Arguably his greatest and certainly his best-known work was his first novel, *Lord of the Flies* (1954), which is now a classic and therefore relatively expensive, while his later works are still reasonable.

British or American 20th-century drama or poetry could equally form the basis of a collection. Both are readily available, with an enormous range of authors to choose from, including Tom Stoppard, Alan Ayckbourn and Harold Pinter. The works of poets such as Sylvia Plath and Poet Laureate Ted Hughes are, similarly, easy to find.

Collecting The 1930s

◀ **W.H. Auden**
Look, Stranger!, Faber, 1936.
£30–55
Spain, wrappers, 1937, £30–75

▲ **Christopher Isherwood**
Goodbye to Berlin, Hogarth Press, 1939. **£400–600**
Without dust-jacket, £40–70

The Russian Revolution of 1917, the General Strike of 1926, the Spanish Civil War of 1936–37, were all contributory factors in creating a generation of writers with a strong sense of history and who were motivated by their political and sociological outlook. Many of them felt guilt at having been too young to fight in the First World War. They felt that the personal and the political were inescapably linked, and struggled to reflect this in their writing. Poets Stephen Spender, Louis MacNeice and W.H. Auden, and novelists Christopher Isherwood and George Orwell, are just a few of those associated with the socialism of the period. There was an intense desire to change society, and many joined the Communist Party for a brief time; several fought in Spain for the Republican Party against General Franco. George Orwell drew on his own experiences for *Down and Out in Paris and London* (1933); a committed socialist, he saw himself as a political writer. He later turned away from Communism, and warned against revolutionary socialism in his adult fable *Animal Farm* (1945) and a totalitarian state in *Nineteen Eighty-Four* (1949). Christopher Isherwood vividly evoked life in the Weimar Republic on the eve of Hitler's rise to power in *Mr. Norris Changes Trains* (1935) and *Goodbye to Berlin* (1939).

Many of the greatest literary names of this century were writing during this historically important period. Some books are scarce and highly sought after, while others are easily obtainable, so there is a wealth of fascinating material available for the new collector.

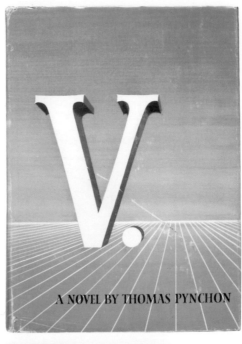

◄ **Thomas Pynchon**
V, Philadelphia and New York, J.B. Lippincott, 1963. The author's first book. **£200–450**
First English edition, £40–60

▼ **Henry Miller**
Tropic of Cancer, wrappers, Paris, Obelisk Press, 1934. The author's first book, banned in England and America for many years. **£400–600**
Sexus, 2 volumes, issued without dust-jackets, Paris, 1949, limited to 3,000 copies, £35–80

▲ **Booth Tarkington**
The Gentleman from Indiana, pictorial cloth, New York, Doubleday & MacClure, 1899. There are numerous issue points to this book relating to the text and the binding. This copy is in what is generally accepted as the earliest binding, with the ear of corn pointing up, not down, and with the earliest text. **£60–120**

► **F. Scott Fitzgerald**
The Great Gatsby, New York, Scribner's, 1925. First issue with "sick in tired" page 205. **£1,500–2,000**
Second issue without dust-jacket, £60–100

Specialist Areas

American authors are an interesting area on which to concentrate. The average collector could probably not afford the great novels by writers such as F. Scott Fitzgerald, Ernest Hemingway or Henry Miller in first edition in fine dust-jackets, but their later works are easy to find and relatively affordable. Others, like Thomas Pynchon with his first novel *V*, had one massive success, which is now hard to find and expensive, whereas their other works are usually more accessible. Earlier writers such as Upton Sinclair or Booth Tarkington are found in pictorial cloth rather than in dust-jackets, giving an added dimension to a collection.

The new collector must be wary of the exorbitant prices demanded for early dust-jackets. Look at alternative areas, such as earlier decorative bindings, which appear on both American and British books. They could form a fascinating collection. One such

◄ Ray Bradbury
Something Wicked This Way Comes, New York, Simon & Schuster, 1962. **£30–60**

▼ M.P. Shiel
The Purple Cloud, pictorial cloth, Chatto and Windus, 1901. **£120–250**

► John Wyndham
The Midwich Cuckoos, Michael Joseph, 1957. **£30–65**

► Michael Moorcock
The Bull and the Spear, Allison and Busby, 1973. One of a trilogy including *The Oak and the Ram*, 1973, and *The Sword and the Stallion*, 1974. The trilogy. **£40–70**

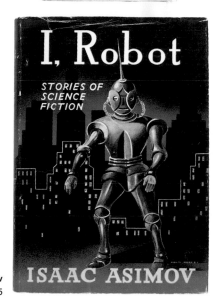

► Isaac Asimov
I, Robot, Grayson and Grayson, 1952. **£80–175**

is that on W. Somerset Maugham's early work *The Making of a Saint* (1898).

For cult followers of the world of fantasy and science fiction there is a great deal to choose from in literature. Collectors focus on different areas, including the texts, the dust-jacket designs, and the texts of seminal films such as Arthur C. Clarke's *2001: A Space Odyssey* (1968). Such a collection should begin with the early works of H.G. Wells, although for a really comprehensive collection one could go as far back as the Gothic novels of the 18th century. Earlier 20th-century science fiction authors such as John Wyndham, Ray Bradbury and M.P. Shiel can be represented alongside current writers; Frank Herbert and Michael Moorcock being two of the best known. Such a specialized field creates a culture of its own and many of the names will be unknown to others outside this field of interest.

Collecting Spy Novels

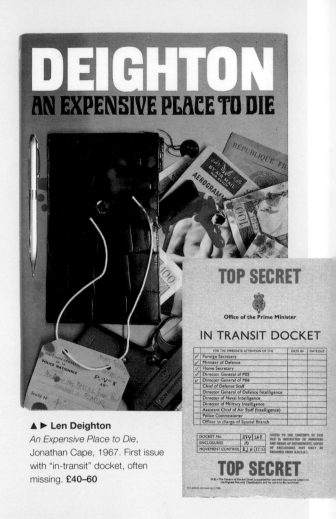

The Cold War ushered in a new genre of spy fiction, which was further popularized by film versions. Ian Fleming's tough yet witty and romantic James Bond is perhaps the most enduring and popular character, first appearing in *Casino Royale* (1953), followed by *Live and Let Die* (1954). The early works by Fleming, if found in fine dust-jackets, now command vast sums, but his later works from the 1960s are extremely affordable and make an attractive collection in their striking dust-jackets. John Le Carré's secret agent, the amiable George Smiley, is a more intellectual hero, and Le Carré's spy thrillers are somewhat less escapist stories of the post-war spy era that has only recently ended. The works of Len Deighton and Frederick Forsyth are also easily found, and for considerably less than works by Fleming.

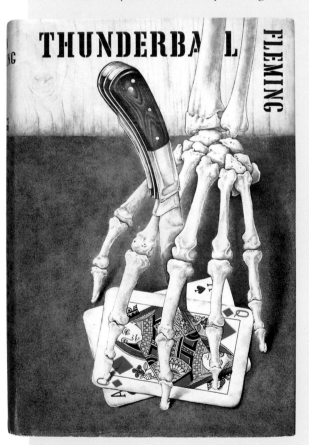

▲ Len Deighton
An Expensive Place to Die, Jonathan Cape, 1967. First issue with "in-transit" docket, often missing. **£40–60**

▼ John Le Carré
Smiley's People, Hodder and Stoughton, 1980. **£30–60**
The Little Drummer Girl, New York, 1983, precedes first English edition, £80–100; first English edition, £30–40

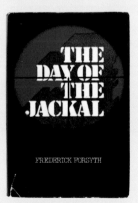

▲ Frederick Forsyth
The Day of the Jackal, Hutchinson, 1971. **£30–60**

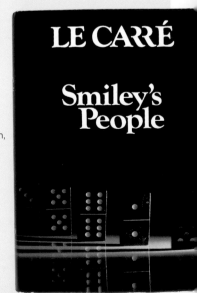

▲ Ian Fleming
Thunderball, Jonathan Cape, 1961. **£80–120**
Casino Royale, 1953, the author's first novel, £800–1,200; without dust-jacket, £100–200; *On Her Majesty's Secret Service*, 1963, £25–50

▶ **Ruth Rendell**
The Lake of Darkness,
Hutchinson, 1980. **£20–40**

▼ **Brian Moore**
The Colour of Blood, Jonathan Cape, 1987. **£15–30**

◀ **Agatha Christie**
Sparkling Cyanide, Collins Crime
Club, 1945. **£120–250**
The Murder at the Vicarage,
1930, without dust-jacket, £80–120;
Third Girl, 1966, £15–30

▶ **Joan Aiken**
Died on a Rainy Sunday, Victor Gollancz,
1972. **£20–40**

A popular and wide-ranging field for new collectors is "Spies and Suspense". The crime and mystery novel has enjoyed extraordinary and abiding popularity, from Victorian times to the present day. Arthur Conan Doyle's eagle-eyed sleuth Sherlock Holmes was active around the turn of the century, and Agatha Christie introduced her Belgian detective Hercule Poirot in 1920 in *The Mysterious Affair at Styles*, the first of her 66 detective novels. Collins, who published her works, were one of the foremost publishers of the crime novel through their Crime Club, alongside Gollancz, who issued novels in distinctive yellow dust-jackets, including those of Joan Aiken (also known for her children's books). A collection of modern first editions will continue to develop with new authors being published, and any collection of crime writers should include those such as Ruth Rendell, Brian Moore and P.D. James, who are writing today.

The ultimate aim of many bibliophiles once their collection becomes complete is to search for "association" copies of their books. These may simply be copies signed by the author, or may contain a more detailed presentation inscription. Most sought after are those from the author to another well-known author, such as Grahame Greene to Evelyn Waugh. Several writers, such as G.K. Chesterton and Henry Williamson, added small drawings to the title-page or a preliminary leaf. Collectors are generally prepared to pay more for books that come from the library of a well-known person; for example, books

on the Cold War from the library of the spy Kim Philby would command considerably more than ordinary copies.

Others are interested in the finer bibliographical points and choose to collect variant issues of books, whether it be American and English first editions of the same books, or variant dust-jackets (George Orwell's *Nineteen Eighty-Four*, for example, existing in red or green). Sometimes a priority has been established by bibliographers, but not always, and part of the enjoyment is in the debate.

One could collect books that were banned or controversial – for reasons often hard to appreciate in today's more liberal climate – and here Henry Miller, James Joyce and D.H. Lawrence, together with *The Satanic Verses* (1988) by Salman Rushdie, could start such a collection.

Uncorrected proof copies, issued by publishers for review or pre-sale, have also created another area for collectors, one which is now perhaps rather out of fashion. Whatever one's interests and however one chooses to collect, this field is one of the most accessible for new collectors, where many have started before moving back in time. Collect what appeals and do not worry if that author is not in vogue; this only means lower prices at the time of purchase.

Prices indicated in this chapter are for copies in good condition in original cloth with dust-jacket, unless otherwise stated. Price ranges for modern first editions are probably wider than for any other area of collecting, determined by condition.

Fine Printing & Typography

The design of the printed page: from grand 20th-century privately printed books to fine commercial printing of the 19th and 20th centuries

▲ **Cranach Press**
William Shakespeare, *The Tragedie of Hamlet, Prince of Denmark*, one of 300 copies on paper, wood-engraved illustrations by Edward Gordon Craig, Weimar, 1930.
£2,500–6,000

A finely printed book must have been well designed, not only well printed. The type used should suit the text, its size suit the page. The inner margins need to be smaller than the outer, to give the facing pages some unity; the upper margins narrower than those at the bottom, to place the text nearer the optical centre. There ought to be adequate space between the lines, and no more than a dozen or so words to the line. Enough, but no more than enough ink should have been used to ensure that the letters print clearly, and the text should have an even colour throughout the book. If the paper is not hand-made it ought at least to be acid-free. The illustrations should be by the finest artists, and in a style appropriate to the text.

The content of the book may be ignored if the book is physically attractive enough, but to begin with, at least, it must be wisest to buy books that can also be read with enjoyment. Without an understanding of Latin or Greek, much from the 15th to 17th centuries can be admired only for its type and layout, and for the illustrations. Books printed by Aldus are desirable indeed, and his *Hypnerotomachia* of 1497 is one of the finest books of any period, but for most of us the Aldine texts are incomprehensible. Plantin printed many fine books in the 16th century, but not in English; and at the turn of the 18th century Bodoni in Italy and Didot in France were even more skilled, but, similarly, are accessible only to those who speak the appropriate languages.

In Britain, in the latter part of the 18th century, Horace Walpole had a series of fine books printed at his Strawberry Hill Press, and many of the finest books produced in this country since then have come from private

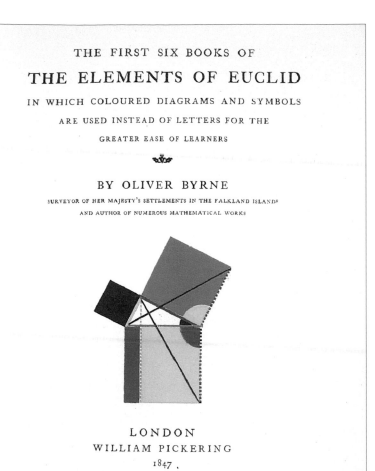

THE FIRST SIX BOOKS OF

THE ELEMENTS OF EUCLID

IN WHICH COLOURED DIAGRAMS AND SYMBOLS

ARE USED INSTEAD OF LETTERS FOR THE

GREATER EASE OF LEARNERS

BY OLIVER BYRNE

SURVEYOR OF HER MAJESTY'S SETTLEMENTS IN THE FALKLAND ISLANDS
AND AUTHOR OF NUMEROUS MATHEMATICAL WORKS

LONDON
WILLIAM PICKERING
1847.

▼ **Curwen Press**
Sir Thomas Browne, *Urne Buriall &
the Garden of Cyrus*, one of 215
copies, illustrations by Paul Nash
coloured through stencils, Cassell
and Co., 1932. **£1,000–2,000**

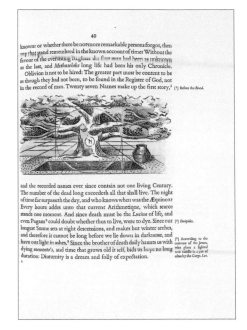

◀ **Chiswick Press**
Oliver Byrne, *The First Six Books of
The Elements of Euclid*, coloured
diagrams, William Pickering, 1847.
£500–1,000

presses – though professionals commonly did the actual work. At the beginning of the 19th century Thomas Johnes had his translations of early chronicles printed at his estate in Hafod, Cardiganshire, in superb quarto and folio volumes. Sir Egerton Brydges employed two skilled printers at his Lee Priory Press, who achieved considerable elegance in their work. William Morris established the Kelmscott Press in 1891, leading the revival of hand-printing upon hand-made paper.

Despite the apparent supremacy of the private presses, a great many fine books have come from commercial printers, among them Foulis, Baskerville, Bensley, Bulmer and the Whittinghams in the 18th and 19th centuries, and in the 20th century, the Oxford and Cambridge University Presses and a good number of private firms. Many of the so-called private presses between the wars used

commercial printers, rather than doing the work themselves. The Nonesuch edition of Shakespeare's *Works* was printed by Cambridge; the Chiswick Press did much for the Golden Cockerel Press. Cassell published a superb *Urne Buriall* with illustrations by Paul Nash, printed at the Curwen Press, and bound in vellum and morocco by Sangorski and Sutcliffe.

Books of this quality can be very expensive, but there is much that can be bought for less than £50 or £100. But before plunging further, you must really become expert enough to know what is finely printed, what is merely vain lavishness. Irrespective of their possible value as investments – and any gain is always uncertain – the most important thing is the pleasure to be had from the books themselves, and that is where their true value lies.

DAVID CHAMBERS

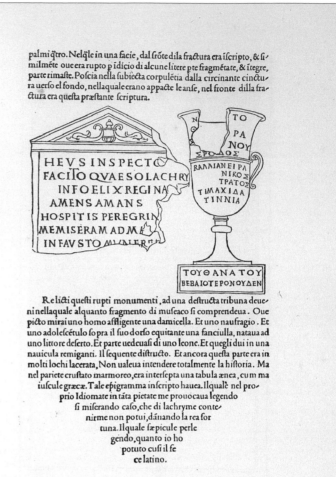

Hypnerotomachia Poliphili, 172 woodcut illustrations, Venice, 1499. The finest book from the press of Aldus Manutius, printed using his new Aldine roman typeface recut and perfected for this work. Printing on commission, he was able to devote considerable time and care to the type, illustrations and press-work.
£40,000–60,000
A facsimile edition published in 1904, £300–400

Fine Printing

The 20th-century typographer and designer Ruari McLean wrote that "typography is the art, or skill, of designing communication by means of the printed word". Some knowledge of the history of typography is important for an awareness of what makes for a well-designed and -printed book, and learning about it can be enjoyable. For many people, the Latin and Greek books of the earliest days of printing are hard to appreciate without a knowledge of the language; this early period is explored more fully later (see pp. 42–7). The most beautiful books up to the 17th century were usually printed in France or Italy rather than in England. Stanley Morison in *Four Centuries of Fine Printing* illustrates 45 books printed in Italy and 77 in France yet not one in England during the 16th century; the 17th century produced few finely printed books anywhere. None of the contemporary editions of the great writers such as Shakespeare and Donne, nor the Authorized Version of the Bible, are beautiful to look at.

Fine printing developed in England during the 18th century, and this should be a rewarding starting point for the new collector. Once a good background knowledge and understanding of fine printing has been acquired, the collector may turn back in time to the great early books of, for example, Christopher Plantin or Aldus Manutius – which are likely to demand a more substantial financial commitment.

▼ **Imprimerie Royale**

Médailles sur les principaux événements du règne de Louis le Grand, avec les explications historiques, engraved title-page, borders and medallions, Paris, 1702. The first use of the "romains du roi" of Philippe Grandjean. By 1745 this series of typefaces was complete (82 in total), which were exclusive to the Imprimerie. **£150–350**

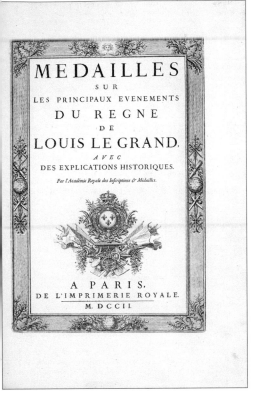

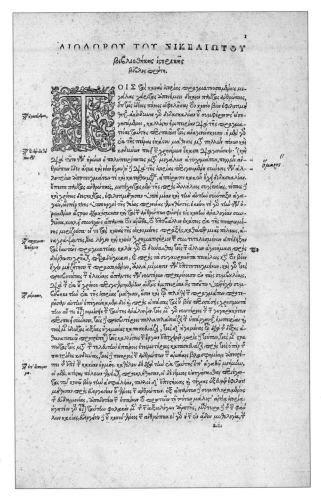

▶ **Robert Estienne**

Dionysius, *Antiquatatum Romanarum Lib.X*, woodcut decorations, Paris, Robert Estienne, 1547. One of the most beautiful Greek books printed, supposedly chosen by François I for publication from a manuscript in his library. **£1,000–2,000**

The average edition of a book printed in the 15th century would probably have been about 200 copies, thus adding rarity value to any surviving today.

Until the 18th century, printing in England was largely concentrated in London; the Stationer's Company was granted a royal charter in 1577 that restricted printing to members of the Company or those under licence. The only body outside London empowered to print legally was the University of Cambridge; in 1586 the University of Oxford was also granted the privilege. Nonetheless, the authorities were unable to stop the flow of books from clandestine presses. It was during the late 17th century that Oxford University acquired its great stock of type, much from Amsterdam, under the auspices of Dr. John Fell, Dean of Christchurch College from 1660 to 1686. Fine printing in France was severely restricted due to religious wars and restrictions imposed by the Crown, but in 1640 Louis XIII created the Imprimerie Royale, to issue religious and political works for use by the government. Run initially by the best printer in France at that time, Sébastien Cramoisy, the press issued its first work in 1640, *De imitatione Christi* by Thomas à Kempis. This could be called the first "best-seller", having been issued in more than 3,000 different editions. Printing was introduced into America in 1638 by Joseph Glover, who took a printing press over from England.

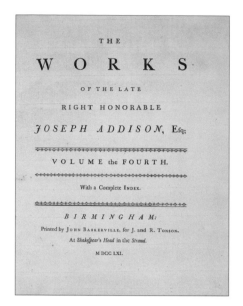

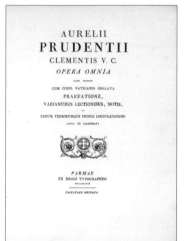

▲ **William Caslon**
A Specimen of Printing Types,
Charles Whittingham, 1796.
£800–1,500

▲ **John Baskerville**
Joseph Addison, *The Works*,
4 volumes, engraved plates,
Birmingham, John Baskerville, 1761.
£100–200

◄ **Giambattista Bodoni**
Aurelius Prudentius Clemens,
Opera omnia, engraved title-vignette,
Parma, Ex folio, Regio Typographieo,
1788. £100–200

Pioneering Typographers

The Press Restriction Act was abolished in England in 1693, allowing a greater freedom of experimentation. The 18th century boasted a number of type-designers whose impact on printing and typography was immeasurable: in Britain, William Caslon and John Baskerville; in France, Louis Luce, Pierre-Simon Fournier and, towards the end of the century, François-Ambroise Didot; and in Italy, Giambattista Bodoni. The style and content of books changed, with religious works becoming less prevalent, and a considerable increase in books for enjoyment. In this time of growing wealth, the rich demanded lavish productions, with fine illustrations and bindings. Typographically, however, books became simpler; for example, title-pages were no longer comprised of a variety of different type-sizes, nor were they decorated to the same degree as those of earlier books.

In England William Caslon, a young apprentice to an engraver of gun-locks and -barrels, took on a new career as a punch-cutter. He designed a roman face which was to become one of the most widely used book types of the next two centuries. Caslon was not a printer himself, but his skill meant that printing houses no longer had to rely on the Dutch firms, such as Enschedé, for type. His foundry continued until 1937, when it was bought by Stephenson Blake. One of the finest printers of 18th century in Britain was John Baskerville. A wealthy man with an early training in calligraphy, he began a new career as a printer in 1750, with the prime aim of printing distinguished books with care and craftsmanship. He spent six years designing the type to be used, and in 1757 his first book, the *Virgil*, was issued to subscribers.

Perhaps his greatest work was his edition of the Bible, issued in 1763, although commercially it was a disaster. For a while after this his interest lapsed, but shortly before his death he issued a series of quarto editions of the classics. The style of Baskerville's books is classical and severe, uncluttered by ornamentation. His influence was probably greater in the rest of Europe than in Britain; his widow sold his punches, matrices and presses to a Parisian printer in

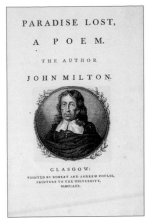

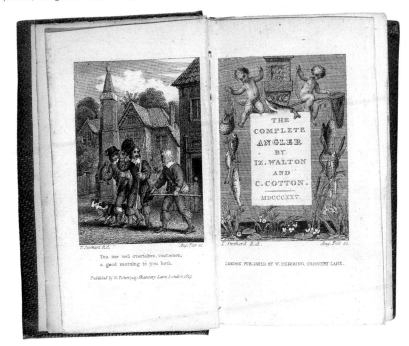

◄ Robert and Andrew Foulis
John Milton, *Paradise Lost*, large-paper copy, engraved
portrait, Glasgow, R. and A. Foulis, 1770. **£100–200**

▲ William Pickering
Izaac Walton and Charles Cotton, *The Complete Angler*,
engraved title and frontispiece, William Pickering, 1825.
One of the Diamond Classics, the majority printed by
Charles Corrall, set in tiny diamond type. The first of
these titles was published in 1820. **£50–100**

◄ William Bulmer
Rev. Thomas Frognall Dibdin, *The Bibliographical
Decameron, or ten days pleasant discourse upon
Illuminated Manuscripts*, 3 volumes, W.T. Bulmer
and Co., 1817. **£300–600**

1779; but his typeface found new markets after it was
recut by the Monotype Corporation in 1924.

Pierre-Simon Fournier published his famous
specimen book *Modèles des caractères de l'imprimerie*
in 1742. He was the first to see the need for a ratio-
nalization of type-size, and introduced the point system of measurement. Printing also continued to
flourish in Italy. Giambattista Bodoni was trained in
Rome, moving to Parma in 1768 to manage the
Stamperia Royale. Initially using Fournier's types,
which can be seen in the first book issued from
Parma, *I voti* (1768), Bodoni later designed and cut
his own types, with much greater contrast between
the thicks and thins of the characters. All the faces
shown in the second version of his *Manuale
tipografico*, published by his widow in 1818, were to
his own design. He printed a number of volumes in
languages other than Italian, Latin and Greek,
including Horace Walpole's *Castle of Otranto* (1791),
and Thomas Gray's *Elegy* (1793) in English.

As the 18th century gave way to the 19th century
there was greater demand for finely printed books,
and printers such as Robert and Andrew Foulis,
John Bell, William Bulmer and Thomas Bensley
flourished using type cast by Caslon and Alexander
Wilson, in what was one of the finest periods of book
production in Britain. Charles Whittingham founded the Chiswick Press in 1811, which continued
under his nephew, also Charles Whittingham; and
in 1828 the younger Whittingham went into part-
nership with an innovative publisher, William
Pickering. They produced fine books, including the
miniature Diamond Classics, the series of Aldine
Poets, the *Book of Common Prayer* with wood-
engravings by Mary Byfield (1853), and great folio
volumes such as Drummond's *Noble Families*
(1846–54). Their early works were printed in modern types, such as Charles Corrall's diamond type,
but they soon turned to old types, including Caslon;
in 1844 they printed their first book wholly from old
typefaces. Books printed in Britain during this
period can be particularly rewarding to collect, as it
is a wide field and titles can be found relatively easily
without involving too great a financial outlay.

Early Private Presses

In 19th-century France, the Didot family of punch-cutters, printers and publishers were prominent. François-Ambroise Didot improved Fournier's point system of measuring type-size. His son Firmin Didot introduced a "modern" typeface, with vertical shading to the letters as opposed to the slanted shading of earlier faces which was based on the broad strokes of a pen. In 1797 Firmin and his brother embarked a project to print a new collection of literary masterpieces, finely printed and illustrated. These de luxe classics were limited to 250 copies, each costing a vast sum for the time.

With the increase of mechanization and the arrival of the iron presses used for printing newspapers as well as books, alongside a substantial increase in literacy and demand for affordable printed matter, the quality of most printing declined. Speed, quantity and cost became key factors. Cheaper paper made by machine and full of acid was used, and stereotyping came into use across Europe. In this process a mould was taken of the type as set for each page, which was then stored, leaving the type free for further use. Although good commercial printers did exist, such as the Chiswick Press and Edmund Evans, much of the work they produced seems dated to us today, and commercial printing went rapidly into decline. It was not until the influence of the pri-

vate press movement came to be widespread that commercial printing improved all over the world, as witnessed in the work of, for example, Bruce Rogers and Daniel Berkeley Updike in America and Oliver Simon in Britain.

At the end of the 19th century those concerned with fine printing chose to turn away from mass publication to smaller, privately printed editions. Private presses had existed for centuries: Cardinal Richelieu set up a press at his chateau in Touraine as early as 1640; and in 1757 Horace Walpole set up a press at Strawberry Hill, Twickenham. Throughout the 19th century individual private presses sprang up: Sir Thomas Phillips created the Middle Hill Press, issuing pieces about his own vast collection of books and manuscripts; Sir Egerton Brydges founded the Lee Priory Press (1813–23) outside Canterbury, Kent; and in 1874 the Reverend C. Daniel printed his first book at Oxford (Daniel had printed as a child, and his Daniel Press imprint first appeared in Frome, Somerset).

It was with the publication in 1891 of *Story of the Glittering Plain*, printed by William Morris at the Kelmscott Press (1891–98), that the private press movement truly began to flourish. All the Kelmscott Press books have a similar feel. Set in one of two typefaces, they are decorated with ornamental

Gregynog Press ▼
Don Antonio de Guevara, *The Praise and Happiness of the Countrie-Life*, one of 400 copies, wood-engravings by Reynolds Stone, Gregynog Press, 1938. £75–150

▼ Eragny Press
Thomas Sturge Moore, *The Little School*, one of 175 copies on paper, wood-engraved illustrations by Lucien Pissarro, Eragny Press, 1905.
£200–400

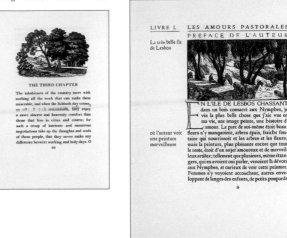

▲ Doves Press
John Keats, *Poems*, one of 200 copies on paper, Doves Press, 1914.
£500–1,000

▲ Ashendene Press
Longus, *Les Pastorales de Daphnis et Chloë*, one of 290 copies on paper, wood-engraved illustrations by Gwen Raverat, initials by Graily Hewitt, Ashendene Press, 1903.
£500–1,000

woodcut borders and initials, and frequently contain wood-engraved illustrations after Edward Burne-Jones and Arthur Gaskin. They look back in time to medieval texts and old German printing and, while often hard to read, they spring from a fundamental concern with the look of the printed page. William Morris's care to find the correct paper and the appropriate ink showed a concern for the finished piece which was to influence generations of printers, and encouraged numerous private presses to set up in defiance of the mechanization of printing. The new presses included Doves Press (1900–16), Ashendene Press (1894–1946), Vale Press (1896–1903), Eragny Press (1894–1914) and Essex House Press (1898–1910). The Kelmscott Press was in existence for only a few years and yet in that short time produced a considerable quantity of books, from its masterpiece of 1896, the grand and costly Chaucer, to less expensive pieces such as Rossetti's *Songs and Lyrical Ballads*.

Books from the Vale and Eragny Presses, set up respectively by Charles Ricketts and Charles Shannon, and by Lucien Pissarro, are quite distinctive: generally slimmer in format, less precious in nature and decorated by the founders themselves. The Vale Press books were printed at the Ballantyne Press, but Lucien Pissarro and his wife, Esther, printed the Eragny books themselves. They remain, as do books from the Essex House Press, more affordable for the collector. The Ashendene Press, run by C.J. St. John Hornby, and Doves Press, founded by Emery Walker and T.J. Cobden-Sanderson, had a more refined and classical feel, often being considered the finest of all private presses. Books from the Ashendene Press were commonly folio in size: large, grand works with prices today to match. Whereas some of the Ashendene books were illustrated, those from the Doves Press rely on simple, beautiful typography with occasional initial letters added by hand in coloured inks.

A book from the Doves Press is the very antithesis of one from the Kelmscott Press, yet both will have been printed with the same premise in mind: the concept of the book as an organic whole, using the best ink, paper, type and binding, imbued with the spirit of the craftsman, not the mechanic. Some people choose to collect simply one example of the different-sized books from the Doves and Ashendene Presses, preferring the illustrative work of the other presses; others collect each work, finding great pleasure in their simplicity. Most of the presses issued a few copies of each book printed on vellum and the prices for these special editions can be ten times the price of the ordinary paper copies.

▼ **Grabhorn Press**
Walt Whitman, *Leaves of Grass*, one
of 400 copies, woodcuts by Valenti
Angelo, New York, Edwin and Robert
Grabhorn, 1930. **£600–1,000**

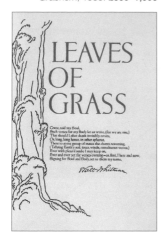

▼ **Rampant Lions Press**
*Books Designed and Printed by
Will and Sebastian Carter at the
Rampant Lions Press, 1982*, 16-page
catalogue, Cambridge, Rampant
Lions Press, 1982. **£5–10**

▲ **Gogmagog Press**
A.R. Philpott "Pantopuck the Puppetman",
Chimneypots, one of 50 copies, coloured elimination
linocut illustrations, Gogmagog Press, 1961. **£200–400**

The 20th Century

Between the wars numerous presses operated in Britain, America and Germany. The finest in Germany was the Cranach Press, founded by Count Harry Kessler in 1913, whose use of great illustrators, such as Eric Gill, Edward Gordon Craig and Aristide Maillol, embellished his fine editions of works by Shakespeare and Virgil – expensive collector's pieces today. The most prolific British press, founded in 1921, was the Golden Cockerel Press at Waltham St. Lawrence, Berkshire. From 1933 to 1959 it was operated by Christopher Sandford, who farmed out the printing to commercial printers such as the Chiswick and Westminster Presses. The numerous publications from this press form one of the easiest ways of starting a collection, being available from a few pounds to several thousand for great works such as *The Four Gospels* (1931), *The Canterbury Tales* (1929–31) and *Troilus and Criseyde* (1927). The Gregynog Press (1923–40) run by sisters Gwendolen and Margaret Davies in Wales, produced fine work, using wood-engravers such as Blair Hughes-Stanton and Agnes Miller Parker to produce some of the best illustrated books of this

period. The Grabhorn Press, founded in 1919 in San Francisco in the United States, by Edwin and Robert Grabhorn, was as prolific in output as the Golden Cockerel. Both issued classic texts and new works; the Grabhorn Press concentrated on American authors or the history of the United States.

Such a concentration of skill within the private press movement opened the eyes of commercial designers and printing houses, and the 1930s saw the quality of commercial book production increase. Commercial printers were used by the private presses to print their publications: the Golden Cockerel Press used the Chiswick Press to print its later books, and publishers Cassell used the Curwen Press to print illustrations and text. The Nonesuch Press was set up by Francis Meynell in 1923, not as a private press but as an imprint, the books actually being printed by the Pelican, Westminster, Oxford University and Curwen Presses. The Nonesuch Press were publishers working within the ideals of the private press movement rather than printers themselves and yet their books remain fine examples of printing, and another good route for the new

▲ Nonesuch Press
Robert Burton, *The Anatomie of Melancholy*, by Democritus Junior, 2 volumes, one of 750 copies, illustrations by E. McKnight Kauffer, Nonesuch Press, 1925. **£150–300**

▼ Hermann Zapf
Typographische variationen, one of 500 copies, 78 pages type specimens, Frankfurt am Main, D. Stempel AG, 1963. **£150–250**

Hermann Zapf **MANUALE TYPOGRAPHICUM 2**

100 typographische Gestaltungen mit Aussagen über die Schrift, über Typographie und Druckkunst, aus Vergangenheit und Gegenwart, in achtzehn verschiedenen Sprachen

¢ 100 typographic arrangements with considerations about types, typography and the art of printing selected from past and present, printed in eighteen languages.

FRANKFURT AM MAIN
NEW YORK · MCMLXIV

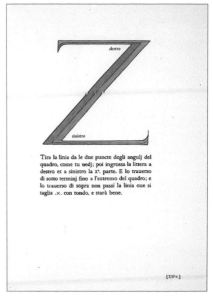

Tira la linia da le due puncte degli anguli del quadro, come tu uedj; poi ingrossa la littera a destro et a sinistro la x°. parte. E lo trauerso di sotto terminj fino a l'estremo del quadro; e lo trauerso di sopra non passi la linia oue si taglia .x. con tondo, e starà bene.

[XII v.]

▲ Officina Bodoni
Felice Feliciano, *Alphebetum Romanum*, one of 400 copies, letters coloured by hand by Ameglio Trivella after the original manuscript, Verona, Officina Bodoni, 1940. **£300–700**

collector to explore. Whilst the major books such as the works of Dickens and Shakespeare are now expensive, the ordinary texts and minor ephemeral pieces are eminently affordable. The tradition of printing on small private presses continues today with the Rampant Lions Press at Cambridge, the Rocket Press, Fleece Press, Gehenna Press and many others in Britain, America and Europe.

Beyond the rather narrow confines of this movement, typographers and designers were encouraged to work within the commercial printing world. Bruce Rogers was the first to earn a living as a freelance typographer, working in America and Britain. Stanley Morison was the most influential designer in Britain during the first half of the century, instrumental in redesigning *The Times* newspaper, among numerous other projects. One could form a substantial collection based on Morison's own writings alongside books he designed. With Oliver Simon, Bernard Newdigate of the Shakespeare Head Press, Francis Meynell and others, Morison was a member of the Double Crown Club, a small group that existed to encourage good design in typography and graphics. In Europe, typographic advances were more avant-garde, being associated with Walter Gropius's Bauhaus movement. Important designers included Jan Tschichold and Hermann Zapf.

There are any number of rewarding areas for the collector, whether one's interest lies in forming a chronological selection or concentrating on a particular century. Many collectors like to make a study of a particular person, such as the publisher William Pickering, who adopted the dolphin and anchor design of Aldus Manutius for his title-pages and was the first to issue books bound in cloth; or the great American printer Theodore Lowe De Vinne who designed the "Century" typeface and wrote *The Practice of Typography* (a four-volume work begun in 1899), the first modern study of the subject. Some might concentrate on the private press movement of the 20th century, or the modern European typographers; on following commercial printing from the Chiswick Press to the Curwen Press; or collecting type specimens from the printing houses. With so extensive a range of choice, any method of collecting will be pleasurably idiosyncratic as well as enjoyable.

Bindings

The book as an object: from fine jewelled bindings to simple, decorative cloth

The primary purpose of a binding is to protect its contents; but binders throughout history have intended that a book could be judged by its covers. The decoration of the surface is designed to reflect the nature and significance of the pages within.

Probably the earliest surviving decorated European binding is on a manuscript of St. John's Gospel, buried with St. Cuthbert at Lindisfarne in AD698, and now on display in the British Library, London. While leather (particularly goatskin, calf and vellum) has traditionally been the favoured material, the medieval "treasure bindings" were set with gold and silver, ivory plaques and jewels; embroidered covers were popular until the 1640s, enjoying a revival in the 19th century.

Islamic craftsmen had long used gold tooling, and this practice reached Venice shortly after 1450. Accompanying the development of printing, the decoration of bindings became ever more spectacular, and was encouraged by bibliophiles such as

Henry II and Diana de Poitiers, Jean Grolier, Thomas Mahieu and Thomas Wotton. If few can afford such provenances, it is quite possible to buy 16th and 17th century bindings, often tooled with the crest or blocked with the arms of the original owner. The period after Charles II's Restoration was the "Golden Age" of English bookbinding, when full use was made of the newly imported brightly coloured goatskin, and designs were taken from Persian rugs. The leading workshop was run by Samuel Mearne and his son, Charles. The attribution of a binding to a particular individual or workshop will certainly enhance its value, but optimistic notes such as "Bound by Mearne" should be treated with great caution. Most binders of this period remain anonymous, although some are known after their clients, such as "the Queen's Binders"; by their use of a distinctive tool, as in the "Small Carnation Binder"; or by a characteristic design, like "the Centre-Rectangle Binder". There have been vast advances in the study and documentation of

◀ **Sangorski and Sutcliffe**
John Keats, *Some Poems*, for
T.J. Gannon, 1912–14. Illuminated
manuscript on vellum with miniatures
and decorations by Ewen Geddes.
This Sangorski and Sutcliffe jewelled
binding comprises 1,027 jewels.
£150,000–200,000

▲ **Embroidered binding**
The Booke of Common Prayer,
Bonham Norton and John Bill, 1629
bound with *The Whole Book of
Psalms*. Imprinted for the Company
of Stationers, 1630, 2 volumes in
one. Contemporary white satin
embroidered in coloured silk, silver
wire and spangles. **£400–850**

binding history over the last 50 years, and books on bookbinding are in themselves a challenging subject to collect.

In the 18th century, some magnificent bindings were produced in Ireland and Scotland, the likes of which were never attempted elsewhere. In England, Roger Payne gained notoriety for his work (and his drinking), and provincial binders such as the Edwards firm of Halifax came into prominence. The market for fine bindings also encouraged an influx of Germans, such as Andreas Linde and Christian Kalthoeber.

From the 1820s publishers began issuing editions of their works in uniform, and increasingly decorative, cloth bindings, ready for the shelves. This by no means spelt the end of the tradition of fine binding, and whilst some designs tended towards retrospection, use was made of new materials, such as papier-mâché, and new methods, such as embossing the covers with large blocks. Great binderies continued to be founded, such as Rivière, established in Bath in 1829, and

Sangorski and Sutcliffe, set up in 1901. These two firms were soon vying with each other over the splendour of their work, much of it for wealthy Americans. Rivière's great series of "Leipzig bindings" survived the First World War, but Sangorski and Sutcliffe's great "Omar" was lost with the sinking of the *Titanic*. This magnificent binding on the *Rubáiyát* comprised 1,051 jewels and over 5,000 pieces of inlaid and onlaid leather.

At the end of the 19th century, T.J. Cobden-Sanderson, a disillusioned lawyer, revolutionized bookbinding design and practices in Britain. He was an inspiration for numerous individuals, including a number of women, such as Sarah Prideaux, Katherine Adams and Sybil Pye. Binders are no longer nameless craftspeople, and French designers in particular, such as Pierre Legrain and Paul Bonet, are regarded as artists, with their works commanding high prices. The techniques of binding and the underlying inspiration remain, however, largely unchanged.

EDWARD BAYNTUN-COWARD

◄ **16th century blind-tooled**
Marcus Fabius Quintilianus, *Institutionum oratoriarum libri XII*, Paris, Robert Estienne, 1542. Contemporary blind-stamped pigskin with clasps. **£300–500**

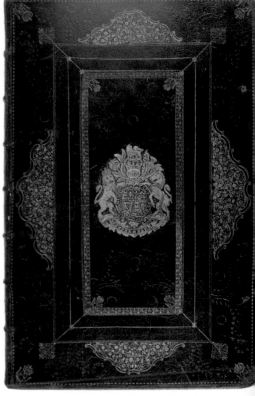

► **"The Devotional Binder"**
Richard Allestree, *The Whole Duty of Man*, R. Norton for Robert Pawlet, 1682. Contemporary red goatskin, tooled in gilt, heightened with black and silver paint. The use of the distinctive large sunflower tool in each corner and at the sides caused this binder, active in London between 1670 and 1685, to be christened the Devotional Binder. **£2,500–3,500**

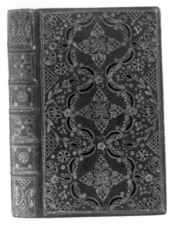

▲ **Late 17th- to early 18th-century English armorial**
The Book of Common Prayer, Oxford, University Printers, 1701. Contemporary calf, tooled in blind and gilt, with the arms of Queen Anne. **£1,000–1,500**

Fine Bindings

The greatest and most beautiful bindings are an exceptionally expensive area to collect. Great collections of bindings formed in the past by bibliophiles like Major Abbey and more recent collections such as the Chevalier Collection of 19th- and 20th-century Rivière and Sangorski and Sutcliffe bindings would take vast resources to put together today. The bindings fashioned for Jean Grolier, one of the greatest patrons ever, are beyond the reach of all but the very rich, if indeed his bindings ever come onto the market; but the aspiring collector should at the very least be aware of Grolier's name and importance. Fine collections of the great 20th-century French binders such as Rose Adler and Pierre Legrain, do exist, but most libraries have only a few representative selections of these bindings costing many thousands of pounds. Major Abbey's collection of fine bindings assembled over many years occasioned a series of sale catalogues from Sotheby's auction house (21 June 1965 to 19 October 1970), as well as two books on the collection, G.D. Hobson's *English Bindings in the Library of J.R. Abbey* (1940) and A.R.A. Hobson's *French and Italian Collectors and their bindings illustrated from examples in the library of J.R. Abbey* (1953), all of which are invaluable reference works.

So how is one to amass a collection of bindings if that is where one's interest lies? There are several paths down which a collector could pass but all should begin with a good knowledge of the techniques of binding, the historical background and a careful study of books, catalogues and institutional

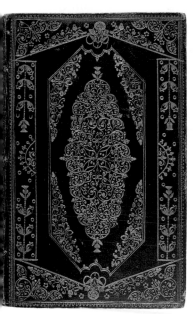

► Edwards of Halifax

Gregorio Leti, *The Life of Pope Sixtus the Fifth*, Dublin, W. Colles, 1779. Contemporary painted vellum, with the arms of the Harrington family on the covers, dated 1778. These painted vellum bindings were revived by Cedric Chivers of Bath at the end of the 19th century, although with significant differences in techniques.
£1,000–2,000

◄ Unidentified early 18th century

Blank book, London, c.1720–30. Contemporary black goatskin, tooled in gilt with an all-over "cottage-roof" pattern. An attractive binding, but like so many of this period difficult to attribute to a specific workshop.
£200–400

▼ Christian Kalthoeber

Augustin, Freiherr von Meyerberg, *Iter im Moschoviam ... ab Augustissimo Romanorum Imperatore Leopoldo*, 1661. Late 18th-century red straight-grained goatskin, tooled in gilt with Greek-key border, a large urn supported by a pair of mermaids. Kalthoeber was one of the finest craftsmen of this period and his distinctive mermaid tools appear on a number of bindings. German by birth, he was drawn to London by the amount of work available and was considered at the time to be the greatest binder of his day.
£3,000–4,000

collections for reference. One should then choose whether to build a representative chronological collection, or a specific and focused collection such as one centred around regional or armorial bindings.

It is still possible to pick up without too much difficulty and for quite modest sums 16th- and 17th-century armorial bindings. Often it is easy to identify the arms, but there is always detective work that can be done. Early blind-tooled bindings can often be found on books whose content is uninspiring – family Bibles, prayer books and other such pious works – hence lowering the price for the collector of bindings. Oldham's *Blind-Stamped Bindings* (1952) and *Blind-Panels of English Binders* (1958), are invaluable reference works for the identification of tools and binders from this period. Generally the greater or

more interesting the content, then the better or more expensive the binding. Fine travel books and the works of the great names of literature will have been owned by the wealthy who could afford to employ the best binders. If one simply desires to collect decorative books then there will be a wealth of pretty calf-bound volumes with ornately tooled gilt spines from the 18th and 19th centuries, the binders unnamed, but the books themselves eminently attractive. Books of blank paper were often bound up, known as "blank books", and particularly attractive examples from the early 18th century can be found for relatively inexpensive sums. As with anything, fashions will also dictate prices: if the fashion at the moment is for Regency morocco grandly and ornately tooled in gilt, or for French red morocco,

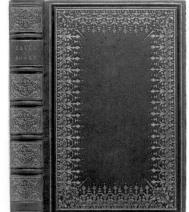

Parables of Our Lord, chromolithographs by Henry Noel Humphreys, Longman, 1847. Original morocco-backed papier-mâché covered boards. **£80–150**

► **Charles Lewis**
Thomas Moore, *Lallah Rookh, an Oriental Romance*, Longman, 1838. Contemporary green morocco, tooled in gilt and blind, dentelle-style border. Charles Lewis was one of the leading English binders in the early part of the 19th century. **£150–250**

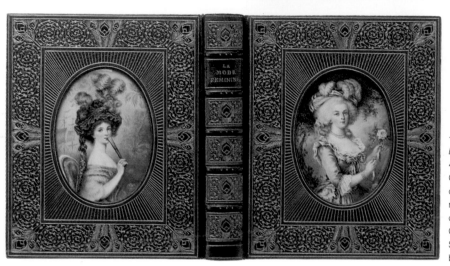

◄ **Rivière & Son**
La mode feminine de 1490 à 1645, 4 volumes in one, Paris, c.1920. Contemporary green morocco ornately tooled in gilt with onlaid red morocco. Each cover has a large oval portrait miniature by Miss C.B. Currie. Competitors of Sangorski and Sutcliffe, Rivière were commissioned by booksellers Henry Sotheran to produce these bindings with onlaid portrait miniatures, the best of which were painted by Miss Currie. **£800–1,200**

then the aspiring collector will probably do well to steer clear for the moment.

A good collection could be amassed of bindings of the Victorian era, about which Ruari McLean has written several books, including *Victorian Publishers' Book-Bindings in Paper* (1983). This was an era of great advances and variety in the covering of books: decorative paper over boards, and decorative cloth, as well as more ambitious techniques such as papier-mâché bindings. These decorative non-leather bindings alone could provide a satisfying collection without too much outlay. Alternatively one could focus on the good 19th-century binders such as Charles Lewis, Francis Bedford or James Hayday, or those who worked with painted vellum bindings such as the firm of Cedric Chivers, following on from the work of Edwards of Halifax (patent

granted 1785) in the late 18th century. These trade bindings were technically almost perfect and highly prolific. At the turn of the century the Glasgow publishers, Blackie, employed some of the finest artists to design their standard covers, including Talwin Morris. This is a neglected area that could provide rich hunting for an aspiring collector; as could the cloth bindings designed by Charles Ricketts, used by Macmillan on their reissues of classic novels; and the decorative trade bindings from 1880s America. Once the pictorial dust-jacket caught the public's imagination these all but disappeared.

The great private presses of the 20th century all employed binders for their special editions. A book bound by Thomas Cobden-Sanderson for the Doves Press will be considerably more than an unsigned binding for the same press (even though the same

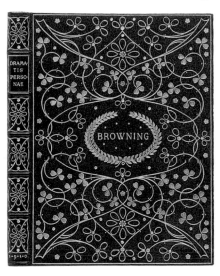

▲ **Sybil Pye**
T. Sturge Moore, *The Little School*, one of 10 copies on vellum, Eragny Press, 1906. Original green morocco, tooled in gilt with onlaid vellum.
£5,000–6,000

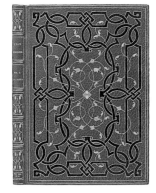

◀ **Henry Stikeman**
Andrew Williams, *Jean Grolier de Servier, Viscount d'Aguisy. Some account of his life and of his famous library*, New York, De Vinne Press, 1892. Contemporary brown morocco tooled in gilt, with onlaid morocco strapwork. This Grolier-style binding was executed by one of America's leading binders. **£600–800**

tools would have been used by an apprentice under his guidance in his workshop), or than those "fakes" of Doves bindings that are slowly being identified.

With judicious searching it is perfectly possible to form a collection of attractive and interesting bindings, simply steering clear of the big names. A little more work will have to be done, but then that is half the fun of collecting, and if eventually after much research one is able to place a name to a binding then all the better. One could form a representative collection of binding throughout the ages by looking for them in miniature format. Miniature books have always been bound to mirror their larger relations and one can find here embroidered bindings, jewelled bindings and painted vellum, all for a fraction of the cost of the full-size works. Try collecting books bound in decorative papers: the embossed papers of Germany and the Netherlands in the 16th to 18th centuries; the marbled papers of Italy and Spain from the 18th and 19th centuries; English marbled papers by the Arts and Crafts designers and artists of the 1920s and 1930s. Women binders have often been overlooked and this could be a good area to develop, although this field is attracting an increasing amount of interest. Historically, great collectors and librarians have concentrated on the grand decorative bindings, but there now appears to be more of a trend towards the actual structure: the materials and tools used take on as great an interest as the design itself. And so, accepting that the great collections will be duplicated with great difficulty, it is quite possible to collect in a different manner, requiring only imagination and not too large a budget.

Illustrated Books

Image versus text:
from Thomas Bewick
to Eric Gill; William
Hogarth to Arthur
Rackham; wood-
engravings to pictorial
dust-jackets

▲ **Gino Severini**
Fleurs et Masques, limited to 125 copies, 16 plates by
Gino Severini, coloured by hand through stencils and
heightened with gold, by J. Saudé, Etchells and
Macdonald, 1930. The illustrations are coloured by
pochoir. **£8,000–12,000**

The earliest form of illustration in
books was essentially decorative:
illuminated borders and initials
were added by hand to manuscripts,
developing into miniature pictures in the great
medieval works of art. With the birth of
printing came the woodcut, the earliest form
of printed book illustration. Although
originally crude and simple, the technique
matured and flourished over the centuries into
a highly effective form of illustration, as seen
in the work of Albrect Dürer, Hans Holbein,
Thomas Bewick, Gustave Doré and Eric Gill,
among others. Copper engraving was first
used in England in 1570, although its finer line
and greater detail was not utilized to the
fullest extent until the 17th century. This
technique was too costly for large editions,
however, and was quickly superseded by steel-
engraving in the 1820s.

Illustration in books during the 17th and
18th centuries, a time of typographic
achievement, was largely confined to a
frontispiece, decorative borders to the title-
page or text (often using printers' ornaments),
and small sentimental and decorative images.
The period also saw ambitious schemes such
as Boydell's Shakespeare Gallery – portraits by
painters which were then engraved; simple
chapbooks – small pamphlets with woodcut
illustrations, sold by travelling pedlars; and the
satirical engravings of Thomas Rowlandson
and George Cruikshank, capitalizing on an
era of political and social flux.

► **David Jones**
Robert Gibbings, *The Book of Jonah*, limited to 175 copies, 13 wood-engraved illustrations by David Jones, Golden Cockerel Press, 1926. **£500–1,000**

At the turn of the century the "illustrated book" really came into being. Two great contemporaries, Thomas Bewick, whose skill transformed the wood-engraving, and William Blake, the great poet, visionary and engraver, created books notable as much for the illustrations as for the text, and it is around this phenomenon that a collection of illustrated books is formed. The technical advances and rapid expansion of literacy in the 19th century led to the greater availability of inexpensive printed matter, which was often illustrated for wider appeal. Annuals and keepsakes with steel-engravings were all the rage from 1820 to 1850, affordable then and still so today. The 1840s saw the birth of the illustrated periodical (including *The Illustrated London News* and *Punch*) and the serialization of novels by Charles Dickens and others; both these factors contributed to the popularity of illustrators such as Richard Doyle, George Cruikshank and John Tenniel. These illustrators, together with the Pre-Raphaelite painters, Birkett Foster and other artists, worked with the Dalziel Brothers and Leighton Brothers, who skilfully transferred their drawings onto wood.

At the end of the 19th century, drawings were being photographed directly onto wood or metal for reproduction by the line-block, leaving artists such as William Morris and Eric Gill, who chose to continue working with wood or copper, to turn to the limited edition of the private press movement.

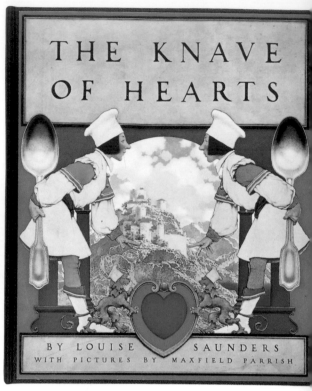

▼ Edward J. Detmold
Aesop, *The Fables*, 25 coloured plates by Edward
J. Detmold, Hodder and Stoughton, 1909. **£150–350**
One of 750 copies signed by the artist, £500–1,000

▲ Maxfield Parrish
Louise Saunders, *The Knave of Hearts*, 26 coloured
plates by Maxfield Parrish, New York, 1925. The last and
most famous book to be illustrated by Maxfield Parrish
and one of the greatest of American illustrated books.
£600–1,000

In the early days, colour had been added
by hand to the finished illustration, but in the
1840s experiments began in printing in colour.
Henry Noel Humphreys, Owen Jones and
George Baxter were some of the early
practitioners. The work of Marcus Ward and
Edmund Evans at the end of the 19th century
once again transformed book illustration and
with the advent of four-colour printing the
illustrative work of Arthur Rackham,
Edmund Dulac and Kay Nielsen could be
appreciated to the full. Publishers such as
Elkin Mathews, John Lane and J.M. Dent
commissioned fine editions of classic works,
often children's texts but intended for adults.
These were de luxe editions bound in vellum

with silk ties, and were limited in number and
signed by the artist. The plates both for the de
luxe editions and the ordinary unlimited trade
editions were printed in colour on glossy paper
and pasted in after the book was finished. The
trade editions were usually the same as the de
luxe editions, simply being bound in cloth and
not signed by the artist, although occasionally
they had fewer illustrations. The limited
editions are very much more expensive than
the ordinary editions, providing two levels of
collecting, according to budget.

Artists such as Claud Lovat Fraser and
William Nicholson were working at this
time with simple woodcuts or pen and ink
drawings, printed in colour or with colour

▼ **William Heath Robinson**
Uncle Lubin, coloured frontispiece and other
illustrations by the author, Grant Richards, 1902.
£150–300
His edition of Shakespeare's *A Midsummer
Night's Dream*, 1914, £50–100

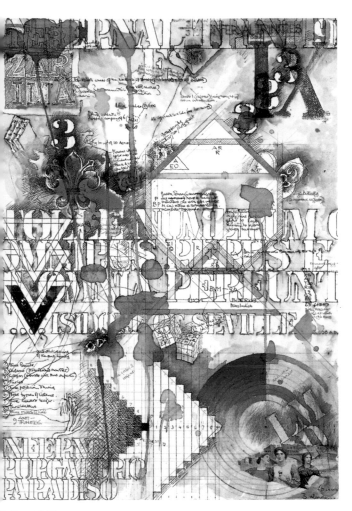

▲ **Tom Phillips**
Dante Alighieri, *The Divine Comedy*, translated by Tom
Phillips, limited to 185 copies, 140 plates by Tom
Phillips, printed from etched plates, lithographs,
screenprints or mixed processes, Talfourd Press, 1983.
£2,000–4,000

► **Edmund Dulac**
Hans Christian Andersen, *Stories*,
28 coloured plates by Edmund
Dulac, Hodder and Stoughton,
1911. **£40–80**
One of 750 copies signed by the
artist, bound in vellum, £300–600

added by hand. The illustrator, as opposed to
the writer, soon became the source of interest
and exhibitions of work completed for a
particular book were often held at venues
such as the Leicester Galleries in London.

From 1930 onward, book production
improved steadily. Many of the artists who
had been working for the small presses (Eric
Gill, Robert Gibbings and Charles Ricketts,
among others) began to turn their attentions to
more affordable books, as publishers such as
the Curwen Press, the Nonesuch Press, Faber,
the Folio Society and the Limited Editions
Club commissioned new works and editions
of classics. Graduates from art schools
(particularly Barnett Freedman, Rex

Whistler, Edward Ardizzone, Edward
Bawden and John Piper), worked on the
pictorial dust-jacket. Books on travel, cookery,
gardening, topography and architecture were
all made more attractive by the inclusion of
their illustrations. More recent artists who
have illustrated books include Andy Warhol,
Jim Dine, David Hockney, Ralph Steadman
and Ronald Searle. Most of these, whilst
issuing a few special copies signed by
themselves, produced the bulk of their work
in ordinary, unlimited, and therefore easily
affordable editions.

CATHERINE PORTER

▲ **William Hogarth**
Les Satyres de Guillaume Hogarth, Oeuvre Moral et Comique en LXIX Sujets, 79 engraved plates by or after William Hogarth, Robert Sayer, 1768. **£1,000–2,000**
Smaller edition of the same year issued by John Trusler for children, *Hogarth Moralized, being a Complete Edition of Hogarth's Works*, £150–300. Complete edition of Hogarth's works, 155 plates, 1822, £300–600

▼ **Francis Quarles**
Emblems, Divine and Moral, facsimile reprint of the first edition of 1635, illustrations, Chiswick Press, 1818. **£30–50**
An edition of 1692, £250–400; of 1736, £50–100

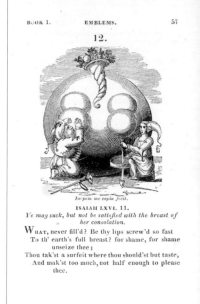

Early Illustrated Books

After the initial flourishing of the printed book with woodcut illustrations, there was a general decline in the illustration of books, ornamentation becoming merely decorative. The increasing use of copper-engraving resulted in portrait frontispieces and engraved title-pages, often historical or architectural in style with elaborate borders composed of columns and archways. The emphasis during the 17th and early 18th centuries was on perfecting the printed page, and ornaments were typographical rather than pictorial. There was at this time, however, a huge demand for emblem books – in which pictures were used as symbolic representation, accompanied by a motto and explanatory verses, all three elements being taken and understood as a whole. There were many religious emblem books in the 17th century; the most famous in English was by Francis Quarles in 1635, and often books for children were issued along the same lines. This is a wide field for the collector, and whilst early Latin examples from the 16th century may be beyond most pockets, later examples can be found with some searching and can provide a challenging study in deciphering the symbolism.

The latter part of the 18th century brought a broad variety of techniques as illustration processes became more sophisticated and artists and publishers more ambitious. The period encompasses the great moral engravings of William Hogarth, Richard Westall's sentimental illustrations for James Thomson's *The Seasons* (1816–17), the neoclassical illustrations of John Flaxman, the fine wood-engravings of Thomas Bewick and the grand copper-engravings of William Blake, making this a rewarding and varied area for the collector.

The birth of the English illustrated book is commonly considered the publication of Samuel Butler's *Hudibras* (1726) in an edition illustrated by William

Hogarth. Hogarth's fame rests, however, on his series of engravings, each of which tells a bawdy, tragic or comic story. His work, reminiscent of stage tableaux whilst full of political or social comment, was immensely popular, and was instrumental in achieving copyright for the engraver. His illustrations were reprinted numerous times during the 18th and 19th centuries in large format (the size of the originals) and scaled down for less expensive publications: the early engravings can be expensive, but these later collections are easier to find.

John Flaxman's simple line-engravings of classical scenes were reminiscent of scenes on Greek vases. He was employed by Wedgwood to supervise their draughtsmen in Rome, and whilst there was commissioned to illustrate Homer's *Odyssey* and *Iliad*, which were published in 1793. It was the widespread circulation of these works that contributed to his fame throughout Europe and his influence over succeeding generations of artists. Possibly not as fashionable today as they once were, Flaxman's books can be found for relatively low prices.

The original editions of Flaxman's great friend and pupil, William Blake (whose first book, *Poetical Sketches*, Flaxman commissioned in 1783), are much more expensive. *Songs of Innocence* (1789) was a forerunner of the later great mystical works in which, engraving his own text and illustrations, Blake tried to escape from what he perceived as the confines of materialism and a narrow Christianity. He died in obscurity, generally regarded as gifted but insane, and it was not until the mid-19th century that his visionary individuality was truly appreciated. The early works, particularly those with contemporary colouring, are extremely rare, but reprints were often made in the 19th and early 20th centuries, and these and the modern facsimile reprints by the Trianon Press in France, taken from original

BRITISH BIRDS. 75

THE RINGTAIL.

(*Falco Pygargus*, Lin.—*Soubuse*, Buff.)

ITS length is twenty inches; breadth three feet nine. Its bill is black; cere and irides yellow: the upper part of the body is dusky; the breast, belly, and thighs are of a yellowish brown, marked with oblong dusky spots; the rump white; from the back part of the head, behind the eyes to the throat, there is a line of whitish coloured feathers, forming a collar or wreath; under each eye there is a white spot; the tail is long, and marked with alternate brown and dusky bars: the legs are yellow; claws black.

THE LANNER.

(*Falco Lanarius*, Lin.—*Le Lanier*, Buff.)

THIS bird is somewhat less than the Buzzard. Its bill is blue; cere inclining to green; eyes yellow; the

K

◀ **Thomas Bewick**
A History of British Birds, 2 volumes, wood-engraved illustrations by Thomas Bewick, Newcastle, Edward Walker for Thomas Bewick, 1821. First published in 1797. **£75–150**

▲ **Richard Corbould**
An original watercolour drawing for an illustrated miniature edition of *Robinson Crusoe*, one in a series of popular novels and classics, c.1820–30. **£150–300**

coloured copies, are a good means of amassing a fine collection of Blake's work.

Whilst London was the centre of the literary and artistic world, it was in Newcastle that Thomas Bewick trained as a copper-plate engraver, and later turning his attention to wood. He proved to be a skilled and perceptive artist, and in *A General History of Quadrupeds* (1790) and *A History of British Birds* (1797–1804), he portrayed rural scenes, birds and animals more accurately and realistically than had ever before been achieved. Bewick's work, including his selections of fables, and excepting only his early and scarce children's books, remains

eminently affordable for the new collector, despite being highly esteemed and the subject of recent academic study. No collection of illustrated books would be complete without an example of his work.

Many of the illustrated books published between 1800 and 1830 were topographical by nature; books on architecture, costume and natural history were also popular and abundant. These are generally known as "colour-plate books", indicating the presence of fine illustrations coloured by hand; they are often sumptuous works and accordingly very expensive. They are dealt with elsewhere in more detail in the relevant chapters.

Collecting
The Caricaturists

▲ George Cruikshank
William Combe, *The Life of Napoleon*, aquatint title and
29 plates after George Cruikshank, coloured by hand,
Thomas Tegg, 1815. **£200–400**

T he golden age of English caricature
stretched from the late 18th to the mid-
19th century. The Grand Tour was at
the height of fashion and the culture of Italy
was the subject of intense fascination: the word
"caricature" comes from the Italian *caricare*,
meaning "to load or exaggerate". Hogarth's
earlier illustrative work typifying "characters"
broadened to include figures in politics and
foreign nationals, and graphic satire developed
into a highly potent force. Many amateur and
rather crude caricaturists merely used the
medium for their own ends, such as Henry
William Bunbury; one of the first to produce
hard-hitting work was James Gillray. His cruel
images and biting wit, applied to politicians and
the royal family to publicize their vices, ensured
he was constantly courted by those hoping to
avoid his attentions. His caricatures of Napoleon
were undoubtedly instrumental in rousing British
patriotism against the threat of invasion. Thomas
Rowlandson and William Combe produced a
series of parodies on the travel books of the
time, the adventures of "Dr. Syntax". George
Cruikshank, particularly prolific, produced a vast
amount of largely political caricature (although
he is possibly best remembered for his
illustrations to the works of authors such as
Charles Dickens, with whom he enjoyed a long
association, and children's books).

The caricaturists provide an insight into this
period of history and can still be found quite
easily today for varying prices, preserved in
simple wrappers, in panoramic form, as loose
prints or more finely bound.

◀ Thomas Rowlandson
William Combe, *The Tour of Doctor
Syntax in Search of a Wife*, engraved
title and 24 plates after Thomas
Rowlandson, coloured by hand,
R. Ackermann, 1821. Volume 3
of a trilogy comprising also *The Tour
of Doctor Syntax in Search of the
Picturesque* (1819) and *The Tour
of Doctor Syntax in Search of
Consolation* (1820). Many editions of
this work were published within a
short time and prices vary according
to the bindings. **£300–1,000**

The Story of Jack and the Giants, wood-engraved illustrations after Richard Doyle, coloured by hand, Cundall and Abbey, 1851. **£50–100**

◀ **L.M. Budgen**
Episodes of Insect Life, by Acheta Domestica, 3 volumes.
9 lithographed illustrations by the author, Reeve, Benham and Reeve, 1849–51. **£200–400**

▶ **Charles Bennett**
John Cragill Brough, *The Fairy Tales of Science*, 16 illustrations by Charles Bennett, 1859. **£50–100**

The 19th Century

Sentimental annuals of light-hearted verses with small steel-engraved illustrations were popular in the 1830s. Inexpensively produced then and generally overlooked now, they are very reasonable in price, and could form the basis of an attractive if not too serious collection. Few of the artists are known today, and only *The Keepsake* and *The Forget-Me-Not* boasted artists such as J.M.W. Turner and John Martin. The latter graduated from decorating china to depicting scenes from the Bible; his images of divine vengeance became immensely popular, the more catastrophic the better. His paintings were reproduced by the mezzotint, suited to his use of black, with shades of grey pierced by shafts of light. The prices of his books today reflect an increase in the value of his original prints and paintings.

The illustrated periodical, so important as a starting point for many artists, came into being under the guidance of the publisher Charles Knight. Aiming to bridge the gap between coarse woodcut pamphlets and learned magazines, he produced a series of journals from the late 1830s such as *The Penny Magazine*. These magazines, along with the illustrated periodicals from the end of the century, could make a demanding area for study and accumulation, often neglected and therefore low-priced. The quality of the illustrations, however, did not improve until the foundation of *Punch* in 1842, which attracted many of the best artists of the 19th century, including Birkett Foster, Alfred Crowquill and H.K. Browne (known as "Phiz"), who would later go on to illustrate books.

Punch's name was really made by the wood-engraved designs of three young artists: John Leech, Richard Doyle and John Tenniel. Leech was an untrained artist whose work was immensely popular,

▲ John Martin
John Milton, *Paradise Lost*, 2 volumes, 24 mezzotint
plates after John Martin, Septimus Prowett, 1827.
£800–2,000

especially his character the "Leech young lady".
Many of the characters he met out hunting appeared
in his illustrations for the Surtees novels *Handley
Cross* (1854) and *Mr Sponge's Sporting Tour* (1853).
Richard Doyle, son of John Doyle the caricaturist
and uncle of Sir Arthur Conan Doyle, designed the
famous cover of *Punch*. Illustrations for his own
works and for John Ruskin's *The King of the Golden
River* (1851) and William Allingham's *In Fairyland*
(1870) are filled with mythology and the fantastical
world of elves and fairies, anticipating the later work
of Arthur Rackham. Both illustrated works by
Dickens: Leech, *A Christmas Carol* (1843) and Doyle,
The Chimes (1845) and *The Cricket on the Hearth*
(1846). John Tenniel was best known for his illustrations to Lewis Carroll's *Alice's Adventures in Wonderland* (1865); much of his other work was political in
content, greatly influenced by Flaxman. His political

cartoons for *Punch* were numerous, two of the best
known being "The British Lion's Vengeance on The
Bengal Tiger" (1857), on the Indian Mutiny, and
"Dropping the Pilot" (1899), when Bismarck was
dismissed by the German Emperor. Although
Tenniel's greatest work in first edition for *Alice* is
known only in a few copies, his other work, as with
that of Leech and Doyle, makes good hunting for a
new collector. This era has often been overlooked,
perhaps because the illustrations are uncoloured and
have been overshadowed by the Edwardian illustrators. For the aspiring collector this means reasonable
prices, which, coupled with greater print runs at the
time of publication, provides wider availability of
some interesting books.

The majority of wood-engraved illustrations
were uncoloured, but change was on its way, with
experiments in printing in colour as the 19th century

▲ **Birkett Foster**

Thomas Hood, *Poems*, large-paper copy, engraved plates by Birkett Foster, E. Moxon, 1871. **£40–100**

▶ **Aubrey Beardsley**

Sir Thomas Malory, *Le Morte D'Arthur*, 2 volumes, limited to 1,500 copies, illustrations and decorations by Aubrey Beardsley, J.M. Dent, 1893–94. **£300–600**
Issued in the same year in 12 parts, £1,500–3,000; an edition of 300 copies on hand-made paper, £900–1,800; an edition published in 1927 including drawings omitted from first edition, £150–300

progressed. Henry Noel Humphreys was one of the first to use the technique of chromolithography, not only for reproductions of illuminated manuscripts but also for his own work; in *The Book of Ruth* (1850) he attempted in the manner of Blake to assimilate text and illustration. Owen Jones, his pupil, issued the first book with real chromolithographed plates, *Alhambra* (1841). Colour printing was also being experimented with by George Baxter, who printed from a mezzotint or aquatint background with colour laid on by means of wood-blocks, although it was not until the end of the century that the process was perfected by Edmund Evans. When one considers how important these early pioneers were, and takes into account the beauty of much of their work, their books today often seem underpriced; this is possibly the result of this whole period being overshadowed by the 1880s to 1930s.

With the advent of the line-block – the photographic transfer of a drawing directly onto wood or metal, a technique first used in 1876 – the artist could work to a much higher standard than had previously been possible, ensuring the quality of the end result. Many of the best illustrators of the 1870s and 1880s worked on children's books, including the designer, illustrator and writer Walter Crane. His art reference books and manuals, which he illustrated himself, are generally less expensive than his children's

books, and essential if one is to form a collection of his work. Crane played an important role in the Arts and Crafts movement, which asserted the value of good design and craftsmanship in the face of the increasing mechanization and mass production; his books provide a good background to the movement.

The final decade of the century produced some of its finest work. The Arts and Crafts movement created a framework for the private presses and the illustrative work of William Morris, Charles Ricketts and Lucien Pissarro, and encouraged the development of Art Nouveau with its decadence and use of the grotesque.

During this period, the illustrated magazine played an important role once again. Titles often lasted for only a few issues, such as the Birmingham Guild of Handicraft's *The Quest* (1894–96), but all determined to be "new", to shock and delight before the new century dawned. The best known, *The Savoy* and *The Yellow Book*, were vehicles for Aubrey Beardsley, whose work encompasses the mythological illustrations for Malory's *Morte D'Arthur* (1893– 94), and the decadence and eroticism in Jonson's *Volpone* (1898) and Wilde's *Salomé* (1893). Beardsley was highly influential over later illustrators; limited editions of his work, often bound in silk or pictorial vellum, command high prices, but ordinary editions are quite affordable.

Collecting
Illustrators of the 1860s

▲ John Everett Millais
Millais's Illustrations, a Collection of Drawings on Wood,
80 wood-engraved illustrations by John Millais,
Alexander Strahan, 1866. **£60–120**

Following the unadventurous years of the 1830s and 1840s, artists looked back to the work of Bewick and Flaxman, and the period from 1855 to 1870 saw a depth of maturity achieved in wood-engraving. The artists were fortunate to have skilled engravers such as the Dalziel Brothers and the Leighton Brothers who were able to translate their drawings onto wood sympathetically. The Pre-Raphaelite Brotherhood of John Everett Millais, Sir Edward Burne-Jones and Dante Gabriel Rossetti all contributed to books, illustrating myths and legends as well as contemporary poetry, as did Arthur Hughes for Christina Rossetti's *Sing-song* (1872).

Parables of Our Lord (1863), is a good representation of the mystical side of this era; illustrated by Millais, this was a labour of love, taking as long as six years to complete. Some of the work of this time is topographical or with a strong rural overtone, with other books concerned with mythology and the fairy-tale, providing a wide range of styles. Many of the books from this period have particularly fine decorated cloth bindings, and whilst some collectors concentrate on these, others form a collection of Pre-Raphaelite book-work, which is still relatively easy to pick up for quite modest sums. A recent exhibition at the British Museum was accompanied by a fine catalogue which will prove to be an invaluable work of reference for those interested in this period.

◄ Sir Edward Burne-Jones
The Flower Book, limited to 300 copies, 38 facsimile reproductions of watercolours by Edward Burne-Jones, Fine Art Society, 1905. **£4,000–8,000**
Burne-Jones's first illustrated book, Archibald Maclaren's *The Fairy Family*, 1857, £150–300

▲ **Arthur Rackham**
Hans Christian Andersen, *Fairy Tales*, 12 coloured
plates and other illustrations by Arthur Rackham,
Harrap, 1932. **£100–250**
One of 525 copies signed by the artist and bound in
vellum, £500–1,000

▼ **E.S. Hardy**
Hans Christian Andersen, *Stories*, 6 coloured plates
and other illustrations by E.S. Hardy, c.1900. **£30–60**

20th-Century Illustrators

The early years of the 20th century are often called "the golden age of illustration". One of the most prolific of the illustrators was Arthur Rackham. Having joined the periodical *The Westminster Budget* in 1892, he concentrated on the illustration of books, in particular those with a mystical or mythological content. His painting often displays a disturbing ambiguity, a mixture of the familiar and the threatening. This is clearly seen in his depiction of trees, the forms of which become strangely human. One of Rackham's most sought-after works is *Peter Pan in Kensington Gardens* (1906).

Edmund Dulac was born in France but settled in London, establishing himself alongside Rackham. His greatest interests and influences lay in the Middle and Far East, reflected in his minute detail and vibrant jewel-like colours, reminiscent of Persian miniatures. Blue, in all its shades, was a particular favourite. Dulac's other work included stamp and bank-note designs, those for the Second World War resistance movement, the Free French, being especially important to him.

Theatre was the inspiration of the Danish artist Kay Nielsen, a set- and costume-designer for the Royal Danish Theatre. He lived briefly in London, and then finally settled in America, where he worked on Walt Disney's *Fantasia*, amongst other films. His reputation rests on four books: Hans Andersen's *Fairy Tales* (1924), *East of the Sun and West of the Moon* (1914), *Hansel and Gretel* (1925) and *In Powder and Crinoline* (1913). His illustrations are theatrical, stylized and full of intricate detail, with figures appearing in ornate costumes set against elaborate backdrops.

The three brothers, William Heath Robinson, Charles Robinson and Thomas Heath Robinson, were all illustrators working in varying styles. Charles worked mostly in black and white, his images encompassing highly decorative borders and lettering, swirling lines circling innocent child faces,

▲ **Willy Pogany**

Johann Wolfgang von Goethe,
Faust, 30 coloured plates by Willy
Pogany, Hutchinson, 1908. **£50–80**
One of 250 copies signed by the
artist, £250–500

▶ **Rex Whistler**

Hans Christian Andersen, *Fairy Tales
and Legends*, illustrations by Rex
Whistler, Cobden-Sanderson, 1935.
One of 200 copies signed by the
artist and specially bound. **£400–800**
Ordinary copy, £50–100

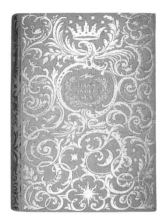

as seen in his edition of Robert Louis Stevenson's
A Child's Garden of Verses (1896). William Heath
Robinson, who is best known for his inventions and
contraptions satirizing the mechanization of the
20th century, also illustrated his own popular stories,
Uncle Lubin (1902) and *Bill the Minder* (1912), as well
as the works of Rabelais and Shakespeare.

Dublin-born Harry Clarke trained as a stained-
glass artist and textile designer, a background that,
alongside the influence of Aubrey Beardsley, helped
shape his illustrative work.

Shading and texture are integral to his designs,
which are often dramatic and sinister, with a powerful use of black and white.

Willy Pogany was born in Hungary and worked
initially in Paris and New York as an interior and
set designer. He went on to join Nielsen in
Hollywood as an art director for Warner and First
National Studios. He illustrated myths and legends
alongside his contemporaries, in particular the

Germanic works of Richard Wagner and Goethe;
his work is usually quite distinctive, with calli-
graphic text and ornamental borders.

The work of twin brothers Edward Julius
Detmold and Maurice Detmold was quite unlike
that of any of their contemporaries. They worked
closely together studying at the Zoological Gardens
in London and at an early age exhibited watercolours of animals and birds, issuing two portfolios
of illustrations *Pictures from Birdland* (1899) and
Sixteen Illustrations from "The Jungle Book" (1903).
Their detailed subjects were often placed against
decorative architectural or landscaped backgrounds
and are marked by their strong use of colour.
Edward's later work, after Maurice's suicide, is reminiscent of Japanese woodcuts or watercolours.

All these artists generally produced work in
ordinary cloth-bound editions, as well as in de luxe
signed and limited editions that were generally
bound in vellum. The price differential can be five or

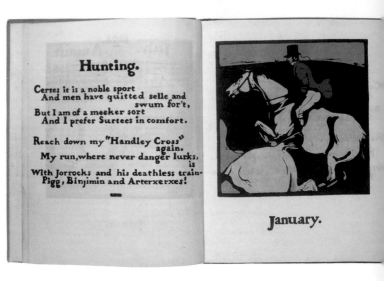

▼ Claud Lovat Fraser
Charles Cotton, *Poems from the Works of Charles Cotton*, illustrations by Claud Lovat Fraser, The Poetry Bookshop, 1922. **£15–40**

▲ William Nicholson
An Almanac of Twelve Sports, with words by Rudyard Kipling, 12 coloured lithographed illustrations after William Nicholson, Heinemann, 1898. The illustrations were reproduced from woodcuts by William Nicholson. **£200–450**
A few copies were printed directly from the woodcuts and coloured by hand by the artist. These are highly sought after. £8,000–20,000

ten times, providing two different levels of collecting, according to budget. One could choose to concentrate on a particular artist, but a comparative collection might be more rewarding. For example, one could concentrate on one author, such as Aesop or Hans Christian Andersen, and collect all the illustrated editions of that author's works. This could create a wide-ranging selection of illustrative work.

Sir William Russell Flint, who was apprenticed to a firm of lithographers in Edinburgh, initially worked as a medical illustrator. His illustrations are quite different from those of his contemporaries, reflecting both classical painting and Mediterranean life. His books and paintings of reclining women were extremely popular during his lifetime, and the prices of the books reflect the level of interest in his paintings.

The private press movement was breathing life back into the old technique of wood-engraving, and at the same time artists such as William Nicholson

and Claud Lovat Fraser experimented with cutting wood rather than engraving it, in styles reminiscent of the early chapbooks and work by Joseph Crawhall in the 19th century. Colour was often laid on by hand. Lovat Fraser's work was frequently reproduced from pen-and-ink drawings, often used simply as vignettes. The fragility of many of these books is not generally reflected in the prices, which have remained low.

Lovat Fraser also designed patterned papers for the Curwen Press and stage sets. Nicholson and his brother-in-law, James Pryde, produced bold and simple posters under the name of J. & W. Beggarstaff, inspired by the French posters of Henri de Toulouse-Lautrec.

Eric Gill was one of the greatest and most influential of all 20th-century illustrators. The majority of his illustrative work was for the St. Dominic's Press and the Golden Cockerel Press. A wood-engraver, sculptor, calligrapher and type-designer,

◀ **Eric Gill**
Robert Gibbings, *The Song of Songs*, limited to
750 copies signed by Robert Gibbings and Eric Gill,
19 wood-engraved illustrations by Eric Gill, Golden
Cockerel Press, 1925. **£350–700**
One of 30 copies coloured by hand by the artist,
£1,500–3,000.

SERENADE.

SOLOMON: How beautiful thou art, my love,
How beautiful thou art!
Thine eyes are like dove's eyes behind thy veil.
Thy hair is like a flock of goats adown the slope of Gilead,

24

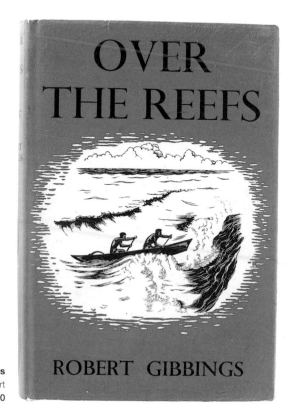

▶ **Robert Gibbings**
Over the Reefs, wood-engraved illustrations by Robert
Gibbings, J.M. Dent, 1948. **£15–30**

he also produced books for mass publication by Faber and Dent. His Perpetua and Gill Sans Serif typefaces have become modern classics. Gill was influenced by the Arts and Crafts movement, and was a convert to Roman Catholicism. His work is frequently a mixture of sensual and erotic imagery accompanying texts of a religious outlook. Gill's friend and contemporary Robert Gibbings founded the Society of Wood Engravers in 1919 and bought the Golden Cockerel Press in 1924, illustrating several of the Press's books himself, the majority of which were for ordinary publication. Inspired by his travels around England and further afield in Tahiti, he wrote and illustrated many works himself. The ordinary books of both Gill and Gibbings cost a fraction of the prices commanded by their limited editions and can provide a satisfactory method of starting a collection.

Book production was improving, and from the 1930s one no longer had to turn to private presses to find good wood-engraving. George Bernard Shaw's *Adventures of a Black Girl in her Search for God* (1932), with wood-engravings by John Farleigh, was the precursor of many books illustrated by, amongst others, Clare Leighton and Reynolds Stone.

The Nonesuch Press, founded by Francis Meynell in 1923, and the Curwen Press, produced remarkable illustrated books, limited in quantity but quite unlike other books from the earlier private presses, enabling fine artists such as Edward McKnight Kauffer, Barnett Freedman and Paul Nash to work freely. They produced a complete range of less expensive books, as well as grander works such as Nash's *Genesis* (1924). Nash's greatest work was Sir Thomas Browne's *Urne Buriall and the Garden of Cyrus* (1932), in which the illustrations were coloured by hand through stencils at the Curwen Press.

The Curwen Press had perfected this process of colouring (*pochoir*), developed in France by Jean

▼ **John Nash**
Walter de la Mare, *Seven Short Stories*, limited to 170 copies signed by the author and artist, illustrations by John Nash, 8 coloured by hand through stencils, Faber, 1931. **£100–200**

▶ **Edward Bawden**
Robert Herring, *Adam and Evelyn at Kew, or Revolt in the Gardens*, limited to 1,060 copies, illustrations coloured through stencils by Edward Bawden, Elkin Mathews & Marrot, 1930. **£50–100**

Saudé, and many of their best illustrated books were finished in this manner; they also coloured books for other publishers, including the Nonesuch Press. Artists such as John Nash and Albert Rutherston worked with stencils, although the majority of John Nash's illustrations were wood-engravings. To list the illustrators who worked for the Curwen Press is to name many of the greatest artists of the period: Edward Ardizzone, John Farleigh, John Nash, John Piper, Graham Sutherland, Edward McKnight Kauffer, Barnett Freedman, Eric Ravilious, Edward Bawden, Paul Nash, Albert Rutherston and Claud Lovat Fraser. A collection of books and ephemeral pieces such as decorated papers from this press would be a stimulating and inexpensive way of collecting many of the best artists of this century. Alternatively, try forming a collection of the series of "Ariel Poems" started in 1927 – each a single poem with one illustration by one of these artists, and issued in wrappers.

Edward Bawden trained at the Royal College of Art under Paul Nash and was a close friend of Eric Ravilious, another great illustrator, who was killed in the Second World War. He gained a Diploma in Book Illustration and continued studying and teaching part-time for many years. The techniques of his book illustrations range from linocuts to the lineblock, the lithograph to the coloured stencil, and include a wide variety of titles, from cookery books to *Gulliver's Travels*. He was an official War Artist in France and the Middle East, producing powerful descriptive images.

The Limited Editions Club in the United States and the Folio Society in Great Britain continued in the tradition of the Nonesuch Press after the Second World War, commissioning artists to illustrate works by living authors as well as classic texts. Barnett Freedman's illustrations to Leo Tolstoy's *War and Peace* (1938) was a fine example from the former. These books have remained relatively inex-

So, 'Fair and softly,' John he cried,
But John he cried in vain;
That trot became a gallop soon,
In spite of curb and rein.

So stooping down, as needs he must
Who cannot sit upright,
He grasped the mane with both his hands,
And eke with all his might.

16

▲ Ronald Searle
William Cowper, *John Gilpin*, limited to 1,600 copies,
illustrations by Ronald Searle, Chiswick Press for Allen
Lane, 1952. Sir Allen Lane issued limited editions of
books at Christmas each year for presentation. **£20–45**

◄ Mervyn Peake
Burgess Drake, *The Book of Lyonne*,
illustrations and dust-jacket by
Mervyn Peake, The Falcon Press,
1952. **£40–80**

► John Piper
J.M. Richards, *The Castles on the
Ground*, coloured plates and dust-
jacket by John Piper, Architectural
Press, 1946. **£30–50**

pensive, and most good booksellers which specialize
in illustrated books will carry some of their titles.

There are many living artists illustrating books
which are both easy to find and a potentially rewarding collecting field for one with a limited budget,
also requiring one to search out new talent – always
challenging and often extremely satisfying.

Many of the best are illustrating children's
books. Ralph Steadman and Ronald Searle are both
humorous illustrators and caricaturists, although
the humour of their work is often balanced by a serious or sometimes even macabre or sinister element.
Both have contributed to *Punch*, amongst many
other periodicals. Searle's illustrations of the infamous schoolgirls of St. Trinian's and for the film
Those Magnificent Men in their Flying Machines
(1965), and Steadman's edition of *Alice's Adventures
in Wonderland* (1967) and more recently his work for
advertising campaigns, have made them both household names.

The dust-jacket as a protective covering
became familiar in the early part of this
century, and was initially plain, featuring only
the title and the author. Publishers soon began
to commission artists to decorate these covers,
making the books themselves commercially
more attractive. Many of the best 20th-century
illustrators have produced pictorial dust-jackets,
and this can be a rewarding and inexpensive way
of collecting their work.

John Piper, one of the most versatile 20th-
century artists – having worked in stained-glass,
with textiles, on stage and set designs, as a
painter and as a book-illustrator – has designed
numerous dust-jackets. The writer and artist
Mervyn Peake is famous in particular as the
author of the fantastical Gothic trilogy
Gormenghast. His best illustrative work is also
fantastical, whether it is interpreting his own
work for children and adults or that of others –
notably Lewis Carroll. Peake's dust-jackets
form a striking part of his work.

A great number of artists, including John
Minton, Edward Ardizzone and Rex Whistler,
can easily be collected in this manner, building
up an imaginative collection of cover designs and
a comprehensive body of artists' work.

Children's Books

Juvenile literature: from Old Mother Goose's Fairy-Tales to Peter Rabbit and Winnie the Pooh

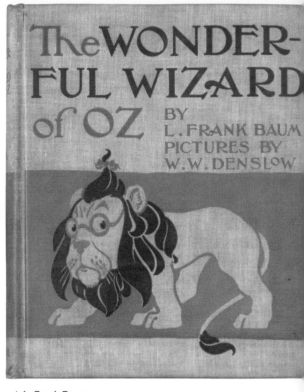

▲ **L. Frank Baum**
The Wonderful Wizard of Oz, Chicago, G.M. Hill, 1900, first edition, first issue, coloured illustrations by W.W. Denslow. There are complex issue points relating to the text and the binding, as well as several later editions, and prices can vary from a few hundred pounds for later issues in poor condition. **£4,000–8,000**
Later Oz titles £50–150

Until the early 18th century there were no books written specifically for children. Alongside the religious works considered suitable, they read works written for their parents, generally fables or mythology, adventures such as *Guy, Earl of Warwick*, Daniel Defoe's *The Adventures of Robinson Crusoe*, biblical tales such as John Bunyan's *The Pilgrim's Progress*, and allegories such as Jonathan Swift's *Gulliver's Travels*. These last three and Aesop's *Fables* were adapted for children many times during the following centuries, and are now considered children's tales. Travelling pedlars sold individual stories; and writing sheets were enlivened with pictures to make them more attractive to children. The French fairy-tales of Charles Perrault and Madame d'Aulnoy were translated into English by 1729, and were

no doubt read by children as well as adults.

It is children's books written for pleasure as opposed to for education that are of interest to most collectors. In 1740 Thomas Boreman published the first in a series of miniature books for children, *The Gigantick History of the Two Famous Giants and other Curiosities in the Guildhall*, in which history was taught through a series of visits to London's famous buildings. The success of these books, together with the changes in society as the English middle classes became more settled and stable after decades of civil war and social unrest, and a slow increase in literacy amongst all but the poorest people, encouraged other publishers to follow suit.

Around 1744 John Newbery published his first children's book, *A Little Pretty Pocket Book intended for the Instruction and*

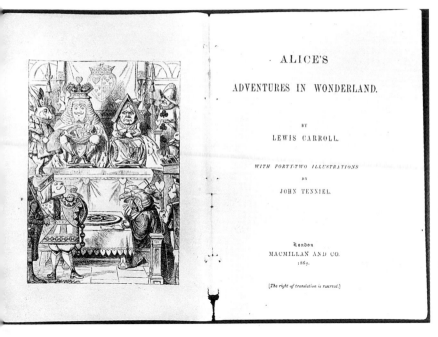

◄ **Charles Lutwidge Dodgson, "Lewis Carroll"**
Alice's Adventures in Wonderland, illustrations after John Tenniel, Macmillan, 1865. The first edition was recalled by Lewis Carroll; only about 25 copies are known of today. **£60,000–100,000**
Reissued with a new title-page for America, D. Appleton, 1866, £2,000–4,000; second (first published) edition, 1866, £1,200–2,000; later editions easily available under £50

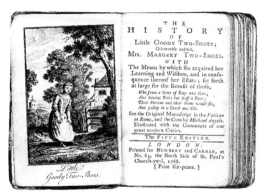

► *The History of Little Goody Two-Shoes, otherwise called Mrs. Margery Two-Shoes*
fifth edition, engraved frontispiece, woodcut illustrations, Newbery and Carnan, 1768. First published in 1765; very few early editions have survived. **£2,000–5,000**
Reprinted many times by numerous publishers; later editions from the early 19th century, under £200

Amusement of Little Master Tommy and Pretty Miss Polly, with an agreeable Letter to read from Jack the Giant Killer, of which the earliest known copy still in existence is dated 1760. It contains a mixture of fables, fairy-tales, romance and education, accompanied by an alphabet, and illustrated with woodcuts of children playing games. 1744 also saw publication of *The Child's Guide to Polite Learning ... for the instruction of Little Master Tommy and Pretty Miss Polly*. Newbery was the founder of an important firm who published many of the best and most important of early children's books. These early children's books are fragile and scarce; immensely popular at the time, it is hardly surprising they have not survived in great numbers. This and the high monetary value of such works makes them difficult for a new collector to find. John

Harris, William Darton, Benjamin Tabart, the Wallis family and John Marshall all came bursting onto the scene as prolific publishers of books for children, whether these were fables, nursery rhymes, fairy-tales or light-hearted educational books.

With the spread of literacy and less expensive printing processes came greater demand for books and an increase in the physical size of the book. Pictorial wrappers were used as covers, and from 1832 the normal binding became cloth, with gilt blocking. Red, blue and green were the favourite colours. Other publishers entered this lucrative market, one of whom, Thomas Dean, survived until the mid-20th century.

There was a resurgence of interest in the fairy-tale during the 1820s with the "discovery" of Hans Christian Andersen,

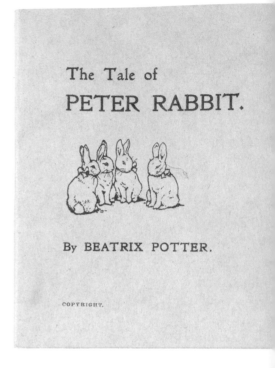

The Tale of Peter Rabbit, first edition, first issue, one of 250 copies, illustrations by author, 1901. **£10,000–30,000**
Presentation copy inscribed by author, £50,000–60,000

◄ **Anna Sewell**
Black Beauty, Jarrold and Sons,1877. There are three known states of the binding. **£1,000–2,000**

and the translation of the tales of the Brothers Grimm. The 1840s ushered in the adventure story, such as Captain Marryat's *Masterman Ready* (1841) and *Children of the New Forest* (1847); the 1850s saw W.G. Kingston, R.M. Ballantyne, Thomas Mayne Reid, Charles Kingsley and ultimately G.A. Henty create the "boy's adventure story". These were quite distinctive in their pictorial bindings depicting adventure and challenge. Robert Louis Stevenson's slightly later books *Treasure Island* (1883) and *Kidnapped* (1886) transcended this narrow field to become accepted as classics. Girls were less well catered for during this period, although the numerous books written by Juliana Horatia Ewing and Mrs. Molesworth were immensely popular from the 1860s onwards.

Two figures who tower over all others in the mid-19th century and who are as important today as then are Edward Lear, whose *A Book of Nonsense* was first published in 1846, and Lewis Carroll. Carroll's *Alice's Adventures in Wonderland* was first published in 1865 but almost immediately withdrawn from circulation owing to the quality of the printing of John Tenniel's illustrations; the book was reissued for 1866. First editions of both titles are extremely rare, therefore highly valuable and beyond the pockets of most people, if indeed they ever come up for sale.

In 1876 education became compulsory in Britain, further increasing the numbers of the reading public, who demanded better-quality books. With improvements in printing, and the process of colour printing perfected by

◄ A.A. Milne
Winnie the Pooh, first edition, illustrations by E.H. Shepard, Methuen, 1926. **£150–300**
With dust-jacket, £300–600; seventh edition from 1928 without dust-jacket, £20–40; *When We Were Very Young*, 1924, without dust-jacket, £400–600

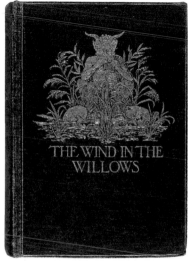

▲ Cicely Mary Barker
Flower Fairies of the Trees, coloured illustrations by the author, Glasgow, Blackie and Son, 1940. **£100–200**

► Kenneth Grahame
The Wind in the Willows, frontispiece by Graham Robertson, 1908. Prices for this edition vary considerably according to the condition of the binding. **£700–1,500**
Illustrated by Arthur Rackham, one of 500 copies, 1951, £500–800; illustrated by E.H. Shepard, one of 250 copies signed by the artist, 1971, £400–600

Marcus Ward and Edmund Evans, the late Victorian era was awash with coloured picture books by Kate Greenaway, Randolph Caldecott and Walter Crane, to name but a few. Other publishers, such as Ernest Nister and Hildesheimer and Faulkner, used colour printers in Bavaria, often producing books with moving pictures or pop-up three-dimensional scenes.

The fairy tale continued to thrive with Andrew Lang's series of *Fairy Books* published at the turn of the century. Animal fantasies became popular, echoing the tales of Grandville in France and Reiner Fuchs in Germany decades before. Beatrix Potter's invention of a rabbit named Peter in 1893 led to Kenneth Grahame's Ratty and Toad in *The Wind in the Willows* (1908), and on to A.A.

Milne's bear named Pooh in 1924. The 20th century has seen many animals as the central character of books, a trend still prevalent today.

Children's books are now a phenomenon in the world of publishing. Some of the best artists turn their hands to book illustration for children, many, such as Nicola Bayley and Alan Aldridge, following in the tradition of Edward Ardizzone and Maurice Sendak by both writing and illustrating their own work . The great classics in first edition of titles such as *Peter Rabbit* and *Alice* are legendary rarities, as are the important early books, and are thus expensive and beyond the reach of most collectors. There is still, however, a wealth of good material from all periods for the new collector to find.

CATHERINE PORTER

FRONTISPIECE

Robinson Crusoe Surprised at the mark of a human foot on the Sand.

▼ **Jonathan Swift**
The Adventures of Captain Gulliver in a Voyage to the Islands of Lilliput and Brobdignag, engraved frontispiece, wood-engraved illustrations, F. Newbery, 1772. First edition of this abridgement, probably the first specifically for children. Rare, even lacking leaves. **£500**
1781 Newbery edition, £1,500–3,000

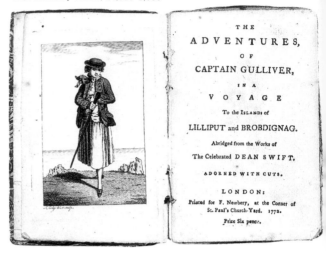

◀ **Daniel Defoe**
The Life and Surprising Adventures of Robinson Crusoe, engraved illustrations, Glasgow, J. Lumsden, c.1818. **£100–200**

The First Books for Children

There was no shortage of toys and games for the children of Tudor and Stuart England, and there are many contemporary references to or paintings of children at play with balls, hoops, tops and rattles. Outdoor games and kite-flying were commonplace, and children made numerous toys themselves. Schooling, however, was limited; most children were sent out to work whilst very young. Reading was not generally encouraged as a form of enjoyment, although the Arthurian legends, Fox's *Book of Martyrs* and similar subjects were favourites, as were Aesop's *Fables*, first translated by Caxton into English in 1484 and reissued numerous times in the following centuries. Sir Roger l'Estrange's new translation of 1692 was the one most favoured, as it was done specifically with children in mind. (In their use of animal characters, these fables have their 20th-century counterparts in Beatrix Potter's tales, and in the stories of characters like Babar or Rupert the Bear, although these do not have the prevailing moral tone of the early fables.) Calvinism and its strong moral stance was still influential in the 18th century and dictated much of the reading matter for a good many years.

Of the books written for adults that were adopted by children as their own, the two most important (and the least moralistic) are Daniel Defoe's *Robinson Crusoe* (1719) and Jonathan Swift's *Gulliver's Travels* (1726) – both still widely read today. Within a few months of first publication *Robinson Crusoe* was pirated and translated into many languages; it was abridged for the use of children in 1722. The elements of adventure and topsyturvyness of both books appealed to children, and anticipate later books. In 1715 Isaac Watts produced the first edition of his *Divine Songs Attempted in Easy Language for the Use of Children*, which became one of the most frequently reissued books; undoubtedly still a moral work, it is far more attractive and simple than anything written before. The first recorded appearance of a nursery rhyme in a book for children was "A was an Archer", which appeared in *Little Book* (1712), written by an author known only by the initials T.W. By 1800 many of the nursery rhymes known to us today had appeared in print for the first time.

It was when the publishers themselves awoke to the need for, and saw the profitable market in, books

Collecting
Chapbooks

THE HORSE AND THE STAG.

THE horse was once a free and a
noble creature, and galloped about the
16

▲ Aesop and others
*Fables Ancient and Modern adapted for the Use of
Children by Edward Baldwin*, 2 volumes, engraved
illustrations, Thomas Hodgkins, 1805. Edward Baldwin
was a pseudonym used by the radical philosopher
William Godwin. The illustrations in this rare adaptation
are possibly by William Mulready. **£500–1,000**

**◄ *The History of Sir Richard Whittington
and his Cat***
Woodcut illustrations, Birmingham,
T. Bloomer. **£100–200**

**▼ *Christmas Tales for the Instruction of
Good Boys and Girls by Mr. Solomon
Sobersides***
Engraved illustrations, Glasgow, J. Lumsden
and Son. **£100–200**
Chapbooks issued by Kendrew, Walker and
many other publishers can be found under
£50

for children, that the scene really changed. From
1770 to 1840 John Newbery, his nephew's wife
Elizabeth Newbery, John Harris and John Marshall
produced many of the best books. These 18th- and
early 19th-century books were issued in a small format, much smaller than today's children's books,
originally in boards covered with Dutch floral paper
(an embossed green and gold or orange and gold
paper), in printed wrappers, or occasionally in boards
with an inexpensive leather known as roan covering
the spine. Around 1780 these publishers began to
commission writers to produce stories for children,
the majority of whom were women. Mrs. Sarah
Trimmer was one of the most prolific writers for
children during this period, most of her books being
strongly moral or educative in tone. Her *Fabulous
Histories, designed for the Instruction of Children,
respecting their treatment of animals*, later known as
The History of Robins, was first published in 1786.
Well known and highly influential, she persisted in
attacking the fairy-tale, in particular "Cinderella", in
her magazine *The Guardian of Education* (1802–6), as
instilling in children "confused notions of wonderful
and supernatural events".

"Chapmen" were travelling pedlars or gypsies
who sold, amongst other things, news-sheets,
ballads, broadsides and inexpensive small books
known now as "chapbooks". Initially published
mostly in London, by the mid-18th century
chapbooks were issued in many provincial towns
for local sale; Newcastle, York, Derby, Glasgow
and Banbury became the most important. Adult
works, such as *Guy of Warwick* and *The Seven
Champions of Christendom,* were available in
inexpensive editions and read by children by the
end of the 17th century. Eighteenth-century
chapbooks usually consisted of 16 or 32 pages
bound in paper wrappers, or simply with the title
on the outer leaf. They had simple woodcut illustrations, were small in format, and cost between
one penny and sixpence. This was the reading
matter of the masses, adopted by children due to
the mixture of adventure, legend and fantasy.
Important publishers were James Kendrew of
York, James Lumsden and Son of Glasgow and
Rusher of Banbury, who all produced fables,
nursery rhymes, versions of *Gulliver's Travels,
Robinson Crusoe* or *Goody Two-Shoes*, and fairy-
tales. The fragility of the books and the attractive
woodcuts make them a rewarding collecting area,
and one that is still relatively inexpensive.

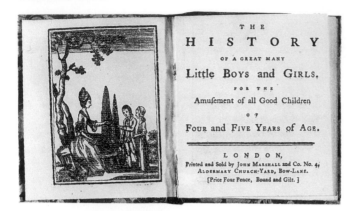

◀ **Dorothy Kilner**
The History of a Great Many Little Boys and Girls, possibly a first edition, wood-engraved illustrations, John Marshall, c.1777. The first editions of the early Kilner stories are notoriously hard to date. **£500–1,000** Later editions from the 1790s, **£200–400**

▶ **Lady Eleanor Fenn**
Mrs. Lovechild's Book of Three Hundred and Thirty-Six Cuts for Children, alphabets, engraved throughout and coloured by hand, Darton and Harvey, 1805. (There were earlier editions by John Marshall and Darton and Harvey of 1797 and 1801.) **£300–600**

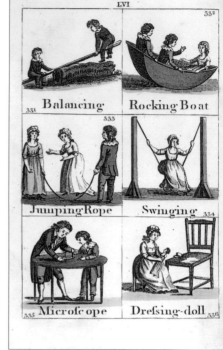

◀ *Cock Robin, a Pretty Painted Toy*
Wood-engraved illustrations coloured by hand, J. Harris, 1819. **£50–100**

19th-Century Children's Publishing

Several of the most popular and less moralistic authors, whose works were reprinted, were Dorothy Kilner, her sisters Mary Ann and Elizabeth Kilner, and Lady Eleanor Fenn, all of whom wrote for the publisher John Marshall under the pseudonyms "M.P.", "S.S.", "S.W." and "Mrs. Teachwell" respectively. The Kilner sisters lived in Essex and each wrote numerous stories, the most popular being *The Life and Perambulations of a Mouse* (?1784) and *The Memoirs of a Peg-Top* (?1781). Another pair of sisters, Jane and Ann Taylor, wrote some charming books of verse, quite natural and unlike anything before, including *Original Poems for Infant Minds* (1804) and later *Hymns for Infant Minds* (1810). It was in their *Rhymes for the Nursery* (1806) that "Twinkle, twinkle, little star" first appeared.

John Harris took over the publishing firm of Newbery in 1802, filled with new ideas, and over the next 30 years he proceeded to publish some of the most attractive books for children. He was one of the first to use the engraved illustration, often with the text engraved as well, employing colourists to enhance the illustrations; such titles were sold plain or coloured. Two of his most important books display this use of fine engraved illustrations, Sarah Catherine Martin's *The Comic Adventures of Old Mother Hubbard and her Dog* (1805), and William Roscoe's *The Butterfly's Ball* (1806). Both titles were reprinted time and time again, with sequels and pastiches pouring out; the sequel to the latter was Mrs. Dorset's *The Peacock at Home* (1807).

John Harris had discovered a formula that kept children amused with no ulterior moralistic or didactic purpose. The firm of Harris continued publishing until 1843, when it merged with Griffith and Farran. By this time many other publishers, such as Dean and Munday, the Dartons, Tabart and Joseph Cundall, had flourishing lists of children's books. Dean and Munday specialized in issuing books of verse with pictures such as *Gaping, Wide-Mouthed,*

◄ Heinrich Hoffmann
The English Struwwelpeter, or Pretty Stories and Funny Pictures, illustrations by the author, coloured by hand, Leipzig, Friedrich Volckmar, 1848, first edition in English. **£2,500–5,000**
The first German edition was published in 1845 and is extremely rare. Later copies published by Routledge and Blackie available for under £50

Collecting Fairy-tales

► Andrew Lang
The Olive Fairy Book, first edition, coloured plates and other illustrations by H.J. Ford, Longmans, Green & Co., 1907. **£60–140**

▼ Edward Lear
A Book of Nonsense by Derry Down Derry, lithographed title and illustrations, Thomas McLean, 1846. First edition issued anonymously in two parts is now rare.
Each part **£2,000–4,000**
Later editions from 1855, £800–1,500; 1862, £200–400

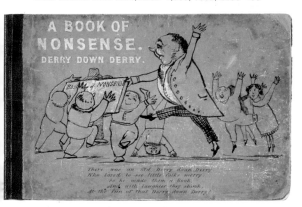

◄ Charles Perrault
Histories or Tales of Past Times, told by Mother Goose, with Morals … Englished by G.M. Gent, woodcut illustrations, J, Harris, c.1803. Rare edition of Perrault fairy tales collected for children.
£2,500–4,000
All editions from 17th and 18th centuries will be similarly priced, but there are numerous selections of Perrault's tales to be found in English and French from the early 19th century, published by Lumsden, Kendrew, Harris and others, £200–600

Waddling Frog and *Dame Wiggins of Lee*. Issued with coloured illustrations, sometimes printed on untearable cloth and larger in format than most of the Harris books, these were precursors of the "toy books" produced in the latter part of the century. The mid-19th century also saw, for the first time, the illustrations becoming as important, if not more so, than the text. In 1845, two different but equally important books of verse appeared, both cautionary and fantastical tales, in which the text and illustrations are interdependent: the German Heinrich Hoffmann's *Struwwelpeter*, and Edward Lear's *A Book of Nonsense*. *Struwwelpeter* was translated into English in 1848. Both volumes were reissued many times before the end of the century and are still widely read today; the later editions are easy to find and form an essential part of any collection of children's books.

Almost 100 years after Thomas Boreman produced his successful miniature books for children in

Fairy-tales were originally written for adults, and the well-loved characters of Little Red Riding-Hood, Sleeping Beauty, Cinderella and Puss in Boots first appeared in Charles Perrault's *Histoires ou contes du temps passé* (1697). Fairy-tales were told at literary salons in France attended by Perrault and Madame d'Aulnoy; a selection were published in 1785 as *Cabinet des Fées*, complete in 14 volumes. These tales were quickly adopted by children and were adapted in chapbook form alongside the English tales of Jack the Giant-Killer, Dick Whittington and Tom Thumb. They were later re-issued by John Harris and other children's publishers. No new fairy-tales appeared until 1812, when the Grimm brothers began to publish their collections. These were translated into English and illustrated by Cruikshank (1823–26). In 1846 Mary Howitt published her translation of Hans Andersen's fairy-tales, *Wonderful Stories for Children*. These four groups of tales have remained the favourites to this day, along with George Macdonald's *At the Back of the North Wind* (1871) and *The Princess and the Goblin* (1872) and followed by Lang's fairy-story collections, of which *The Blue Fairy Book* (1889) was the first. No collection of children's books would be complete without fairy-tales, and they are to be found at all prices.

◄ Kate Greenaway
A Day in a Child's Life, coloured illustrations by the author, George Routledge, 1881. **£50–100**

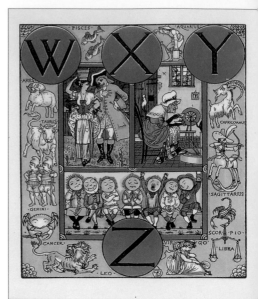

► Goody Two-Shoes Picture Book
coloured plates by Walter Crane, George Routledge, 1875. **£100–200**

the 1740s, the categories into which children's books are still conventionally divided had been firmly established, with authors and publishers realizing that boys and girls liked different books. Between 1841 and 1849 Henry Cole and Joseph Cundall issued their "Home Treasury" series, echoing the earlier tales of romance and adventure and adult books by the likes of Sir Walter Scott and William Ainsworth. These small books, on good paper, illustrated and bound in decorative wrappers or boards, were popular; they reissued tales of adventure and history alongside fairy-tales and fables.

Captain Frederick Marryat's *Masterman Ready* (1841) was the first of many adventure stories for boys; numerous authors turned their hand to this genre during the latter part of the 19th century. James Fenimore Cooper's tales of American frontier and pioneer life were avidly taken up in Britain, *The Last of the Mohicans* (1826) being the best known. The most popular writers of this genre were William Kingston, R.M. Ballantyne (whose *Coral Island* was published in 1857) and George Henty. Henty, a war correspondent, wrote over 35 stories for boys, many reissued several times in his life. The adventure books, set in the contemporary era or the past, were full of action and honourable ideals, with heroes who were always honest and trusting in God; in their attractive pictorial bindings they make fascinating collecting. Robert Louis Stevenson took this genre to the end of the century; *Treasure Island* (1883), the best of his stories and the first adventure story with no overtly didactic aim, is enduringly popular and his most collectable work today. His other books can be picked up at a fraction of the cost.

Another dominant theme of the middle of the century was fantasy (already seen in *Struwwelpeter* and *A Book of Nonsense*), explored with spectacular success by a Cambridge lecturer in mathematics, the Reverend Charles Lutwidge Dodgson – better known as Lewis Carroll. The story of Alice was told on a boat-trip on the river to three young girls from the Liddell family and written out later for the eldest, Alice; at first entitled *Alice's Adventures Under Ground*, it was illustrated by Carroll himself. He later altered the story and expanded it into *Alice's Adventures in Wonderland* (1865), with wood-engraved illustrations after drawings by John Tenniel; one of the most scarce and expensive of children's books in first edition.

The initial printing of the drawings was unsatisfactory, and Carroll recalled all the copies printed in 1865, reissued them with a new title-page and shipped them to America with the title-page dated 1866. Another printing was done and the first published edition in England came out in December 1865, dated for 1866. Only about 25 copies of the book with the 1865 title-page are known, the majority now in libraries. Despite other books such as *The Hunting of the Snark* (1876), and *Sylvie and Bruno* (1889–93), Carroll's fame rests on *Alice* and its sequel *Through the Looking-Glass* (1872); both have been reissued many times and with numerous accomplished illustrators, from Arthur Rackham to Salvador Dali, Barry Moser to Ralph Steadman.

In the last few decades of the 19th century adventure stories continued to be produced; school stories, family sagas and animal tales were popular for girls, with authors including Mrs. Molesworth, Juliana

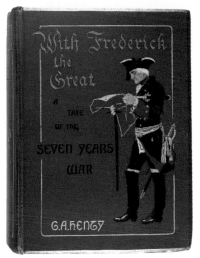

▲ G.A. Henty
With Frederick the Great, first edition, plates by
Wal Paget, Blackie and Son, 1898. **£40–80**

◄ Lothar Meggendorfer
Look at Me!, coloured illustrations,
the moving parts operated by levers,
H. Grevel & Co., c.1900. First
published in Germany and quickly
brought out in England, many have
survived in working order. **£400–800**

► Sweets from Fairyland
Chromolithographed illustrations,
each with a lever operating
sliding slats which change the
image, Ernest Nister, c.1895.
£300–600

Horatia Ewing and E. Nesbit (whose greatest success was *The Story of the Treasure-Seekers*, 1899).

This is, however, the era of the picture book or "toy book", epitomized by three people, Kate Greenaway, Randolph Caldecott and Walter Crane. In the 1860s, publishers began to sell books to children mainly on the basis of the illustrations. Walter Crane, trained as a wood-engraver, illustrated toy books for several publishers between 1865 and 1900. The earliest was *The House That Jack Built*, published by Ward Lock and Tyler in 1865, with a further 29 titles issued before 1874. These toy books were based on fairy-tales and nursery rhymes, with striking, full-page coloured illustrations. Issued in a larger format than children's books to date, they were immediately successful and encouraged publishers such as George Routledge to commission Kate Greenaway and Randolph Caldecott.

The success of the toy books was largely a result of the advance in colour printing achieved by Edmund Evans, a wood-engraver and also printer employed by the publishers to execute the complete book from drawings to final completed version. It was with the work of Greenaway that Evans really excelled. The Kate Greenaway girls and boys first appeared on greetings cards and later in books, the first being *Under the Window* (1878). The entire first edition of 20,000 copies sold immediately – an extraordinary success. The freshness and innocence of children playing in period costume has appealed in varying degrees ever since. Randolph Caldecott also illustrated nursery rhymes and fairy-tales, producing a series of 16 picture books from 1875 to 1885, each, like Crane's, bound in pictorial wrappers.

Booksellers in the 18th century offered novelties, fans, spinning-tops and dolls, and printed games alongside their books to tempt children. Once the juvenile market was established publishers continued to offer these profitable novelties. Robert Sayer took over a print shop in Fleet Street in the middle of the 18th century and began to issue "harlequinades", books with coloured illustrations composed of flaps which lifted up to reveal an alternative illustration, so named due to Sayer's summaries of the pantomimes, or harlequinades, at the London theatres. These were popular for about 40 years, and other publishers soon adapted the concept of books with changing images. Dean & Son published some of the best moveable books from 1840, with flaps being moved horizontally or vertically; tabs or levers to pull slats were introduced. Lothar Meggendorfer in Germany was the skilful creator of a series of books in which figures or animals would move by means of hinged levers behind the image, operated by tabs. Ernest Nister, of Nuremberg, produced many books with beautifully printed colour illustrations, often three-dimensional pop-ups or dissolving views with sliding slats. Both publishers issued English editions. Due to the popularity and fragility of any moving picture book they are uncommon in fine working condition, but are well worth looking out for.

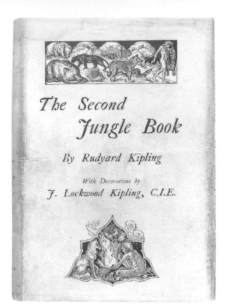

◄ **Rudyard Kipling**
The Second Jungle Book, first edition, illustrations by
J. Lockwood Kipling, Macmillan, 1895. Scarce in dust-
jacket. **£1,000–1,500**
Without dust-jacket, £50–100. Normally found with *The
Jungle Book* as a pair, without dust-jackets, £200–400

◄ **Carlo Lorenzini, "Carlo Collodi"**
*The Story of a Puppet, or the
Adventures of Pinocchio*, illustrations
by C. Mazzanti, T. Fisher Unwin, 1892,
first edition in English. First published in
Italy in parts and then in book form in
1883. **£1,000–2,000**

▲ **Beatrix Potter**
The Tailor of Gloucester, first published edition,
coloured illustrations by the author, Frederick Warne,
1903. **£200–600**
Prices for the first published edition vary according to
condition; a poor copy will be £50–200, and later issues
of the first edition also less. Issued privately in 1902 in
an edition of 500 copies, £1,500–3,000

Animal Characters & Fantasy Tales

The influence of the three major illustrators, Crane, Greenaway and Caldecott, was enormous, and lightened the tone of children's books. Once again, three main genres, found in the earliest of children's books, stand out in the late 19th and 20th centuries: the animal story, the fantasy and the fairy-tale. In 1877, a year before her death, Anna Sewell wrote her one and only book, *Black Beauty*, in which a horse was the main character. Rudyard Kipling turned back to Aesop with *The Jungle Book* (1894) and *Just So Stories* (1902). Of his many books, several written for children, these are his most widely read today and usher in an era of animal characters. Beatrix Potter was born in London and had no formal schooling; she taught herself to draw small natural objects. She wrote picture letters to the

children of friends, often miniature in format, and one, written in 1893 to Noel Moore, the son of her former governess, introduced the rabbits Flopsy, Mopsy, Cotton Tail and Peter. In 1901 this became a book, *The Tale of Peter Rabbit*: she privately printed 250 copies herself, before Frederick Warne took over publication in 1902. Potter wrote over 25 books, many depicting her pets and neighbours in the Lake District where she had made her home. Here, she also devoted much of her time and money to the newly set-up National Trust.

The importance of a sympathetic artist is shown by the fact that neither Kenneth Grahame nor A.A. Milne found fame until the artist E.H. Shepard provided the illustrations to their works. Grahame's *The Wind in the Willows* (1908) was not a success at

◄ Walt Disney

The Adventures of Mickey Mouse, Book 1, coloured illustrations by the Walt Disney Studios, Philadelphia, David McKay Company, 1931. **£100–200**
The Disney books from the 1930s featuring Mickey Mouse, Donald Duck and Snow White are the most sought after; those from the 1940s and 1950s can be found under £50
© DISNEY

▼ A.E. Bestall

The Rupert Book, coloured illustrations by the author, Daily Express, 1948. **£40–80**
The most sought-after annuals are those from 1936 to 1939, the first being over £400 and the others around £200 each; the later annuals from the 1950s onwards can be found for £20–40

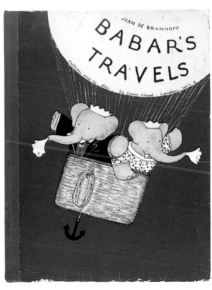

▲ Jean de Brunhoff

Babar's Travels, third English edition, Methuen and Co., 1941. **£20–40**
The first title *Histoire de Babar le petit elephant*, published in Paris, 1931, £150–300

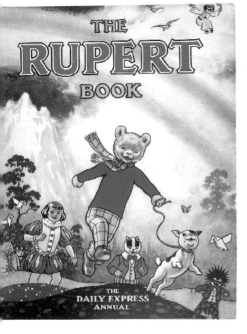

◄ J.M. Barrie

Peter Pan and Wendy, coloured plates and other illustrations by Mabel Lucie Attwell, Hodder and Stoughton, 1955. **£40–80**

the time of publication, when it appeared with only a frontispiece, but upon being illustrated by Shepard in 1931 and Arthur Rackham in 1940, Rat, Mole and Badger became classic childhood characters. Milne's verses *When We Were Very Young* (1924), introduced Christopher Robin and the Bear, who reappeared as Winnie the Pooh in the book of that name in 1926. With the expansion of his character came a whole host of animal companions, including Tigger, Eeyore and Piglet.

Jean de Brunhoff's elephants Babar and Celeste and their Peaceable Kingdom paved the way for Rupert the Bear and his adventures, first dreamt up by Mary Tourtel in 1920 and published in a series of small yellow books. But it was not until A.E. Bestall's comic strip drawings in the *Daily Express*

newspaper and the first annual in 1936 that Rupert became the cult figure that he remains today.

Walt Disney produced short cartoon films of original stories before turning to classic fairy-tales such as *Snow White*, but his most famous characters are animals, Mickey Mouse and Donald Duck. The books of the films featuring these characters are still easily affordable. Contemporary children's literature features numerous animals, including the rabbits of Richard Adams's *Watership Down* (1972).

Another memorable Disney film was based on Carlo Lorenzini's *Pinocchio* (1883; English translation 1892), the story of a puppet who is changed into a real boy. Pinocchio was the precursor of many fantasy figures based on playthings who came to life, such as Florence and Bertha Upton's Golliwogs.

▼ Edward Ardizzone
Little Tim and the Brave Sea Captain, first edition, coloured illustrations by the author, Oxford University Press, 1936. The first title in the Little Tim series and the most scarce. **£80–170**
Later titles, under £50

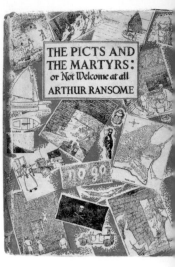
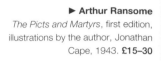

► Arthur Ransome
The Picts and Martyrs, first edition, illustrations by the author, Jonathan Cape, 1943. **£15–30**

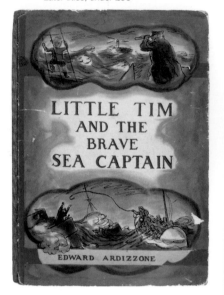

◄ Hugh Lofting
Doctor Dolittle's Puddleby Adventures, first edition, illustrations by the author, Jonathan Cape, 1953. **£15–30**

20th-Century Children's Books

In 1900 L. Frank Baum's *The Wonderful Wizard of Oz* was published, the first of many fabulous adventures for Dorothy, the Tin Man and their friends; stories of playthings come alive. But it is another fantasy figure who is perhaps the enduring image of childhood: Peter Pan, the boy who would not grow up. His creator, J.M. Barrie, was born in Scotland and wrote a number of novels and plays before turning the stories he had made up for the five sons of Arthur and Sylvia Llewellyn Davies into a play, *Peter Pan*. First performed in 1904, it was not published as a play until 1928; but in 1906 a story version appeared, *Peter Pan in Kensington Gardens*, with illustrations by Arthur Rackham. This tale, Lewis Carroll's *Alice's Adventures in Wonderland* and Hans Andersen's *Fairy Tales* are considered by many to be the three most influential children's books.

There was great interest in fairies at the turn of the century, several elaborate hoaxes encouraging the belief of many that they really existed, and Cicely Mary Barker produced a series of small books dur-

ing the 1920s depicting the "Flower Fairies". These fairies of the flowers and trees were very popular and quickly reissued, and are still in print today.

A major genre of children's books in this century is a continuation of the adventure books of the late 19th century, generally written for older children. The journalist and writer Arthur Ransome (who married Trotsky's former secretary) published a collection of Russian fairy-tales, but is best known for his classic adventure stories, the first of which, *Swallows and Amazons*, appeared in 1930. His love of the countryside, fishing and sailing are reflected in the adventures of the Walker and Blackett families set in the Lake District, Suffolk and the Norfolk Broads. Similarly, the adventures of a family or group of children were recounted by Enid Blyton in her *Famous Five* stories, books which have divided authorities and critics ever since their first publication, but which remain popular; her numerous titles are readily available to the collector.

The scholar, critic and novelist C.S. Lewis (like

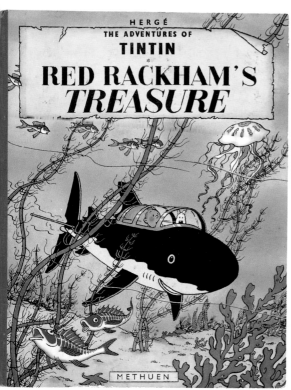

◀ **Hergé**
The Adventures of Tintin. Red Rackham's Treasure, first English edition, coloured illustrations by the author, Methuen, 1959. **£40–80**

▼ **Maurice Sendak**
Outside Over There, first English edition, coloured illustrations by Maurice Sendak, Bodley Head, 1981. One of the most important and prolific of American illustrators for children. **£20–30**

authors such as A.A. Milne, Lewis Carroll, Rudyard Kipling and J.M. Barrie) wrote serious books for adults, often reflecting his strong moral and religious feelings, but is now probably best remembered for his work for children. The seven great "Narnia" stories (1950–56) begin with the adventures of the Pevensies in *The Lion, the Witch and the Wardrobe*; pure fantasy, they also contain spiritual nuances.

The child as lone adventurer is epitomized by Edward Ardizzone's boy, Tim. Ardizzone is one of the most enduring and best loved of 20th-century writer-illustrators. *Little Tim and the Brave Sea Captain* (1936), was the first of many adventures, mainly at sea. The earlier books had handwritten text and illustrations by Ardizzone, lithographed in colour in a large format, but during the war the size was reduced and the text set by letterpress. Another famous 20th-century boy was Charlie, whose adventures were recounted by Roald Dahl in *Charlie and the Chocolate Factory* (1972) and illustrated by Pauline Baynes.

Ardizzone's Tim was often accompanied by his black cat. Hergé's boy hero, Tintin, had a white dog called Snowy to share his adventures. Tintin first appeared in France in 1929 in *Tintin au pays des Soviets*, in the comic-strip format used for the Rupert Bear stories, each crammed with action, colour and humour. *Tintin* was rapidly translated into English and many other languages, and new titles came out for the next 35 years. This format is still used today, notably by Raymond Briggs in his powerful books, many of which have an underlying moral theme and, although picture books, are perhaps more for adults. *The Snowman* (1978) is a moving story of a lonely boy befriending a snowman, but ultimately realizing he cannot bring him into his own world.

Children's book publishing is one of the strongest growth areas of the moment, with many new authors and illustrators for the aspiring collector to look out for, and the themes that produced much of the greatest literature through the centuries still enduring.

Natural History

Studies in natural history: collecting images and texts

▲ **Charles Darwin**
On the Origin of Species by Means of Natural Selection,
folding diagram, John Murray, 1859. One of the most
important books ever published, this controversial work
was successful from the day of publication and
reprinted many times. First edition in original cloth.
£6,000–12,00
Rebound, £2,000–3,000; third edition, 1861, the first
to include Darwin's textual additions, £500–700

Booksellers would like you to believe
that book collecting is a game with
secret rules. Do not believe them.
You make the rules. This is especially
so if you are resolved to collect somewhere
in the huge field (or jungle) of the biological
arts and sciences: you can pick your patch
historically, topographically, taxonomically or
thematically and cultivate it how you will. You
may choose to study the natural history of
Perthshire or of Persia, of perching birds or
percherons, of the Permian or the permafrost;
you can study the theories of nest-building, or
nutrition, or natural selection, or Nathaniel
Grew. Some collectors in this area are bird- or
beetle- or begonia-watchers; others never go
out of doors. Some collect illustrated books of
evident beauty; others want gloomy tracts in
forgotten languages. Many are practising
scientists or historians of science, otherwise
logical persons who have persuaded
themselves – and who am I to argue? – that
owning the first edition of Galton or Wallace
or Hooke will make their work go better;
others are committed collectors, immune
to logic.

There is a complication about collecting
the records of great discoveries. Most
biological reporting and debate takes place
in the pages of learned journals. It would be
wearisome to collect the annual volumes,
ethically and aesthetically disgusting to extract
the few interesting pages. Customarily, at
least since the 18th century, authors receive a
number of separately printed offprints which
they circulate among their friends: this is

THALURANIA REFULGENS, *Gould*

◀ **John Gould**
A Monograph of the Trochilidae, or Family of Humming-Birds, 6 volumes including supplement, 418 hand-coloured lithographed plates after and by Gould, H.C. Richter and W. Hart. By the Author, and Henry Sotheran, 1849–87.
£40,000–60,000

reckoned the desirable way – sometimes impossibly desirable – to possess Mendel on heredity or Darwin and Wallace on the tendency of organisms to form varieties. Yet less epochal offprints – which often contain fine illustrations – are sold, if at all, at derisory prices: even 17th-century theses, full of curious lore, are considered awkward, hard for the proud owner to display or for the librarian to catalogue (and usually found under the name not of the obscure scholar who wrote it, but of the *praeses*, the chairman of the board of examiners).

Other kinds of publication are more obviously collectables, and this field includes monographs, expedition reports, travellers' (or "stay-at-homes") journals, theological or ecological polemics, catalogues from museums of cabinets of curiosities, guides to zoos, arboreta, or game parks.

Alternatively you can collect whatever epoch your tastes and means permit. The earliest printed natural histories, conforming closely to manuscript precursors, were woodcut-illustrated books of wonders; herbals that concentrated on plants of real or imaginary medical use; and bestiaries – histories of fabulous animals and fabulous histories of real animals, exemplars of morality or theological emblems: the pelican in its piety; Christ the tiger; the beasts of the evangelists and of the apocalypse.

In the 17th century the fables and the faunistics gradually drew apart: gentlemen of leisure, no longer content with legends, using their eyes or their microscopes, constructed

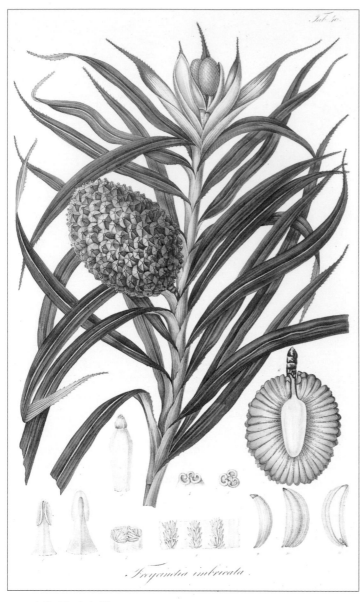

Trigonia imbricata.

▲ **Carl Ludwig Blume**
*Rumphia, sive commentationes botanicae imprimis
de plantis Indiae Orientalis*, 4 volumes, 3 lithographed
portraits and 210 plates, 150 hand-coloured, Leiden,
1835–49. **£5,000–7,000**

▼ **Carolus Linnaeus**
*Systema naturae, siva regna tria naturae systematice
proposita per classes, ordines, genera, & species,*
Leiden, Joannes, Wilhelm de Greet for Theodor Haat,
1735. Printed for private circulation, this important work
on the classification of plants and animals consisted of
12 leaves only. A unique copy on 7 leaves sold for
$165,000 (£110,000) in 1989.
The 10th edition, Stockholm, 1758–59, £1,200-1,800

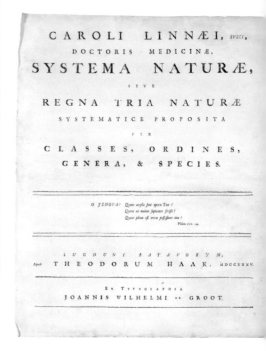

herbaria, menageries, or cabinets of
curiosities: imaginative woodcuts gave way
to meticulously engraved anatomies. In the
18th century began the flood of superbly
illustrated monographs of favoured groups,
the systematic faunas and floras of newly
surveyed territories. In the 19th century the
name and calling of scientist came to be: and
with the professionals came new techniques
of illustration: the lithograph and the

chromolithograph, steel-engraving and
revived wood-engraving: colour printing
replacing hand-colouring. (Photographically
illustrated natural history books are still
hardly collected.) The old sciences budded
new sciences and divided and subdivided like
yeast cells.

In all these fields the unfrequented paths
are less costly and more rewarding. If you
specialize in aphids instead of butterflies,

▲ Albertus Seba

Locupletissimi rerum naturalium thesauri accurata descriptio, 4 volumes, engraved title and portraits, 449 engraved plates of natural curiosities, 175 double-page, Amsterdam, Jannson-Waesberg, Wetsten and Smith, 1734–65. The work was issued uncoloured and is a record of the second cabinet of natural curiosities formed by this German-born apothecary. This copy has contemporary hand-colouring. **£40,000–50,000**

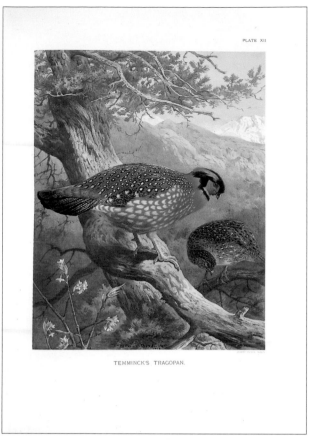

TEMMINCK'S TRAGOPAN.

▲ William Charles Beebe

A Monograph of the Pheasants, 4 volumes, 90 chromolithographed plates after Archibald Thorburn and others, 88 photogravure plates after photographs, for the New York Zoological Society by Witherby & Co., 1918–27. One of the greatest ornithological works of this century. **£1,500–2,000**

earthworms (or even better tapeworms) instead of snakes, tubers instead of fruits, you will shake off most of the competition and discover unexpected beauties. Second editions; flowerless plants; losers of great debates; drab fish; non-winners of Nobel prizes; failed popularizers; second mates to great navigators: all these offer great economy, elbow-room, and the excitements of the unexplored.

It is a question of character as well as cash.

Do not collect Charles Darwin unless you are prepared to spend something between the cost of a large car and a small house on two or three high spots, or unless you can cheerfully contemplate life without them. Modest treasures await on the path less travelled.

Eric Korn

▼ **William Salmon**
The English Herbal, engraved title, woodcut illustrations, H. Rhodes and J. Taylor, 1710. **£300–500**

▲ **Elizabeth Blackwell**
A Curious Herbal, engraved head-pieces and title, 500 hand-coloured engraved plates, 1737–39. One of the first English botanical books with hand-coloured plates. Blackwell undertook this work at the suggestion of Sir Hans Sloane in order to release her husband from the debtor's prison. **£4,000–8,000**

Botany

Early botany was intertwined with medicine, and the first printed botanical books were herbals. Apprentices to the Society of Apothecaries, founded in London in the 16th century, had to visit botanical gardens to study and draw plants. As these early illustrations were copied over the years they tended to alter and end up bearing little resemblance to the original. Strange specimens were being brought back from voyages overseas and there was soon a need for some kind of classification to avoid great confusion. Leonhard Fuchs's important herbal *De historia stirpium* (1542) illustrated the largest number of species known at the time. The work was immediately successful and was reprinted several times. Whilst only 500 plants were listed in this work, the immense growth in floriculture meant that by 1623, more than 6,000 were recorded.

A passion began to develop for beautiful rather than useful plants, and with the subsequent demand by the wealthy for sumptuous picture books depicting these flowers, the grand *florilegia* were born. These fine, coloured botanical books were first produced in the early 17th century, but the greatest appeared during the late 17th and 18th centuries. They were expensive productions at the time, often being issued for subscribers only, and have remained so today, usually beyond the reach of the ordinary collector, unless acquired in later reprint or modern facsimile. They are easy books to appreciate with their skilled and beautifully coloured plates, and prices have climbed steadily.

One of the finest libraries ever amassed of these great botanical books, that of Robert de Belder, Vice-President of the Royal Horticultural Society,

▼ **James Bolton**
An History of Funguses, growing about Halifax,
4 volumes, first English edition, engraved title and
182 hand-coloured plates, Halifax and Huddersfield,
1788–91. **£3,000–5,000**
An uncoloured copy, £1,200–1,800

▲ **Pierre Joseph Redouté**
Les Liliacés, 8 volumes, 488 stipple-engraved plates
printed in colours and finished by hand, Paris, Didot
jeune, 1802–16. This was Redouté's largest and most
ambitious work and is generally regarded as his
masterpiece. **£100,000–150,000**
Facsimile editions of his work can be acquired, for
example *Alburn de Redouté* by Sacheverell Sitwell,
Collins, 1954, £75–100

was sold at Sotheby's in 1987 for an impressive
£5,910,465. The 388 books in the library were used as
a reference tool in order to document botanical illustration from 1600 to 1900. A new collector interested
in this field should attempt to find a copy of the sale
catalogue, for most of the great names are represented, recording the progress of illustration from
the woodcut technique to the more delicate engraving: Basil Besler, Nichols Robert, John Martyn,
Georg Dionysius Ehret and Christoph Jacob Trew
to name but a few.

It was at the end of the 18th century that a young
Belgian stage-designer began his career under the
patronage of Charles Louis L'Héritier de Brutelle, a
wealthy botanist. Pierre-Joseph Redouté mastered
the technique of stipple-engraving to produce some
of the greatest botanical books ever.

This was also the era of the botanical periodical.
Flora Danica was published over the period 1761 to
1883; perhaps the greatest was *Botanical Magazine*,
founded by William Curtis. This periodical, sought
after today because of its fine plates, was started in
1787 and is still being published today. Whilst long
runs are expensive, it is possible to find odd volumes
for quite modest sums.

Women artists played a greater role in illustrating botanical books than in any other field of natural
history, often unacknowledged at the time. Clara
Maria Pope produced fine plates for Samuel Curtis's
A Monograph of the Genus Camellia (1819), and Ellen
Willmott's The *Genus Rosa* (1914), is probably one of
the best flower books of this century.

It was with the arrival of the 19th century that
botany developed into a popular pastime for more

▼ **Robert John Thornton**
New Illustrations of the Sexual System of Carolus von Linnaeus ... The Temple of Flora, or Garden of Nature, 3 volumes, engraved portraits and titles, 31 colour-printed aquatint and mezzotint plates finished by hand, 91 uncoloured engraved plates, 1799–1810. One of the most famous English botanical plate books, first issued in parts. **£40,000–60,000**
Later editions issued with the plates reduced in size but inferior in quality, 1812, £1,500–3,000

▲ **James Sowerby and Sir Edward James Smith**
English Botany, or Coloured Figures of British Plants, hand-coloured engraved plates, 1790–1814. 36 volumes were issued in total.
Complete set. **£2,000–4,000**
Volumes 1–11 only, with approximately 790 plates, £500–800

▲ **Colin Milne**
A Botanical Dictionary or Elements of Systematic and Philosophical Botany, 25 hand-coloured engraved plates, H.D. Symonds, 1805. Third edition. **£250–350**

than just the leisured classes or the adventurous, and numerous books were issued with lithographed and, later, chromolithographed plates. Some of these were grand productions, but most were popular in tone, and this is where the new collector will find a wealth of material. Numerous botanical periodicals were spawned and many of the artists of this century produced work for the *Botanists' Repository, Botanical Cabinet, The British Flower Garden,* and *Florists' Magazine.*

With the advent of the lithograph came one of the finest botanical books – and certainly the largest – James Bateman's *Orchidaceae of Mexico and Guatemala* (1837–41), illustrated by this medium. One of the most prolific artists of this period was

Walter Hood Fitch, who worked for Sir William and Sir Joseph Hooker, the father and son botanists who created Kew Gardens as it is known today. Fitch's work included contributions to the *Botanical Magazine*, the Hookers' *A Century of Orchidaceous Plants* (1851) and *Illustrations of Himalayan Plants* (1855), and H.J. Elwes's *Monograph of the Genus Lilium* (1877–80).

The revival of the woodcut and the development of chromolithography in the early 19th century permitted mass production of botanical books for the ever-growing market. Anne Pratt was a prolific artist who was able to flourish in this popular market, and the collector on a limited budget will be able to acquire her works such as *The Flowering Plants*

▼ *The Florist and Garden Miscellany 1849*
13 hand-coloured engraved plates by Joseph Andrews, woodcut illustrations, Chapman and Hall, 1850. One of a series issued 1848–61, **£200–300**

PLUMBAGO LARPENTE.

► **Paul Jones**
Flora Superba, one of 406 copies, 16 coloured plates by Paul Jones, Tryon Gallery, 1971. **£150–300**

Datura arborea

and Ferns of Great Britain (1855) for a relatively modest sum. There was an increased interest in wild flowers and the wild, as opposed to formal, classical gardens, and here books such as Mrs. Loudon's *British Wild Flowers* (1845) illustrated by Henry Noel Humphreys, or journals such as William Robinson's *The Garden* (1871–1927) and *Flora and Sylva* (1903–5), are of interest. One of Robinson's artists was Henry Moon, who produced the plates for *Reichenbachia* (1888–94), Frederick Sander's great series of folios on orchids.

This interest in botanical books has continued throughout the 20th century. However, much of the best illustrative work is now in periodicals and journals. Many of the 20th-century illustrators, such as

John Nash, have turned their attention to plants and gardening. One can quite easily find Nash's own *English Garden Flowers* (1948), William Dallimore's *Poisonous Plants* (1927), Patrick M. Synge's *Plants with Personality* (1939), and Robert Gathorne-Hardy's *Wild Flowers in Britain* (1938). Wood-engravers such as Clare Leighton, Agnes Miller Parker and Gertrude Hermes have all turned their hand to botanical illustration, using the wood-engraving. The collector can choose to search for sentimental works such as Sacheverell Sitwell's *Old Fashioned Flowers* (1939), illustrated by John Farleigh, or more specialized, scientific works such as Carl Lindman's three-volume *Bilder ur Nordens Flora* (1901–5; reprinted in 1921).

▲Conrad Gesner

Historiae animalium; Icones avium omnium; Icones animalium quadrupedum, De serpentium natura, 4 volumes in one, wood-engraved illustrations, later hand-colouring, Zurich, C. Froschoverus, c.1550–60. Second edition.
£1,500–2,000

▲ Daniel Giraud Elliot

A Monograph of the Felidae, or Family of Cats, 43 hand-coloured lithographed plates after Joseph Wolf, By the Author for Subscribers, 1878–83. One of the finest colour-plate works on mammals.
£20,000–30,000

▼ Thomas Bewick

A General History of Quadrupeds, fifth edition, wood-engraved illustrations, Newcastle, 1807.
£150–300

Zoology & Ornithology

Some of the earliest printed writings on animals were by the philosopher Aristotle, tutor to the future Alexander the Great. His depictions of animals and birds often seem absurd and fanciful today, and yet he was extraordinarily knowledgeable for his time. Writers for centuries based their studies on his work. The early naturalists attempted to identify and classify animals according to species already known rather than to depict them accurately; however, by the 16th century, there was a need for correct attribution. It was a Swiss, Conrad Gesner, who produced the first large-scale illustrated books on zoology, *Historia animalium* (1551–58). The four volumes featured woodcuts worked from dead animals or their skins and, although he still based his work on Aristotle, Gesner's books contained enough new material to mark the transition from the world of medieval bestiary to modern zoological science.

Few zoological books were published in the 16th century and what was published was often still a mixture of fact and fiction, as seen in Edward Topsell's *Historie of Four-footed Beasts* (1607), and *Historie of Serpents* (1608), reissued together in 1658

as *The History of Four-footed Beasts and Serpents*. These immensely popular books provide a fascinating insight into science at the time and can be found quite readily today.

It was not until the latter part of the 17th century, with the writings of Francis Willughby and John Ray, that the relatively chaotic studies to date were replaced with a more precise classification of birds and animals. They planned a vast "History of the Natural World" and set out on a series of travels to explore, note and record everything from birds to plants, geology to insects, both at home and abroad. Ray studied comparative anatomy, physiology and animal behaviour. His many books are not expensive, and are worth searching for, because he laid the foundations for subsequent scientists.

As with botanical illustration, the early works had been illustrated by the woodcut, soon superseded by the finer engraving. It was not unusual for books to be coloured after publication, but Eleazar Albin's *A Natural History of Birds* (1731–38) was the first to be issued for subscribers with plates coloured at source. Some of these illustrations were taken

▼ **James Barbut**

The Genera Insectorum of Linnaeus,
exemplified by various specimens of English
insects drawn from nature by John Dixwell,
engraved title and 22 plates, all but 2 hand-
coloured, 3 folding, J. Dixwell for J. Sewell,
1781. **£400–800**

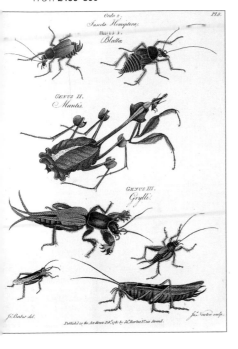

▲ **Archibald Thorburn**

British Mammals, 2 volumes, one of
155 copies, 50 coloured plates and
other illustrations in the text,
Longmans, Green and Co., 1921.
£800–1,500

▼ **Maria Sibylla Merian**

Histoire générale des insectes de
Surinam et de toute l'Europe,
volume 2: Des plantes de l'Europe,
184 hand-coloured engraved plates
on 47 sheets, Paris, L.C. Desnos,
1771. **£5,000–8,000**

from live specimens, but this work still contains imaginary birds, notably one with no feet. Whilst the subscribers' copies of this book are scarce, Albin's other works on songbirds and spiders are still relatively inexpensive.

The 18th century

With the dawn of the 18th century and the Age of Reason, such an imaginative attitude to zoological illustration waned and the supreme age of natural science began. Many artists still had to rely on their imagination or on dead specimens in the museums, but the age of travel was also dawning. One of the earliest to draw direct from life was Maria Sibylla Merian, who set sail in 1698 with her daughters for the colony of Surinam in South America; she remained there for two years collecting and studying insects, flowers and animals. Merian's most glorious work was published in 1705, *Metamorphosis insectorum Surinamensium*. Two of her contemporaries were Mark Catesby, whose *Natural History of Carolina* (1731–43) provides an invaluable record of the flora and fauna of North America, and George

Edwards, known as "the father of British Ornithology". Edwards painted more than 900 zoological watercolours and published extensive works such as *A Natural History of Uncommon Birds* (1743–64) and *Gleanings of Natural History* (1758–64).

The second half of the 18th century was an age of great colonial expansion coupled with huge strides ahead in general knowledge. Explorers brought back specimens to be studied and illustrated, and naturalists themselves began to undertake expeditions. Collecting became an obsession amongst the wealthy, some of whom financed voyages or even travelled themselves. Sir Joseph Banks accompanied Captain Cook to the South Seas, and employed Sydney Parkinson to produce numerous watercolours. The copper plates for these illustrations languished in the British Museum and were not finally published until 1988. Later exploratory voyages took a great interest in the wildlife encountered and almost always employed natural scientists. The subsequent journals make fascinating reading; they were often reprinted over the years and modern editions are readily available.

THE BLUE AND YELLOW MACCAW.

Macrocercus Ararauna, Vieill.

In describing the Red and Blue Maccaw, at page 13 of the present volume, we gave a brief indication of the characters by which the Maccaws are distinguished from the rest of the Parrots. The present species exhibits all these characteristic marks as completely as any of the group, of which it is one of the most conspicuous examples. In size it is somewhat inferior to the species formerly described, the male bird measuring little more than two feet and a half in total length when fully grown and in fine condition. Its colours are remarkably distinct. All the upper parts, from the forehead to the extremity of the tail, including the sides of the head and the upper surface of the wings, are of a bright blue, with a slight tinge of green; the under parts, from the breast downwards, are of a light orange

◄ E.T. Bennett
The Gardens and Menagerie of the Zoological Society delineated, 2 volumes, woodcut illustrations, Charles Whittingham and Thomas Tegg, 1830. Amongst the numerous woodcut illustrations are some of Edward Lear's earliest illustrations, including a macaw signed with his initials. **£60–120**

► Hermann Schlegel and A.H. Verster van Wulverhorst
Traité de fauconnerie, lithographed title and 16 hand-coloured plates after J. Wolf, Leiden and Dusseldorf, 1844–53. The life-size illustrations in this, the finest book on falconry, established the reputation of Joseph Wolf. **£3,000–6,000**

MALLARD or WILD DUCK. ♂ & ♀.
Anas boschas, Linn.

▲ Thomas Littleton Powys, Fourth Baron Lilford
Coloured Figures of the Birds of the British Islands, 7 volumes, 421 chromolithographed and hand-coloured plates after A. Thorburn, J.G. Keulemans and others, R.H. Porter, 1891–98. Second edition. **£1,500–2,000**

The 19th and 20th centuries

By the end of the 18th century, general zoological books were making way for more specialized studies, of which there had been a few already, notably on insects, serpents and fish. As accuracy and specialization developed, so the books accordingly followed those lines. Between 1790 and the 1840s hundreds of books on natural history were published, and this would be a good period for the new collector to start looking at.

One of the most prolific of writers was Edward Donovan, collector, naturalist, author and artist, who produced nearly 50 volumes on birds, of which *Natural History of British Birds*, begun in 1799, was one. His works were immensely popular at the time, and whilst first editions tend to be expensive now, the later printings can be found more easily. It was Donovan's great contemporary, Thomas Bewick, however, who really popularized natural history and marked a turning point in animal art. Reverting to illustration techniques using wood, Bewick's skill in cutting produced the most realistic and sensitive pictures of birds and animals to date. *A General History of Quadrupeds* (1790) was followed by *A History of British Birds* (1797–1804). His works were

reprinted many times and should be found in any natural history collection.

The 19th century ushered in the golden age of bird illustration. These great names will be beyond the reach of most new collectors in the original, but they have often been reprinted, or can be found in facsimile editions published in the 20th century. The leading ornithological artist at this time in England was Prideaux John Selby, who drew most of his specimens life-size. His great works were expensive at the time and are still so today.

Selby and the botanist Sir William Jardine supported and encouraged one of the greatest natural history artists of all time: the American John James Audubon. Unable to find an American publisher for his ambitious work, Audubon went to Britain, exhibiting his first paintings in Edinburgh in 1827. Renowned for his bird portraits, as in the four-volume *The Birds of America* (1827–38), he was also one of the greatest of animal artists, as seen in *The Viviparous Quadrupeds of North America* (1849), which was completed by his son after his sight failed in 1846. Both these works were reduced in format for wider publication. Audubon worked on his portraits of birds and animals, set against realistic and

▲ **C.F. Tunnicliffe**
Shorelands Summer Diary, 16 coloured plates and
other illustrations in the text by Tunnicliffe, Collins,
1952. One of the most popular names in 20th-century
natural history books and one of the most accessible
for new collectors. **£70–140**

► **John James Audubon**
Audubon's Birds of America, by
Roger Tory Peterson and Virginia
Marie Peterson, coloured plates,
some folding, New York, Abbeville
Press, 1981. This facsimile edition
of Audubon's work is an affordable
means of obtaining these
illustrations. **£20–40**
First edition of 7 volumes, 1840–44,
£10,000–15,000

◄ **David Bannerman**
*The Birds of West and Equatorial
Africa*, 2 volumes, 54 plain and
coloured plates, other illustrations
in the text, Oliver and Boyd, 1953.
One of the major names in late 20th-
century ornithology. **£60–120**

highly detailed backgrounds, through the complete
process from original drawing to overseeing production of the final aquatint plates.

By contrast, another of the greatest names in
ornithological art rarely saw beyond the original
drawing: John Gould. He would leave the detailed
drawings, lithography and colouring to be carried
out by others, often his wife, Elizabeth Gould, and
Joseph Wolf, another great artist in his own right.
Gould and his artists produced works arranged
according to country: *The Birds of Europe* (1832–37),
The Birds of Australia (1837–38), *The Birds of Great
Britain* (1862–73); or by species, *Humming-Birds*
(1849–61), *A Monograph of the Trogonidae* (1835–38).
Joseph Wolf developed into one of the greatest
painters of animals ever, as seen in the two folios of
plates produced for the London Zoo, *Zoological
Sketches* (1867), setting his subjects within convinc-
ing and dramatic settings.

The preliminary sketches that Wolf carried out
for Daniel Giraud Elliot's great *A Monograph of the
Phasianidae or family of the pheasants* (1864–65), were
finished by his protégé, John Keulemans, one of the
best illustrators working during the latter part of the
century. Of the many Victorian books published on

natural history, often with chromolithographed
plates, it is worth looking out for those illustrated by
Keulemans. His plates were more traditional than
those of Gould or Audubon, with the birds being the
dominant feature and the scenery being relegated to
a mere background. Another name to look for is
Archibald Thorburn who, with Keulemans, provided the plates for Lord Lilford's *Coloured Figures
of the Birds of the British Islands* (1885–97), as well as
himself producing some of the finest animal illustrations of this century.

The 20th century has seen a return of interest in
bird books, and some of the most important books in
the field come from this century, with far more
detailed identification than ever before. With species
dying out all the time these become invaluable.
Contemporary artists work in varying styles, some
simply recording, others setting their subjects
amongst dramatic settings: Peter Scott, David
Shepherd, Terence James Bond and Peter Hayman
are just a few of the names to look out for. One may
choose to collect new monographs, such as John
Harrison's *Birds of Prey*, or hunt for the work of the
great names of previous centuries in the excellent
facsimile editions being published today.

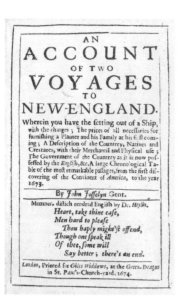

▲ **John Josselyn**
*An Account of Two Voyages to New
England*, for Giles Widdows, 1674.
The first complete description of the
flora and fauna of the Middle Atlantic
and New England states. £500–800

▶ **James Ellesworth de Kay**
Zoology of New York, or the New York Fauna, part 3
Reptiles and Amphibia, engraved title and 23 hand-
coloured lithographed plates, Albany, 1842. £150–200

◀ **Jacob Bigelow**
*American Medical Botany, being a
Collection of the Native Medicinal
Plants of the United States*, 3
volumes, 60 coloured engraved
plates, some partly hand-coloured,
Boston, Cummings and Hilliard,
1817–20. This was one of the first
American botanical books with
coloured illustrations, and the first
book published in the United States
to have the plates printed in colour.
£1,000–2,000

America

Whilst some may choose to concentrate on botanical illustration or animal and ornithological art, others may wish to study a particular country. Such a collection would encompass botany, zoology, ornithology, geology, and also important texts relating to the history and development of that country. Once again many of the early texts will be impossible to own, unless available in later editions, but the 19th century will provide a mass of material for consideration.

If America is chosen as the specific area then Mark Catesby's *The Natural History of Carolina, Florida and the Bahama Islands* (1731–43) will be an essential book to acquire. The original editions are very expensive, even though reprinted, and so most collectors will have to be content with the 1974 facsimile reprint. It is the first comprehensive collection of coloured plates of North American natural history. George Edwards painted a series of warblers from North America in his *Gleanings of Natural History* (1758–64), which contain some of the most important of early American illustrations.

The first really great American ornithological book was Alexander Wilson's and George Ord's *American Ornithology*, or *The Natural History of the Birds of the United States* (1808–14). It is John James Audubon, however, who is generally regarded as the greatest American naturalist and whilst his works are only available to most in facsimile, his *Ornithological Biography* (1831–39) is more affordable and provides a fascinating picture of an untamed eastern America. Another interesting book to acquire in this context would be Charles Waterton's *Wanderings in South America, the North-West of the United States and the Antilles* (1825). This Yorkshire country squire, who later turned his estate into a wildlife sanctuary, spent years exploring Guiana. He insisted on obtaining specimens himself, even a large live black cayman alligator, and the poison used by local Indians to coat their arrowheads.

A young Scot, David Douglas (after whom the giant Douglas fir is named), was sent by the Royal Horticultural Society on a botanical expedition to North America in 1823, his first priority being to

▲ William C. Harrls
The Fishes of North America that are Captured on Hook and Line, 40 chromolithographed plates, other illustrations in the text, New York, The Fishes of North America Publishing Co. 1893–98. **£600–800**

▲ William Paul Barton
A Flora of North America, 3 volumes, 106 hand-coloured engraved plates, Philadelphia, 1820–24. These plates are the first successful use of stipple-engraving in America. **£2,000–3,000**

◀ John G. Goodman
American Natural History, 3 volumes, second edition, engraved titles and 50 plates, Philadelphia, Stoddart and Atherton, 1831. **£100–200**

collect specimens of American fruit trees. Douglas's *Journal* makes for compulsive reading, vividly depicting the harshness of life in the wilderness during that period, and at the same time informing the reader as to the plant and animal species he encountered. His visits were to the east coast and to the north-west of the country – which he reached by sailing round Cape Horn in 1824.

Works such as those by Douglas and Waterton are generally much easier to find for the new collector than the great plate books, and are in many ways much more interesting in providing a detailed and personal picture of the period.

The Auk, published in Boston between 1884 and 1968, could be of great interest, being the principal ornithological journal in America; it was itself a continuation of *The Bulletin of the Nuttal Ornithological Club* (Cambridge, Mass., 1876–83). A popular work reprinted many times into the 20th century, and hence not too difficult to find, is Thomas Nuttall's *A Manual of the Ornithology of the United States and of Canada* (1832). Its illustrations were based on those of Thomas Bewick. Nuttall also issued a supplement to Francois Michaux's *The North American Sylva* (1852), again reprinted several times.

It was as early as 1803 that the first American botanical text-book was issued – Benjamin Smith Barton's *Elements of Botany* – and the English edition of 1804 can be found for very little. If one cannot afford the great plate books such as *A Monograph of the Felidae, or Family of Cats* (1878–83) by Daniel Giraud Elliot, then his *The Life and Habits of Wild Animals* (1874), would be worth looking for. John Gould's extensive research for *A Monograph of the Odontophorine, or Partridges of America* (1884–50), resulted in 24 species being added to the 11 previously recorded. This work would perhaps appeal more to someone interested in America than would many of Gould's other works, and whilst expensive, it does not command the huge sums his other works require. William C. Harris's *The Fishes of North America that are Captured on Hook and Line* (1893–98) is a fine work and one that is not too expensive, considering the quality of the plates.

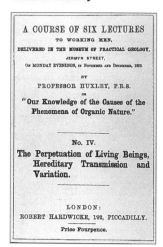

A COURSE OF SIX LECTURES
TO WORKING MEN,
DELIVERED IN THE MUSEUM OF PRACTICAL GEOLOGY,
JERMYN STREET,
On Monday Evenings, in November and December, 1863.

BY

PROFESSOR HUXLEY, F.R.S.

ON

"Our Knowledge of the Causes of the
Phenomena of Organic Nature."

No. IV.

The Perpetuation of Living Beings,
Hereditary Transmission and
Variation.

LONDON:
ROBERT HARDWICKE, 192, PICCADILLY.

Price Fourpence.

▲ **Thomas Henry Huxley**
*On our Knowledge of the Causes
of the Phenomena of Organic
Nature*, Robert Hardwick, 1862.
First edition in the original parts.
£700–1,200
First edition as book, £200–400

▼ **Francis Morris**
All the Articles of the Darwin Faith,
Moffat Paige & Co., 1876. **£50–80**

▲ **Philip Henry Gosse**
The Romance of Natural History, 2 volumes, first and
second series, 21 pates, James Nisbet and Co.,
1860–61. **£30–100**

Natural History Texts

So far we have looked at collecting books about natural history from the illustrative point of view, which is the basis upon which many collections are formed. However, natural history is a science and as such breaks ground, formulates theories and constantly advances. Such theories are written down and one could therefore choose to collect texts important to the field of natural history: the written word as opposed to the pictorial aspect.

Carolus Linnaeus

Early natural history studies were vague and rather chaotic. The early naturalists – Aristotle, Ray, Gesner – had attempted to classify and identify, but it was only with the 18th-century Swedish naturalist, Carolus Linnaeus, that order was brought to the chaos. Linnaeus demonstrated that the reproduction of plants had a sexual basis, pollination being carried out by male and female organs, and classified his plants according to the number of stamens. He applied these principles of taxonomy to all branches of nature, and his *Systema Naturae* became a comprehensive catalogue of all known living things, and was not finalized until it had gone through many editions. The tenth edition (1758–59) is more important scientifically and textually than the first (1735), although many collectors would prefer the first – extremely expensive – edition. It is from the date of this tenth edition that taxonomists officially recog-

nized the standard Latin names: all names before that date were to be ignored. Linnaeus wrote many other works on the classification of plants, as well as his *Tour of Lapland*, in Swedish, which was not published until long after his death.

Charles Darwin

During the 19th century, natural history began to divide into various fields of study, with the appearance of specialized scientific work written by the professional scientist for his peers, and separate popular natural history books written for the layman. Nevertheless, a few scientists continued to pursue interests across a wide field, the most renowned of whom is probably Charles Darwin. Darwin's body of published work is both botanical and zoological, although he is best remembered for his, at the time, radical theories on evolution. Darwin's major works, *On the Origin of Species* (1859), *Narrative of the Surveying Voyages of His Majesty's Ships Adventure and Beagle* (1839), and *The Zoology of the Voyage of H.M.S. Beagle* (1839–43) with its accompanying folio of plates by John and Elizabeth Gould, are the best known and most expensive of the numerous books he wrote. However, one can acquire his works in later edition, or copies of his lesser-known works for more reasonable sums.

A collection of Darwin should also include the works of those associated with Darwin. This would

Collecting
Books on Gardening

▲ William Alexander Forbes
The Collected Scientific Papers of the late William Alexander Forbes, edited by F.E. Beddard, etched frontispiece portrait and 25 lithographed plates, 15 hand-coloured, R.H. Porter, 1885. Forbes was a member of the Zoological Society of London and these scarce papers are on the muscular structure and voice organs of birds. **£200–400**

◄ Humphry Repton
Observations on the Theory and Practice of Landscape Gardening, 27 aquatint or engraved plates, 9 hand-coloured, 14 with overlays, T. Bensley for J. Taylor, 1803. The use of overlays was employed to show the scenery before and after being landscaped. **£2,500–5,000**

► Clare Leighton
Four Hedges, a Gardener's Chronicle, wood-engraved illustrations, Victor Gollancz, 1935.
£40–60

mean friends and collaborators such as Alfred Russel Wallace, Thomas Huxley and Henry Walter Bates. The latter's *The Naturalist on the River Amazons* (1863) confirmed Darwin's theories through the study of butterflies. It could also mean looking for the works of opponents to the theory of evolution, such as Francis Orpen Morris, better known for his *A History of British Birds* (1851–57) and similar series on moths and butterflies. His vitriolic and fundamentalist pamphlet *All the Articles of the Darwin Faith* was published in 1876, and is a fascinating historical piece and quite affordable.

Philip Henry Gosse, an associate member of the Linnean Society, believed that Darwin was terribly, blasphemously wrong. He tried to reconcile his firm religious beliefs with the scientific facts of geology, propounded in *Omphalos* (1857). Despite his passionate beliefs and the confusion caused thereby, he was first and foremost a fine naturalist and popular with his contemporaries, writing books on birds as well as his classic text, *A History of the British Sea-Anemones and Corals* (1860). It was Gosse's experiments with fish and aquatic plants that led to the Zoological Society's installing a marine tank filled with plants and fish in Regent's Park, followed by the world's first "marine aquavivarium" in 1853. The works of the early geologists such as Sir Charles Lyell who wrote *The Principles of Geology* (1830), could also make an interesting area of study.

The most famous gardening book of the 17th century was John Parkinson's *Paradisi in sole paradisus terrestris, or a Garden of all sorts of pleasent flowers which our English ayre will permitt to be noursed up* (1629). Parkinson's book was based on the content of his own garden, and even the first edition is not as expensive as one might have assumed. It was reprinted several times and there is a facsimile reprint from 1904. John Evelyn's *Sylva, or a discourse of forest-trees* (1664) was the first important book on the subject published in England. It is also an important gardening book, containing as an appendix the first edition of one of Evelyn's most popular books, the *Kalendarium hortense*, a gardener's almanac that has been often reprinted. As with Parkinson's book, *Sylva* is not expensive, especially the numerous later editions; it had been published four times by 1706.

The great era of the landscape garden came with Lancelot "Capability" Brown and Humphry Repton. Repton produced a "Red Book" in which he set out the design for each garden he worked on; these are now mostly lost in the original. The Basilisk Press published a facsimile reprint in 1976, which is a good work for the new collector to look for and more affordable than his great colour-plate book based on the Red Books, *Observations on the Theory and Practice of Landscape Gardening* (1803). During the late 19th century the garden became less structured and ornamental, and filled with wild flowers. These ideas were propounded in the books of Gertrude Jekyll, including *Some English Gardens* (1904).

◄ **Oliver Goldsmith**
*An History of the Earth and
Animated Nature*, 8 volumes, 100
engraved plates, 1774. **£150–300**

The Ant Bear.

► **George Louis Leclerc,
Comte de Buffon**
*Natural History, General and
Particular*, 9 volumes, engraved
frontispiece and 307 plates,
A. Strahan and T. Cadell, 1791.
Third English edition.
£300–500

ANONYMOUS ANIMAL

Populist Nature Books

The great natural history books, whether botanical, zoological, or ornithological, were lavish and expensive productions at the time of publication, often being issued for subscribers only, and their strong visual appeal has made them highly sought after today, often resulting in exorbitant prices. There is, however, a strong popular side to natural history books which is one area that today's new collector, especially on a limited budget, can quite happily explore.

One of the earliest of popular natural history books was *A Description of Above Three Hundred Animals* (1782), illustrated with woodcuts. The quality of these illustrations was poor and were seen as a child by Thomas Bewick, who determined to produce more accurate images of animals and birds. Bewick's own books were popular and reprinted several times and are easy to find today. His wood-engravings of birds and quadrupeds, and his vignettes of country scenes, are highly attractive as well as being some of the earliest accurate depictions of wildlife. The Reverend Gilbert White was another who contributed to this mass appeal. He was neither naturalist, artist nor scientist, but an observant and knowledgeable rural cleric who loved the countryside. He wrote a series of letters to Thomas Pennant describing life around his parish, which were published in 1789 as *The Natural History and*

Antiquities of Selborne. This has appeared in more than 80 editions, illustrated by many different artists up to the present day. White's descriptions of the everyday events in the countryside appealed to ordinary people and prepared the way for the mass of popular natural history books during the following two centuries. Many of the major natural history books were reissued in less expensive, smaller format with chromolithographed plates, to cater to this desire for knowledge. Edward Donovan's small octavo editions of his books with coloured plates of birds, fish and insects were immensely popular and went through many editions. William Yarrell continued in the tradition of Bewick with his three-volume *A History of British Birds* (1837–43), which became the standard bird book for many years. These books were readily available then and still are so today, for modest sums.

These works were still uncoloured, and it was with the advent of chromolithography that inexpensive coloured books proliferated. Often initially rather garish, the colour printing did improve later. There was a vogue for sentimental books on flowers, with floral pictures accompanied by verses or excerpts from the Bible; and also for books illustrated with real flowers: *Wild Flowers and Their Teachings* (1845) is a good example of this, and although not more than a thousand copies can have

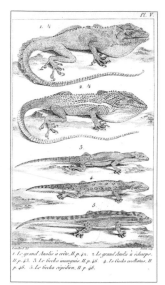

◄ **Georges L.D., Baron Cuvier**
Le règne animal distribué d'après son organisation,
4 volumes, 15 engraved plates, Paris, Deterville, 1817.
This work served as the standard zoological manual for
most of Europe during the first half of the 19th century.
£800–1,500

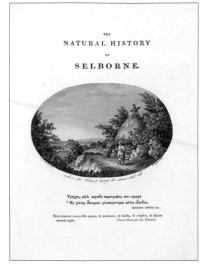

▶ **Gilbert White**
*The Natural History and Antiquities
of Selborne,* engraved title and
12 plates, White & Cochrane
& Co., 1813. **£100–200**
The first edition of 1789, £500–800

▲ **W.B. Tegetmeier**
*Pigeons: their structure, varieties,
habits and management,* 16
chromolithographed plates and
wood-engraved illustrations in the
text by Harrison Weir, George
Routledge, 1868. **£70–150**

been issued, such works proved popular for a while. Nature-printing had been around since the end of the 18th century, a process in which the actual plant was used to make the printing plate from which the final impression would be taken, but it was in the 19th century that its popularity was greatest. The most famous nature-printer was Henry Bradley who prepared *The Nature-Printed British Sea-Weeds* (1859–60), for W.G. Johnstone and A. Croall, an inexpensive and fascinating book. Such works accompanied the fashion for pressed flowers and chromolithographed scraps of flowers to be bought and pasted into albums.

Copy-books and pattern books, textbooks and gardening books were all aimed at the mass market. The publisher Henry G. Bohn would buy up original copper plates, lithographed stones or wood blocks, and reissue cheaper reprints of more expensive works. The quality was often not as good, but he was aiming to bring otherwise expensive books within the reach of the less fortunate. He also occasionally sold remainder stock at greatly reduced prices under his imprint. Oliver Goldsmith's *History of the Earth and Animated Nature* was originally published in 1744, but was reprinted numerous times during the 19th century.

The numerous popular encyclopedias and books for children on natural history with wood-engraved illustrations were usually the result of collaboration between a variety of authors and illustrators and have escaped the attention of many serious collectors, remaining easy to find. Philip Henry Gosse's works were immensely popular, particularly his *Naturalist's Rambles on the Devonshire Coast* (1853). Charles Kingsley, best known for *The Water Babies,* published *Glaucus; The Wonders of the Shore* in 1855, which went into many editions, as did the books of Reverend J.G. Wood, particularly those on the seashore and fish. His *Common Objects of the Country* reputedly sold more than 100,000 copies in its first week of publication, with attractive illustrations printed in colour by Edmund Evans.

In the 20th century, series such as the *New Naturalists,* and publishers A. & C. Black's guides to birds and flowers, have helped bring a specialist knowledge within the reach of the general reader. Publication of fine facsimile reprints of classic books has contributed to the popularization and spread of knowledge: these include Redouté's *Les Roses* (1974–78), Jardine's *British Salmonidae* (1979), Audubon's *Birds of America* (1981), and books such as Wilfrid Blunt's *The Art of Botanical Illustration* (1950), Sacheverell Sitwell's and Wilfrid Blunt's *Great Flower Books* (1956) and Sitwell's and Handasdyde Buchanan's *Fine Bird Books* (1953), all invaluable reference books now collected in their own right.

Travel & Topography

The exploration of the world: maps and voyages, guide-books and tales of adventure

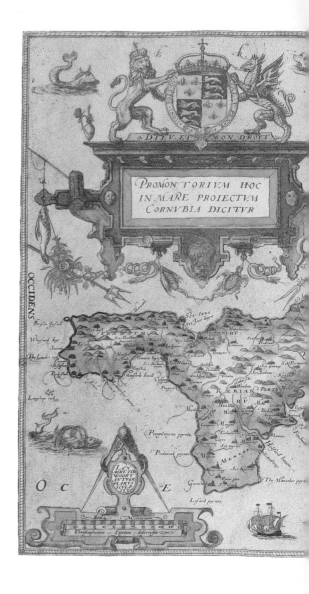

In his *Advice to an Author* (1710), the third Earl of Shaftesbury referred to travel books as "the chief materials to furnish out a library". Travel, with the sister literature of topography (the study of different regions), provides an immense range. Here are works by scientists, explorers, scholars, artists and architects, geographers, diplomats, spies, merchants, military and naval men, missionaries, eccentrics, the merely curious, and those who, like R.L. Stevenson, travelled "not to go anywhere, but to go".

Most collectors focus on one or a few areas for collection, broadly divided by region, period, or language (foreign sources offer similarly broad scope for study as books in English, and the collector of books on the Far East, for example, will not neglect Dutch and Portuguese authors, in the original or in translation), or a combination of the three. The works of a single author like Sir Richard Burton, who travelled widely in a variety of roles, may form one's sole object. The field extends to maps and atlases (such as those by the great cartographers of the past, Ortelius, Blaeu, Speed, *et al*), and is cross-fertilized by works chiefly known under other headings: natural history in particular. Some works are valued chiefly for their narratives, others, like Kip's *Britannia Illustrata* and Roberts's *Holy Land*, for the quality of their plates; yet others are fine narratives with plates and maps as an integral ingredient.

In their contemporary contexts, the impact

◀ ▲ **Christoper Saxton**
An Atlas of England and Wales, engraved frontispiece,
2 plates and 35 double-page or folding maps, with
contemporary hand-colouring, 1579. Several engravers
were used on this fine atlas, one of the earliest national
surveys of any kind and the first uniformly conceived
cartographic survey of England and Wales.
£50,000–70,000
Individual maps are also scarce and will cost £1,000+

of many travel books was utilitarian.
Travellers from Ralegh to Burton offered
insights of a political and economic nature,
providing the grounds upon which to trade
and colonize; in a more immediate and
practical context, one can picture Fletcher
Christian, having seized the *Bounty*, poring
over Bligh's copy of Hawkesworth's *Account
of Cook's first voyage*. There is moreover the
attraction of the way travellers relate their
adventures, and their enormous value as
educational tools for the desk-bound. Thus
Defoe's *Compleat English Gentleman* might
"make the tour of the world in books, he
may make himself master of the geography
of the universe in the maps, atlases, and
measurements … [and] go round the world

with Dampier and Rogers". Defoe's career,
indeed, expresses the contrasts found in travel
literature: his *Tour thro' the Whole Island of
Great Britain* (1724–27, frequently revised
and reprinted) is a utilitarian and exhaustive
compilation of facts, figures and critical
opinions. *Robinson Crusoe*, on the other hand,
romances the imagination wonderfully, with
Crusoe himself drawn from Woodes Rogers's
Cruising Voyage around the World (1712).
In Coleridge's experience, travel literature
provided the essential ingredients of
imaginative stimulation, from the albatross
episode in Shelvocke's *Voyage round the World*
(1726) to the origins of *Kubla Khan* in Samuel
Purchas's *Purchas his Pilgrimage* (1613 and
subsequent editions).

▼ **Rudolph Ackermann**
A History of the University of Oxford, its Colleges, Halls, and Public Buildings, 2 volumes, portrait, 70 hand-coloured aquatint plates on 64 sheets by J. Buck and others, after A. Pugin and others, 17 hand-coloured engraved costume plates, R. Ackermann, 1814.
A companion volume on Cambridge University was issued in 1815. **£2,000–3,000**

Antarctic (Discovery) Exp.   Birds. Plate 1.

▶ **National Antarctic Expedition 1901–1904**
12 volumes, 1907–13. The 12 volumes record Robert Scott's first Antarctic Expedition in the *Discovery* and contain fine coloured plates after Edward Wilson, including the first report of a nesting colony of Emperor penguins, and reproductions of photographs by members of the expedition. Individual volumes can be found, but a complete set is rare. **£3,000–6,000**

Furnishing a library of travel books is a voyage of discovery in itself. Early accounts, and many of the later ones, present difficulties in terms of condition and availability, but Richard Hakluyt's great 16th-century collection contains the most important narratives and is reasonably accessible, either in the originals or reprinted. Later collections (Purchas, Churchill, Harris, Pinkerton) are excellent ways of obtaining the highlights, still quite easy to obtain, and have been popular and esteemed from their first appearance. Among the best and relatively common 16th-century voyages, though not published until 1622, is Sir Richard Hawkins's *Observations … in his Voiage into the South Sea*. This was reprinted in 1933 by the Argonaut Press, who also reprinted the accounts of Drake and other early voyagers. The early editions of the great

18th-century accounts, such as those of Anson and Cook, though sought after and relatively expensive, are still readily available; so that the Cook collector owning Beaglehole's edition of the voyages, which presents the most accurate texts, would ultimately seek the early editions.

The 19th century was the great age of the geographer, particularly within central Africa (Livingstone, Speke, Stanley), central Asia (participants in the "Great Game"), Australia (Sturt, Mitchell, Leichardt) and the Arctic (Franklin, Ross, Parry); it was also the age of scientific exploration (Humboldt and Bonpland, Darwin and Wallace), and archeology (Leake, Schliemann). With the spread of literacy and longer print runs, some excellent travel works of the 19th century are quite easy to find: Livingstone's important *Missionary Travels and Researches* (1857),

▼ John Claude Nattes

Bath, illustrated by a series of Views, 28 hand-coloured aquatint plates by I. Hill and F.C. Lewis after John Claude Nattes, William Miller and William Sheppard, 1806. **£3,000–5,000**

▲ David Roberts and Louis Haghe.

The Holy Land, Syria, Idumea, Arabia, Egypt and Nubia, 6 lithographed titles and 241 lithographed plates, F.G. Moon, 1842-1849. Issued in parts, this great 6-volume work on the Middle East with the plates coloured by hand, **£70,000–80,000**
The 6-volume quarto edition, 1855–56, £1,000–2,000; the 3-volume quarto edition of the first part only, *The Holy Land, Syria, Idumea, Arabia, Egypt and Nubia*, 1879–84, £400–800

◄ Edward Dodwell

Views in Greece, text in English and French, 30 hand-coloured aquatint plates, Rodwell and Martin, 1821. Dodwell made several visits to Greece between 1801 and 1806 and was amongst the first generation of 19th-century British travellers to the country. The work was expensive to produce, remaindered and re-offered for sale a few years later. **£6,000–8,000**

though difficut to find in good condition, is a reasonably common example. The 20th century has seen the development of Antarctic literature, with the romantic heroism of Scott and Shackleton, and an increasing wealth of Middle Eastern and Central Asian material, all fruitful areas for collection. The easier it becomes to travel, the harder it is to be a pioneer. But modern travellers, Sir Ranulph Fiennes for example, explore the possibilites, and best-seller lists prove that travel writing remains popular.

The price range of travel books is as wide as the fields covered, and in common with all collectables, different copies of the same book vary in value according to such factors as condition and association. Prices fluctuate with fashions and may be driven up by the sale of a major collection. If your interests are within less collected areas – perhaps such narratives as the under-rated *Views of Society in France, Switzerland and Germany* and *in Italy* by Dr. John Moore, confidant of Smollett and Burns, or some better idea of your own – then collections can be formed on a very modest budget. It is up to the individual. Patience mingled with opportunism and a degree of determination enables every collector to form an interesting and cohesive library. Arrange it as idiosyncratically as you wish. Alastair Cooke mimics geography in his bookcase of Americana, with books on New England in the upper right-hand corner, and California on the left, or Pacific Coast. Given an acute eye, eclecticism and the essential ingredient of taste, a library with its own integrity will tend to develop naturally.

ALAN GRANT

▲ John Cary
New and Correct English Atlas,
47 engraved county maps, hand-
coloured in outline, 1812. **£400–800**
Individual maps will be under £50

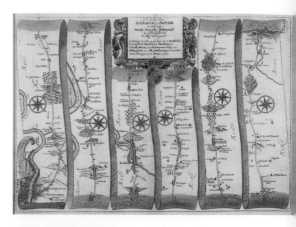

▲ J. Ogilby
The Road from London to Dover,
double-page engraved strip road
map, hand-coloured, 1675. Taken
from *Britannia*, 1720, these road
maps were the first of their kind and
quickly copied by others. **£70–120**

◄ H. Hondius
Galliae, French text, double-page
engraved map, contemporary hand-
colouring, Amsterdam, 1631.
£100–150

Maps & Atlases

The earliest printed maps were made from designs cut on metal, with wood quickly taking over to become the favoured medium for many years. Copper-engraving came back into fashion and in the early 19th century steel-engraving provided a more durable surface for printing the quantities of maps then required. Lithography was also used in the mid-19th century. Maps were issued uncoloured, and were coloured up later at the request of the purchaser, usually by the map-maker. Contemporary colouring is desirable, and one should be aware of colours that look too fresh and bright, which may have been added recently. Green that has oxidized to a muddy brown is an indication of early colouring.

Claudius Ptolemy's *Geographia* (c.AD125) was first printed in Bologna in 1477. The 27 maps in this edition were compiled from earlier manuscript maps drawn up using Ptolemy's system of co-ordinates. Its publication in the 15th century coincided with greater exploration and knowledge of the world's geography and subsequent improvements in cartography. It was reprinted regularly up to the 18th century, with two facsimile reprints in the 20th century. In 1569 Gerard Mercator produced his first map according to new projections in which the lines of latitude and longitude are set at right-angles; maps drawn up on the old and new principles

existed side-by-side for several years. In 1570 Abraham Ortelius published his *Theatrum orbis terrarum* in Antwerp, composed entirely of new maps drawn up from the latest information: 14 different editions were published before 1575, each varying as to the number of maps included.

The Spanish and Portugese, dominant at sea, produced relatively few charts, for fear of imparting their knowledge. Before long it was the Dutch who were travelling farther than any other nation of voyagers, and Amsterdam became the cartographic centre of the world. The pre-eminence of the Dutch culminated in Joannes Janssonius's *Novus atlas* (1658–61) and in the works of his rivals, the Blaeu family, arguably the greatest cartographers of all time. Their earliest work centred around terrestrial and celestial globes, and their first atlas was of the sea; their finest work was Johannes Blaeu's 11-volume *Atlas major* (1662), issued hand-coloured.

In 1570, Christopher Saxton instigated a survey of England and Wales, and his great atlas, published in 1579, was the first of its kind, consisting of detailed maps of individual areas of the country. William Camden's *Britannia*, an historical survey immensely popular for over two centuries, was first published in 1586. It was revised in 1607 to include maps after Saxton in reduced form and also after

▼ Johannes Blaeu
Atlas maior, sive cosmographia blaviana, 11 volumes, Latin text, 10 engraved titles, 593 engraved maps, plans, views and plates, Amsterdam, Johannes Blaeu, 1662. The greatest atlas produced, with contemporary hand-colouring. **£80,000–100,000** Individual maps by the Blaeu family, £150–2,000+

Collecting John Speed

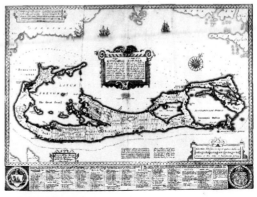

▲ John Speed
A Mapp of the Sommer Island called the Bermudas, engraved map, descriptive text, Humble, 1631. **£300–500**

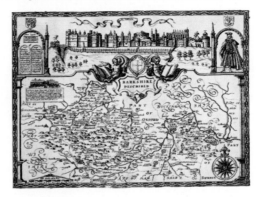

▲ John Speed
Barkshire Described, double-page engraved map, J. Sudbury & G. Humble, 1614–16. **£250–400**

those of John Norden. As the Saxton atlas is exceedingly rare and expensive, these become the earliest form of acquiring these maps for most collectors.

Herman Moll's *The World Described; or a New and Compleat Atlas* was one of the most important of 18th-century atlases, the maps of America being the most sought after. Other names to look for include John Seller, Richard Blome, Robert Morden, Moses Pitt, Edward Wells, Emanuel Bowen, Thomas Kitchin, Christopher and John Greenwood, Thomas Moule and John Cary.

While the complete atlases themselves are rare and expensive, copies broken up over the years yield individual maps and these can be eminently affordable, although the Saxtons are expensive and Blaeu more so than John Speed. The most sought after maps today are of the World, the Americas, Japan and the Far East, Australia and the Pacific. Price fluctuations are often dictated by an influx of collectors from one particular country or area, and in the mid-1990s interest is high in areas such as Poland, Greece and Turkey, but not in France or Yugoslavia. Early decorative sea charts are also highly sought after. English county maps are relatively inexpensive, the Home Counties and Cornwall being the most popular, but many good early maps can regularly be found for under £100.

John Speed's maps are easily distinguished by their detailed town plans and descriptive texts. They were the most up-to-date maps available, immensely popular in their time and still so today. Reissued time and again and therefore not hard to find or generally expensive, they are made very attractive for the collector by their fine engraving and ornamentation. Born in Cheshire in 1552, Speed was a tailor by profession; it was not until his fifties, when Sir Fulke Greville became his patron, that he was able to devote time to research. Saxton, Norden and Camden were his references, but much of the new information was his own. His maps began appearing in 1606, and in 1610–11 *Theatre of the Empire of Great Britaine* was published, followed by *A Prospect of the Most Famous Parts of the World* in 1627. Numerous editions exist of both, and while complete they are expensive, it is not difficult to acquire individual maps for quite modest sums.

▼ **Johann Theodore de Bry and Johann Israel de Bry**
Lesser Voyages, Part II: Relation of the Voyage of Jan Huyghen van Linschoten to Africa and the East Indies, 3 double-page or folding engraved maps, one plate and 38 illustrations, Frankfurt am Main, Wolffgang Richter, 1599. **£800–1,500**

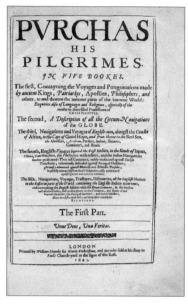

▼ **Maximilianus**
Epistola, de admirabili & novissima Hispanoru[m] in orientem navigatione, woodcut border, Rome, Franciscus Minitius Calvi, 1524. **£10,000–15,000**

▲ **Samuel Purchas**
Purchas his Pilgrimes, 4 volumes, engraved and woodcut illustrations, William Stansby for Henrie Fetherstone, 1625. With *Purchas his Pilgrimage*. **£6,000–8,000**

Historic Voyages

Some of the earliest travel books are accounts of voyages by land or sea. Whereas those from the 16th and 17th centuries may require an outlay of a few thousand pounds, later works can be found for a few hundred pounds, such as Richard Walter's *A Voyage Round the World…* (1748), by George Anson, one of the most popular maritime books of adventure in the 18th century.

The earliest books were often general compilations of numerous voyages, avidly read at the time and reprinted on several occasions. There may be very little price difference between a first or later edition, more important factors being condition and completeness: the lack of maps or volumes can greatly reduce the price. Several of the earliest and most important collections were reprinted by the Hakluyt Society at the end of the 19th or beginning of the 20th century, and these often contain useful scholarly introductions or essays.

One of the most famous of all such collections is Richard Hakluyt's *The Principall Navigations Voiages and Discoveries of the English Nation* (1589; reprinted 1903–5; Hakluyt Society, 1965). This work describes all the major early maritime voyages, and as such is an invaluable reference of early circumnavigation and travel in Africa, America, Asia, and the Arctic. Samuel Purchas continued Hakluyt's work, acquiring his manuscripts after his death, and his *Purchas His Pilgrimes* (1625; Hakluyt Society,

1905–7), was one of the most popular and complete collections of voyages in the English language. Johann Theodor de Bry issued a highly desirable collection, generally known as *Grands voyages* and *Petits voyages*, issued in parts between 1590 and 1634, with text in German or Latin. Complete sets are rare and extremely expensive, although individual parts can be found for a few hundred pounds.

The 18th century saw a great increase in the number of voyages undertaken, with subsequent reports becoming widely read at the time and more readily available today. Awnsham and John Churchill published four volumes of *A Collection of Voyages and Travels, some now first printed from original manuscripts, others now first published in English* in 1704, supplemented by two volumes in 1732 and by Osborne's two further volumes in 1745. Other early names to look for are William Dampier, whose *New Voyage* (1697), recounts the rescue of Alexander Selkirk, the model for Daniel Defoe's Robinson Crusoe; Thomas Salmon, whose *The Universal Traveller* (two volumes, 1745), contains fine maps by Moll and Kitchin; also John Harris, John Pinkerton and Thomas Osborne.

Circumnavigation – a voyage by sea encircling the entire globe – has always held enormous fascination, especially in the days when the world was thought by many to be flat (indeed it is still regarded as quite a feat today), and the names of Ferdinand

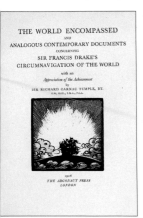

Collecting
Captain James Cook

Magellan and Sir Francis Drake are known to everyone. Accounts of their voyages were published in the early compilations but separate printings are rare: Antonio Pigafetta's account of Magellan's voyage, *A Briefe Declaration of the Voyage of Nauigation made abowte the Worlde*, was first published in English in 1525 (Hakluyt Society, 1874; Cleveland, 1906). Drake's circumnavigation of 1577 to 1580 was first recorded by Francis Pretty and printed in some copies of Hakluyt's 1589 collection, reprinted in 1618. The more interesting and lively version, however, is that written by his nephew from the notes and recollections of the chaplain, Francis Fletcher: *The World Encompassed by Sir Francis Drake* (1628; Hakluyt Society, 1854; Argonaut Press, 1926). A collected edition of his travels was published in 1653, *Sir Francis Drake Revived … being a Summary and true Relation of foure severall Voyages*.

Less expensive in the original are William Dampier and Woodes Rogers, buccaneers who tormented the Spanish in the South Seas, whose journals and writings are lively and highly entertaining without sacrificing scientific accuracy; and George Shelvocke, who was charged with piracy but got off on a technicality. It was Shelvocke's *A Voyage Around the World by Way of the Great South Sea* (1726), in which he recounts the shooting of an albatross, that was the inspiration for Samuel Taylor Coleridge's *Rime of the Ancient Mariner*.

Collecting material relating to Captain James Cook's voyages can be fairly complex, but there is a good bibliography published by the Public Library of New South Wales, edited by M.K. Beddie. There are individual accounts of each of his three voyages, as well as collected editions, all issued in French and English. John Hawkesworth wrote the official account of the first voyage, *An Account of the Voyages undertaken … for making Discoveries in the Southern Hemisphere and successfully performed by Commodore Byron, Captain Wallis, Captain Carteret and Captain Cook 1764–1771* (1773): written from the journals but partly fabricated by himself, it was an immediate success and was reprinted several times.

The same year saw publication of *A Journal of a Voyage to the South Sea in His Majesty's Ship the Endeavour*, from the papers of the draughtsman Sydney Parkinson, who died on the homeward voyage. This is more expensive than Hawkesworth's account because of its inclusion of fine hand-coloured engraved plates. The rarest account, however, is one published anonymously and surreptitiously two months after Cook's return, and attributed to James Matra or Magra, one of the crew: *A Journal of a Voyage Around the World in His Majesty's Ship Endeavour* (1771). William Anderson compiled *A New, Authentic and Complete Collection of Voyages round the World by Captain Cook* in 1784, reprinted as six volumes in 1790, and this is one of the best means of acquiring an account of the voyages, as is the four-volume abridged edition of 1784 published by John Stockdale.

▲ N. de Fer
Cette carte de Californie et du nouveau Mexique
engraved, Paris, 1700. This map shows California as an
island after the map in *Purchas his Pilgrimes*. **£150–250**

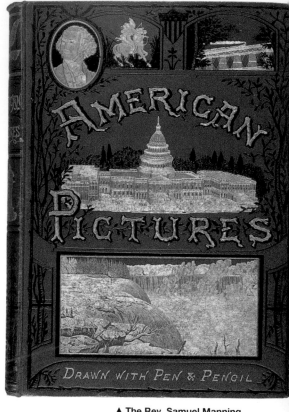

◄ James Henderson
A History of Brazil, 2 lithographed
maps and 28 plates, 1821. This is
a useful background volume and
becoming scarce. **£400–600**

▲ The Rev. Samuel Manning
*American Pictures drawn with Pen
and Pencil*, illustrations, Religious
Tract Society, 1880. One of a series
of "Pen and Pencil" views from
different countries. **£30–50**

The Americas

Books and maps on the exploration and discovery
of America have a strong emotive interest for
many collectors, with the early accounts being
highly sought after: expensive or impossible to
obtain in the original, often known only in one or
two copies in institutional libraries.

The first printed work relating to America is
Christopher Columbus's Letter or report of his voyage (1493), with similar reports following each of his
voyages (19th- and 20th-century reprints by the
Hakluyt Society and Argonaut Press). Columbus's
achievements were overshadowed by the publication of the voyages of Amerigo Vespucci, after
whom the continent was named, although it is
accepted today that only the voyage to Brazil actually took place. Contemporary accounts being
beyond the reach of most collectors, the Grabhorn
Press *Letter describing his Four Voyages to the New
World* (1925), is a good alternative.

The first general history of the early landings
was by Peter Martyr, *De nouo Orbe, of the History of*
the west Indies ... comprised in eight Decades (first
complete edition in English, 1612; reprinted 1912).
For accounts of the early English voyages, the Hakluyt Society editions of James Alexander Williamson's *The Cabot Voyages and Bristol Discovery under
Henry VII* (1962) and *The Voyages of the Cabots and
the English Discovery of North America under Henry
VIII* (1929), and their 1878 edition of the works of
Hawkins, are worth acquiring. The exploits of Sir
John Hawkins summon up the days of buccaneer-
ing, and his *A True Declaration of the troublesome
Voyage ... to the Parties of Guynea and the West Indies*
(1569) is one of the great rarities. It is the earliest
book written and printed in English relating the
adventures of an Englishman in the New World.

The earliest accounts of travels and settlements
in the interior are equally rare, such as *The Discoveries of the Large, Rich and Beautiful Empyre of Guiana*
(1596; Argonaut Press, 1928) by Sir Walter Ralegh,
or *Generall Historie of Virginia, New Engand and the
Summer Isles* (1624), by the first historian of Virginia,

◄ Eugène Duflot de Mofras
Exploration du territoire de l'Orégon, des Californies et de la Mer Vermeille, 3 volumes including Atlas, 8 engraved plates in text volumes, folding engraved map and 25 engraved or lithographed views, maps, charts and plans, Paris, Arthus Bertrand, 1844. This important voyage of 1840–42 extended from Central America to Alaska. **£2,500–5,000**

▼ Alexander von Humboldt and Aimé Bonpland
Researches concerning the Institutions and Monuments of the Ancient Inhabitants of America, 2 volumes in one, facsimile reprint, maps and plates, Amsterdam and New York, Theatrum Orbis Terrarum Ltd, & Da Capo Press, 1972. **£40–60**

► Manuel Rodriguez
El marañon y Amazonas, Madrid, Antonio Gonzalez de Reyes, 1684. First edition of this rare and important book on the discovery and early history of the Amazon. **£1,500–3,000**

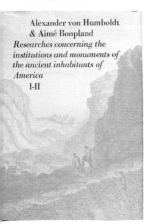

◄ Jonathan Carver
Travels through the Interior Parts of North America, 4 engraved plates, 2 folding maps, for the Author, 1778. First edition. **£500–800**
A Philadelphia edition of 1796, £150–250

John Smith (whose complete works were edited by Edward Arber in 1884).

As travel accounts from the late 18th and 19th centuries are more accessible, it is to this period that most new collectors will be drawn. There is a wealth of material available: general histories such as Cadwallader Colden's *The History of the Five Nations of Canada* (New York, 1727); county histories such as *History of Dallas County, Texas, from 1837 to 1887* by John Henry Brown, the first history of the county; Frank Edwards's *A Campaign in New Mexico with Colonel Doniphan … with a map of the route* (Philadelphia, 1847), an important description of the early days of Texas. The 19th century is rife with accounts by individual explorers, missionaries or Quakers that provide a fascinating insight into American life, such as Mrs. Frances Trollope's *Domestic Manners of the Americans* (1832). The Quaker preacher Thomas Chalkley, who settled in Philadelphia after preaching throughout the British Colonies, West Indies and British Columbia, had his *Collection of the Works* printed by Benjamin Franklin in 1749, providing an invaluable picture of people and events during his travels. An early account of the first settlers of Oregon is that by Thomas J. Farnham, *Travels in the Great Western Prairies, the Anahuac and Rocky Mountains, and in the Oregon Terrritories* (Poughkeepsie, 1841).

As the century progressed and more settlers moved west, guide-books for aspiring travellers were issued describing the journey, proposing routes and warning of the dangers; one such is Randolph Marcy's *The Prairie Traveller: a Handbook for Overland Exhibitions* (1859), which was re-issued several times.

One may choose to collect books on slavery, the Jesuits, the American Indians, early surveyors and traders, or books of views; although early colour-plate books will be costly, later steel-engravings will be more affordable, such as Nathaniel Parker Willis' *American Scenery* and *Canadian Scenery* (1840 and 1842 respectively).

◄ Edward Lear
Views in the Seven Ionian Islands,
facsimile reprint, one of 1,000 copies,
plates, Oldham, Hugh Broadbent,
1979. **£100–200**

▼ William Turner
Journal of a Tour in the Levant,
3 volumes, 2 engraved folding maps,
22 plates, 6 hand-coloured aquatints,
John Murray, 1820. **£1,500–2,500**

◄ Le Rhin de Bâle à Dusseldorf
18 maps, 16 plates, Leipzig, Karl Baedeker, 1854.
A reprint of the first title issued by Karl Baedeker in
1832. The early bindings were in boards; only later was
the red cloth used that is more commonplace today.
£300–600 Baedekers can be found for a few pounds
for later reprints, and some countries will be more
sought after than others, notably Russia (particularly for
1914) and Greece.

► William Beattie
Switzerland Illustrated, 2 volumes, engraved
additional titles, double-page map and 106 plates after
W.H. Bartlett, James S. Virtue, 1836. **£250–500**

Europe & the Middle East

European and Middle Eastern travel and topographical books can be collected from many
aspects: books of views; works on archaeology and
antiquities; those of decorative and architectural
interest; literary narratives; books of costume; letters; of exploratory, geographical or historical interest. One's interest may lie in forming a comprehensive collection based on a particular country,
whether it be France or Switzerland, Egypt or
Greece; in collecting general views of European
countries; or in following architectural and decorative trends throughout the ages across Europe. The
English-speaking collector may choose to concentrate on books in English (although some of the most
interesting will be in other languages).

Early and unillustrated accounts of travels can
provide an fascinating view of 17th-century Europe.
A marvellous and relatively affordable early work
which provides a good social picture of Europe is
that by Fynes Moryson, *An Itinerary Written by Fynes
Moryson, Gent ... containing his Ten yeeres Trauell
through the Twelve Dominions of Germany,
Bohmerland, Sweitzerland, Netherland, Denmarke,*
*Poland, Italy, Turky, France, England, Scotland and
Ireland* (1617; Glasgow, 1907–8). Other early travellers were William Lithgow, whose *Travels and
Voyages through Europe, Africa and Asia for nineteen
years* (1632) includes the first account of coffee-
drinking in Europe; and Thomas Coryate, who
found it almost impossible to interest a publisher in
his work *Coryats Crudities* (1611; 1776; Glasgow,
1905). This legendary and eccentric traveller produced what was the first, and for a long time the
only, handbook for continental travellers.

More commonplace during the 18th and 19th
centuries, such accounts become quite easy to obtain.
Edward Daniel Clarke's *Travels in various Countries
of Europe, Asia and Africa, 1790–1800* (six volumes,
1810–23), is a remarkable account of his extensive
travels, a work which inspired Byron and others of
the Romantic movement.

The earliest illustrated books were composed of
simple and often crude woodcuts, such as Hartmann
Schedel's *Liber chronicarum* (1493), more often
called the "Nuremberg Chronicle", but the late 18th
and early 19th century brought the great age of the

▼ S.L. Bensusan
Morocco, 74 coloured plates by
A.S. Forrest, Adam & Charles Black,
1904. **£40–80**

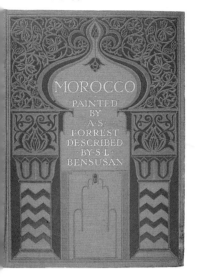

LE MUSÉE   LE THÉÂTRE

▲ Vues du Havre
24 lithographed scenes joined to form continuous strip,
coloured by hand, Paris, F. Sinnett, c.1840. **£40–80**

► Fr. Bianchi Noe
Viaggio da Venetia al Santo Sepolcro et al Monte Sinai,
woodcut illustrations in text, Venice, Alessandro Vecchi,
1619. One of the oldest Italian travel books, this work
first appeared in 1500 as an anonymous pilgrim's
handbook and guide to Palestine and was not attributed
to Father Noe until the 1566 edition. **£800–1,500**
An edition of 1690, £300–500; of 1770, £150–250

illustrated travel book. Many of the finest artists were English, tempted abroad by the prospect of the Grand Tour, and by interest generated in Europe as a result of the Napoleonic Wars. The grandest of these books contain superb colour-plates and are highly desirable and subsequently expensive, such as Edward Dodwell's *Views in Greece* (1821) and Thomas and William Daniell's *A Picturesque Voyage to India* (1810). One of the greatest of these colour-plate books is David Roberts's and Louis Haghe's *The Holy Land, Syria, Idumea, Arabia, Egypt and Nubia* (1842–49). The original hand-coloured folio edition is extremely expensive, but the later quarto edition with tinted plates can be found under £1,000. Less expensive are books of views engraved on steel, as well as later lithographed or wood-engraved works, traditionally neglected in favour of the hand-coloured or early engraved books.

As is the case with collecting maps, fashion is a factor in dictating which countries are the more sought after. For example, when the library of Henry M. Blackmer II, devoted to books associated with the Ottoman Empire (Greece, Cyprus, Turkey and the Levant) came up for sale accompanied by its fine catalogue (itself an invaluable reference work), interest in and prices for those areas rose accordingly. Politics and the movement of people may also affect prices: for example, in the mid-1990s interest in Poland is strong, and there is also a demand amongst Lebanese living in France and elsewhere for books on their country.

By reading catalogues to obtain a feel for prices and trends, one should then be able to look for neglected areas. These could be chromolithographed or wood-engraved guide-books other than those issued by Baedeker, and often rather quaint local publications; or accounts of the earliest motorized journeys, written at the beginning of this century, and still not seriously collected, although this was the age when mass travel really began. Alternatively, at the begining of the 20th century, publishers like A. & C. Black and Dent issued series of topographical books and guide-books, usually illustrated by respected artists. These were mass-produced, are often found in decorative bindings, and are still reasonably priced.

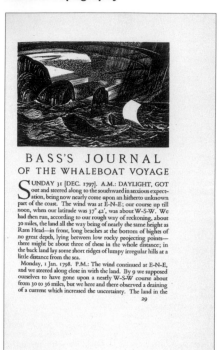

BASS'S JOURNAL
OF THE WHALEBOAT VOYAGE

SUNDAY 31 [DEC. 1797]. A.M.: DAYLIGHT, GOT
out and steered along to the southward in anxious expect-
ation, being now nearly come upon an hitherto unknown
part of the coast. The wind was at E-N-E; our course up till
noon, when our latitude was 37° 42′, was about W-S-W. We
had then run, according to our rough way of reckoning, about
30 miles, the land all the way being of nearly the same height as
Ram Head—in front, long beaches at the bottom of bights of
no great depth, lying between low rocky projecting points—
there might be about three of these in the whole distance; in
the back land lay some short ridges of lumpy irregular hills at a
little distance from the sea.
  Monday, 1 Jan. 1798. P.M.: The wind continued at E-N-E,
and we steered along close in with the land. By 9 we supposed
ourselves to have gone upon a nearly W-S-W course about
from 30 to 36 miles, but we here and there observed a draining
of a current which increased the uncertainty. The land in the
29

▲ Matthew Flinders
Narrative of his Voyage in the Schooner "Francis",
limited to 750 copies, 7 wood-engraved illustrations by
John Buckland Wright, Golden Cockerel Press, 1946.
£150–250
Flinders was the first to circumnavigate Australia and his
own work *A Voyage to Terra Australis ... 1801, 1802
and 1803*, 2 volumes and Atlas volume, 1814, is
extremely important, and expensive. £8,000–10,000

▼ Ernest Peixotto
Pacific Shores from Panama, illustrations, New York,
Charles Scribner's Sons, 1913. **£20–40**

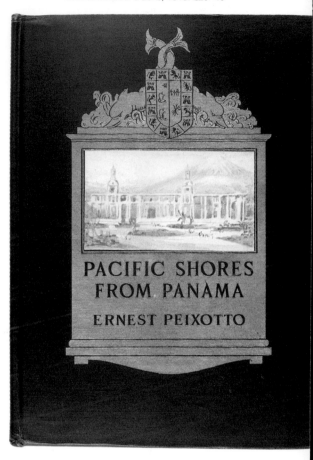

Australasia & the Pacific

Europe, the Middle East and Africa have long
been the subject of travel books, whereas the
history of books on Australia and New Zealand is
relatively recent. Early accounts of the exploration
and settlement of these countries are rare and even
19th-century accounts are uncommon, especially in
original bindings. Inextricably linked with the earliest accounts are voyages to the South Seas, the exploration of the Pacific and the East Indies. Many of the
earliest voyages can be found in collections such as
Purchas, Churchill and Hakluyt, from which they
can also be acquired as extracts.

The earliest account in English of Abel
Tasman's voyage in 1642, during which he discovered Tasmania and New Zealand, appeared in *An
Account of the Several Late Voyages and Discoveries to
the South and North* (1694; second edition 1711).
Although edited by Tancred Robinson, it is usually
catalogued under the name of Sir John Narborough,
whose voyage of 1669 to 1671 was the first English

journey into the Pacific since that of Hawkins in
1594. Other names worth looking for are Alexander
Dalrymple, who was turned down in favour of Cook
to lead the *Endeavour*'s voyage to find *Terra Australis*;
Louis Antoine de Bougainville, who sighted the
Great Barrier Reef and visited Tahiti; and works by
or about Jean François de la Pérouse, who landed in
Botany Bay hours after the First Fleet but disappeared on his homeward voyage. One of the most
famous names associated with the South Pacific is
that of William Bligh, whose own accounts of heroic
journeys by long-boat – *A Narrative of the Mutiny*
(1790) and *A Voyage to the South Seas* (1792) – will be
sought after in first edition, but have been reprinted
several times in the 20th century by the Golden
Cockerel Press and the Limited Editions Club.

Useful catalogues to acquire would be "The
Longueville Collection of Voyages and Travels to
Australia and the South Seas" (Sotheby's, 1992), and
those from booksellers Bernard Quaritch and

A
NARRATIVE
OF THE
EXPEDITION
TO
BOTANY BAY;
WITH AN ACCOUNT OF
NEW SOUTH WALES,
ITS PRODUCTIONS, INHABITANTS, &c,

TO WHICH IS SUBJOINED,

A LIST of the CIVIL and MILITARY
ESTABLISHMENTS at

PORT JACKSON.

BY CAPTAIN WATKIN TENCH,
OF THE MARINES.

LONDON:

PRINTED FOR J. DEBRETT, OPPOSITE
BURLINGTON-HOUSE, PICCADILLY.
1789.

▲ Watkin Tench
A Narrative of the Expedition to Botany Bay, for
J. Debrett, 1789. First edition of first published account
of the settlement of Australia. **£1,500–2,000**

Hordern House, which will provide details of books on the first European discoveries of Australian territories and exploration and settlement there, including settlers' own accounts of life in general and of the gold rushes in particular, as well as guide-books. Although much may be beyond the pocket of many collectors, catalogues will provide useful background information. The earliest accounts of settlement by Watkin Tench, Arthur Philip, John White and George Barrington, a famous pickpocket who was sent to New South Wales and became chief of police in Parramatta, were quickly reprinted and translated into French and German, making them more affordable for the collector today. Books on the overland exploration of Australia begin to appear from 1813 onwards, although once again these early works can be extremely hard to find. Charles Sturt, Joesph Cross, Thomas Livingston Mitchell, and John McDougall Stuart are all names associated with these early exploratory days.

Collecting
Books on the Arctic and Antarctic

Sir Ernest Henry Shackleton ▼
The Heart of the Antarctic being the story of the British Antarctic Expedition, 1907–9, 2 volumes, plates, William Heinemann, 1909. First edition. **£100–250**
3-volume de luxe signed edition, £1,000–2,000

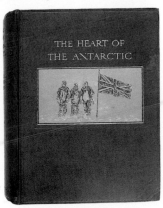

▲ Apsley Cherry-Garrard
The Worst Journey in the World, Antarctic 1910–13, 2 volumes, 63 plates, 5 maps, Constable and Co., 1922. Tale of Scott's last expedition. First edition. **£300–700**

The romance of the North-West Passage has long exerted its influence: early books are scarce, but there are titles from the 18th and 19th centuries well worth looking for, such as William Edward Parry's *Journal of a Voyage for the Discovery of a North-West Passage from the Atlantic to the Pacific* (1821). The Arctic and Antarctic conjure up for most people tales of extraordinary daring, truly brave explorers and terrible loss. Romantic heroes such as Scott and Amundsen still exert a powerful hold over the imagination. Books on these adventures are quite easy to find, are usually well illustrated and often bound in decorative cloth; and even earlier works such as Sir John Franklin's *Narrative of a Journey to the Shores of the Polar Sea* (1823) are not expensive. At the end of the century Fridtjof Nansen wrote several books and the best known, *Farthest North* (1897), is quite easily found in excellent condition.

The Antarctic has been the subject of more recent books, many quite modestly priced. One of the most unusual exceptions is *Aurora Australis* (1908), edited by Sir Ernest Shackleton, which was written, illustrated, printed and bound by members of Shackleton's expedition team, at the winter quarters of the British Antarctic Expedition. All copies are avidly sought after.

▼ **J. and R. Fairfax Blakeborough**
The Spirit of Yorkshire, 51 illustrations, B.T. Batsford, 1954. One of the easily obtainable Batsford County books. **£20–30**

▲ **Tourists Guide to the Trossachs**
24 chromolithographed plates and other illustrations, Thomas Nelson, c.1880. **£30–40**

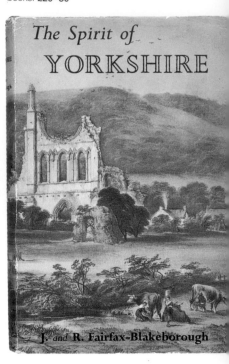

The British Isles

The majority of British topographical books published before the end of the 18th century were illustrated surveys, the best known being William Camden's *Britannia* (1610) and John Stow's *The Summarye of the Chronicles of England* and *A Survay of London* (1598). Among the earliest county surveys was William Lambard's *A Perambulation of Kent* (1576). All of these have been printed in many different editions and hence can be found without too great a financial outlay.

The cult of the picturesque, fashionable at the turn of the 19th century, focused attention on topography. Landscape and buildings were picturesque if they had the qualities of composed paintings, as seen in the engraved plates in Humphry Repton's landscape garden books. Many of the greatest topographical books of the 19th century were architectural, with buildings depicted as part of a social environment. The publisher, Rudolph Ackermann, thrived on this fashion for topographical illustration: his *Microcosm of London, or London in Miniature, the Architecture by A. Pugin, the Manners and Customs by Thomas Rowlandson* (1808), and his two-volume work on the colleges of Oxford and Cambridge, are fine and well-known examples. John Britton worked as an architectural draughtsman, publishing

county surveys of architectural antiquities, *The Beauties of England and Wales* (1801–21), containing 700 illustrations. Under his tutelage a whole school of topographical illustrators flourished, including Samuel Prout, Frederick Mackenzie, W.H. Bartlett and the watercolourist George Cattermole.

The Napoleonic Wars focused interest on foreign countries and the greatest artists often worked abroad, several returning ultimately to the English landscape. William Daniell's great work *A Voyage around Great Britain* (1814–25) followed the works undertaken in conjunction with his brother Thomas Daniell depicting the Orient and India.

With the advent of steel-engraving, far more durable than copper, artists could see their work reaching wider audences, and topographical illustration spread over into decoration in literature, annuals and periodicals. Topographical and architectural artists learnt to draw for the engraver. John Sell Cotman, a natural landscape painter whose hands were tied by the publishers' demands for antiquarian views, worked on a series of architectural views of Norfolk and Suffolk before embarking on a series of poorly engraved scenic views, *Excursions through Norfolk* (1818–19). J.M.W. Turner produced many landscape drawings to be reproduced as

Collecting Books on London

▼ **Samuel Ireland**
Picturesque Views on the River Thames, 2 volumes, large paper copy, engraved frontispieces, 2 maps and 52 aquatint plates, other illustrations in the text, T.&T. Egerton, 1792. **£200–300**

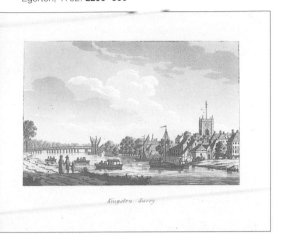

▼ **John Bowles**
Britannia Illustrata. Several Prospects, of the Royal Palaces, & Publick Buildings of England, engraved title incorporating panoramas of Westminster and London, and 22 plates, John Bowles, c.1731. **£200–400**
John Bowles published two earlier volumes of engraved views of England, the first in 1720, copying earlier plates in books by John Stow and Johannes Kip. The three parts can be found separately or bound as one volume and were re-issued several times.

Thomas Lord Busby ▲
Costume of the Lower Orders of London, hand-coloured engraved frontispiece and 23 plates, Baldwin & Co., 1820. **£300–600**

engravings for annuals and keepsakes of this period, but it was his first large-scale project, *Liber Studiorum* (1807–19) which brought prestige to steel-engraving, followed by the landscape *Picturesque View of the Southern Coast of Engand* (1814–26), which was illustrated by Turner, William Westall, Samuel Owen and William Havell. The 1830s and 1840s saw a series of books of picturesque views and landscape scenery, such as *Heath's Picturesque Annual*, whilst the development of the lithograph during the 1820s created a more atmospheric medium for views and architecture, particularly notable in the works of Thomas Shotter Boys, whose *Original Views of London* was published in 1842.

The mid-19th century brought books on railways, the Great Exhibition and the Thames Tunnel, technological achievements becoming of great interest generally. Guide-books were being published by local booksellers as travel became more accessible to a wider class of people. It was this mobility that created the demand for series such as the Highways and Byways, the Batsford and Robert Hale County books, and the Shell Guides. Twentieth-century illustrators such as John Piper turned once again to the landscape, portraying the countryside in its own right or as decoration for poetry or novels.

Interest in topography is often sparked by collecting books relating to one's home area. Ancient cities such as Bath or York could inspire a fine collection, with many books having been published on the history of such cities, their buildings and landscape. A still richer area is London itself. The early maps of London were often simple bird's-eye views of the City with crude representations of the buildings and the river. The earliest books were illustrated surveys, including that carried out by John Stow in 1598. The 17th and 18th centuries saw the publication of many volumes depicting the buildings of London, engraved after W. Hollar, Johannes Kip, Thomas Sandby and many others. The Great Fire, displays of fireworks, waterworks and executions have all been depicted through the years, forming a remarkable social history. A collection of such books brings to life the London that has all but disappeared. Many volumes containing plates depicting the trades or "cries" of London were published during the late 18th and 19th centuries, for both children and adults. Panoramas were also popular during this time; whether less expensive wood-engraved views for the popular market or fine engraved and hand-coloured examples, these can be a particularly satisfying means of building up a collection.

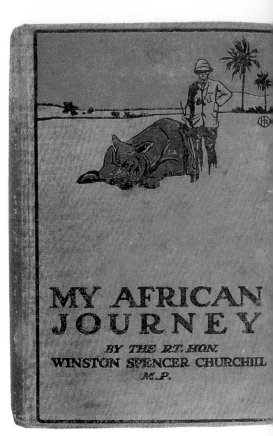

► **Winston Churchill**
My African Journey, Hodder and
Stoughton, 1908. First edition.
£100–200

◄ **David Livingstone**
*Missionary Travels and Researches
in South Africa*, 1857. First edition,
rebound. **£100–200**
A fine copy in original cloth,
£300–400

Other Collecting Areas

The collector of travel books may choose to concentrate on a particular country, yet others prefer to concentrate on the human element. By choosing to collect books by or about individual travellers one can acquire first-hand accounts of heroic adventures and tales of escapism. The Arctic and Antarctic have heroes such as Scott, Amundsen, Shackleton and Franklin, but it is possibly Africa and the Middle East which have most inspired the romantic traveller, and provided the background to some of the most vivid travel books. The majority are from the 19th and 20th centuries, are quite reasonable in price and often lead to a wider, more in-depth collection of travel books.

Sir Samuel White Baker was an early explorer of the Nile and also undertook an anti-slavery expedition to Africa. His several books include *The Albert N'Yanza, Great Basin of the Nile* (1866) and *The Nile Tributaries of Abyssinia and the Sword Hunters of the Hamran Arabs* (1867). The African Association was formed in the 19th century to explore the heart of Africa, later becoming the Royal Geographical Society. One of its early members was Mungo Park, who explored the source of the Niger, and wrote several classic accounts of his expeditions. Arguably the best-known name associated with Africa is David

Livingstone: a missionary who spent 30 years travelling in Africa and wrote several books about his experiences, including *Missionary Travels and Researches in South Africa* (1857). One of the greatest names associated with the Middle East and Arabia is that of T.E. Lawrence ("Lawrence of Arabia"). His *The Seven Pillars of Wisdom* is now extremely expensive in the 1926 privately printed first edition, but the first trade edition of 1935 is relatively common; and his other works such as *Crusader Castles* (1936) and *Secret Despatches from Arabia* (1939) are more readily available. Charles Doughty, Harry St. John Bridge Philby (father of the spy Kim Philby) and Wilfred Thesiger are other names of this century worth searching for, and whilst Charles Doughty's *Travels in Arabia Deserta* in the first edition of 1888 will cost a substantial amount, the 1936 edition should be found for less than £100.

Perhaps a more unusual way of collecting invidual travellers would be to concentrate on women writers. An early example could be Marie Catherine, Countess d'Aulnoy, whose *The Ingenious and Diverting Letters of the Lady —'s Travels into Spain* (1691), was immensely popular and reprinted 16 times before 1800. The Victorian and Edwardian women were resourceful travellers in India and

Africa, often accompanying their husbands, but writing their own accounts and providing a different perspective from those written by men. Isabella Lucy Bird travelled to the United States and Canada, Australia and New Zealand and the Sandwich Islands, studied medicine and founded hospitals in Kashmir and the Punjab. A prolific writer and the first lady fellow of the Royal Geographical Society, she wrote, among other works, *The Hawaian Archipelago* (1875), *A Lady's Life in the Rocky Mountains* (1879) and *Journeys in Persia and Kurdistan* (1891). A recent explorer of Arabia is Freya Stark, whose works can be found under £50.

Books on travel and topography can be collected in order simply to obtain new images of lands and people, or with the aim of broadening one's horizons and understanding of other races, but equally one could choose to concentrate on a more narrow field. Navigation and naval expeditions, tales of disasters and shipwrecks, guide-books, or architectural studies, all could form inexpensive and unusual areas of interest. These types of books have always been popular with the armchair traveller, and possibly never more so today, as sales of the works of popular living travel writers, such as Patrick Leigh Fermor, Gavin Young, Colin Thubron and Eric Newby testify.

Remembered by many primarily for his translation of the *Arabian Nights*, Sir Richard Burton was, as well as a fine translator, an explorer, linguist, soldier, writer and anthropologist. One of the most flamboyant characters of his day, he left Oxford without graduating, and joined the Indian army in 1842. He left in 1849, and travelled (in disguise) to the forbidden city of Mecca, to Africa, the Crimea and Salt Lake City; he also spent time as Consul in Brazil, Damascus and Trieste. His travels resulted in over 40 volumes, including collections of folklore, poetry and translations of erotica, notably the *Kama Sutra* (1883). Most of his works in first edition in original cloth will be extremely expensive, the most scarce titles often costing upwards of £1,000; prices will be lower for rebound copies, and most have been reprinted and can be found in more affordable editions. His books range from *Ultima Thule, or a Summer in Iceland* (1875), to *Zanzibar, City, Island and Coast* (1872), from *Explorations of the Highlands of Brazil* (1869) to *Vikram and the Vampire, or Tales of Hindu Devilry* (1870). On his death his wife, Isabel, herself a traveller and writer, destroyed his papers and diaries, many of which explored his interest in sexual deviancy and erotica.

Americana

Collecting a national literature: from the Declaration of Independence to 1930s public works pamphlets

▲ **Prince Maximilian Alexander Philipp zu Wied-Neuwied**
Reise in das innere Nord-America in den Jahren 1832 bis 1834, 2 volumes, text and atlas, 81 aquatint plates coloured by hand after Karl Bodmer, folding engraved map, woodcut illustrations, Coblenz, J. Hoelscher, 1839–41. The finest work on American Indian life and the American frontier. **£80,000–100,000**

The field of Americana is a broad and exciting area of book-collecting. In its largest sense, it encompasses all of the Western Hemisphere and any related works in history, geography, travel, politics, cartography, and the arts and sciences which fall therein. It also encompasses a variety of printed genres, ranging from broadsides (such as the Declaration of Independence) to visual images, as well as books. However, only a few libraries have the resources to collect on this exceptional scale, and most collectors pursue some smaller aspect of the field. To many the term "Americana",

has a more limited meaning, describing books and maps relating to the part of North America that is now the United States of America. This has gained currency because the bulk of active collectors are focused on the history of the United States. Both uses are accurate, but materials relating to other areas are usually, and more strictly, called Latin Americana, Canadiana, and so on, to distinguish them. The bibliographer Wright Howes suggested "U.S.iana" as an alternative and more accurate term, but this infelicitous phrase has never caught on.

In whatever sense Americana is used, it

In CONGRESS, July 4, 1776.

A DECLARATION

By the REPRESENTATIVES of the

UNITED STATES OF AMERICA,

In GENERAL CONGRESS ASSEMBLED.

[Full text of the Declaration of Independence, in period typography]

Signed by Order and in Behalf of the Congress,

JOHN HANCOCK, President.

ATTEST.
CHARLES THOMSON, Secretary.

PHILADELPHIA: PRINTED BY JOHN DUNLAP.

◀ **The Declaration of Independence**
In Congress, July 4th, 1776. A Declaration by the Representatives of the United States of America in General Congress Assembled … signed by Order and in Behalf of the Congress, John Hancock, President, Philadelphia, Printed by John Dunlap, 4 or 5 July 1776. This folio broadside is the first printing of the Declaration of Independence, one of only 23 known surviving copies, the majority now in institutional hands. The evening of the actual declaration a fair copy was taken to the printing office of John Dunlap where copies were printed overnight, probably no more than 100 in total. The last copy sold at auction, 1991, fetched **$2.1million (£1.3million)**

▲ **Giovanni Battista Ramusio**
Brasil, double-page woodcut map orientated west to the top, 265mm by 362mm, Venice, Giunti, c.1560. A map from the earliest collection of voyages, *Delle navigationi et viaggi*, first published 1554. **£300–500**

begins in 1493, with the publication of Columbus's Letter, or report of his first voyage, written to inform the Spanish Court of his discoveries, and published in several forms immediately after his return. The *Epistola…* is best known in its Rome 1493 edition, of which two copies appeared at auction during the quincentenary year of 1992. Each fetched about $330,000 (£180,000) for the small 8-page pamphlet, making it word-for-word one of the most valuable printed works.

Most Americana collectors have chosen to collect either geographically (often the state or country in which they live), by topic (such as

early exploration and discovery, the American Revolution, the western fur trade, presidential politics, or the career of a hero like Simon Bolívar), or by genre (maps, prints, broadsides, imprints or photographs). These themes often logically become combined. Any collector of books on the exploration of the American West will almost certainly become interested in the related maps, while politics will as readily relate to political cartoons. The new collector will do best by picking the niche which is of most interest to themselves and trying to familiarize themselves with the relevant reference works. This will give a

► **R.M.**

Newes of Sr. Walter Rauleigh. With the True Description of Guiana, woodcut portrait, H. Gosson and J. Wright, 1618. **£500–700**
Even an incomplete copy of this early work on Ralegh's discovery of Guiana would be of interest. His own book, *The Discoverie of the Large, Rich, and Bewtiful Empire of Guiana,* first published in 1596, £3,000–4,000. The Argonaut Press edition of 1928, £60–100

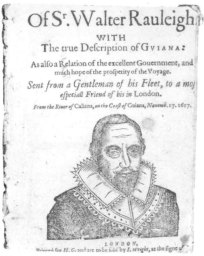

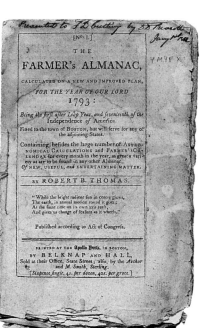

◄ **Robert Bailey Thomas**
The Farmer's Almanac, Boston, Belknap and Hall, 1792. The first issue of the most popular and most enduring of all American almanacs.
£600–1,000
Other almanacs include *Poor Richard Improves, being an Almanack,* a collection of Benjamin Franklin's proverbs, sayings and aphorisms written and published over several years from 1733. The earliest and last titles are extremely rare, the others are usually £2,000–4,000. The Limited Editions Club produced a facsimile reprint of the series in 1964, £100–200

► **Isaiah Thomas**
The History of Printing in America, 2 volumes, 5 engraved plates, Worcester, Thomas, 1810. First edition in original boards.
£800–1,200

better idea of the scope of the field and the books to look for. Thus a collector of Indian captivities would do well to read R.W.G. Vail's *The Voice of the Old Frontier,* while an interest in travel in the American West would lead to *The Plains and the Rockies* by Henry R. Wagner and Charles L. Camp. For books related to the United States, the handiest guide is Wright Howes' *U.S.iana,* which lists almost 12,000 titles. There are numerous state and genre bibliographies which provide useful background material.

Americana has been a collecting field since the 1840s, when gentlemen such as John

Carter Brown and James Lenox began to gather books on the topic with a vigour which had previously been reserved for the literature of early printed books. Their collections now form the basis of the John Carter Brown Library at Brown University in Providence, Rhode Island and the Americana material at the New York Public Library, two of the greatest institutional holdings in the field. The first collectors generally focused on the very early periods of discovery and exploration. By the late 19th century colonial material and the American Revolution had become fashionable to collect, and in the mid-1920s, Western

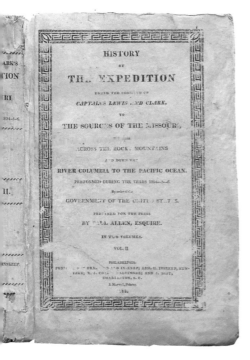

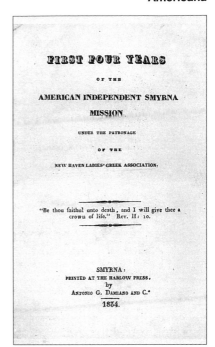

◀ Meriwether Lewis and William Clark

History of the Expedition under the command of Captains Lewis and Clark, to the Sources of the Missouri, thence across the Rocky Mountains and down the River Columbia to the Pacific Ocean, performed during the years 1804–5–6, 2 volumes, 6 engraved maps and plans, one folding, Philadelphia, Bradford and Inskeep, 1814. The definitive account of the most important exploration of the North American continent, funded by Congress with the aim of establishing trade ties with the Indians. First edition in the original boards. **£15,000–20,000** Rebound, £5,000–8,000. First English edition, 1814, £2,000–5,000. New York, 1893, £200–400. An earlier unofficial "Apocrypha" account of their voyage, *The Travels of Capts. Lewis & Clarke*, 1809, £400–700

▲ Josiah and Emilia Brewer and Mary Reynolds

First Four Years of the American Independent Smyrna Mission, under the Patronage of the New Haven Ladies' Greek Association, Smyrna, Harlow Press, 1834. A collection could be formed on the influence of Americans abroad; this work documents the history of a school for Greek girls run by American missionaries. In later years the mission became the headquarters for all American missionary work in the Levant. **£400–800**

◀ Lewis A. Tarascon

Petition of Lewis A. Tarascon (and others) praying the opening of a Wagon Road from the River Missouri, North of the River Kansas to the River Columbia, Washington, 1824. Documents issued by the government are often repositories of important material. Tarascon's memorial is the first proposal for a road to the Pacific Ocean. **£150–200**

Americana emerged as a field. Since then a number of speciality areas have developed, ranging from the Civil War, to guidebooks issued by the Works Progress Administration during the Great Depression.

While generally speaking the earlier fields are more expensive and difficult to collect, areas more recent in date often remain quite affordable. In a field such as early travel, where many books may be too costly for most collectors (or simply unavailable because all known copies are in libraries), the scholarship of the last century or so has made many of them available in new editions, some of which are themselves collectors' items. For example, the 12-volume set of Hakluyt's *Principal Navigations* published in Glasgow in 1903–5 will cost a few hundred pounds; a copy of the 1589 edition complete with the Ortelius map, might cost one hundred times as much.

There are opportunities to collect at almost every level of the market, and in the late 19th- and 20th-century material there are numerous collecting possibilities as yet little explored. Americana remains a broad and open field with numerous genres and topics for the collector to explore.

WILLIAM REESE

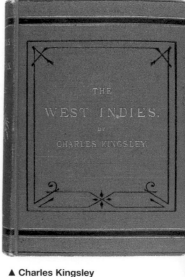

▼ Admiral Raphael Semmes
Memoirs of Service Afloat during the War between the States, Baltimore, Kelly, Piet and Co., 1869. The Civil War is an active area of collecting, and this narrative by the commander of the Rebel-raising ship *Alabama*, has both naval and biographical interest. **£200–300**

▲ Charles Kingsley
At Last, a Christmas in the West Indies, illustrations, New York, Harper Brothers, 1871. **£30–70**

▲ Thomas Loraine McKenney and James Hall
History of the Indian Tribes of North America, 117 lithographed portraits and 3 landscapes, coloured by hand, Philadelphia, Edward C. Biddle and others, 1833–44. First issued in 20 parts printed by four different publishers and over more than a decade, this work has been reprinted upon numerous occasions in various formats. The original parts. **£15,000–20,000** Edition of 1933–34, published in Edinburgh, £150–300

► Samuel Warner
Authentic and Impartial Narrative of the Tragical Scene ... when Fifty-Five of its Inhabitants ... were inhumanly Massacred by the Blacks, New York, Warner & West, 1831. A description of the famous Nat Turner slave rebellion. A gruesome and dramatic frontispiece showing the massacres is usually missing; if present, the price could be five times as much. **£500–800**

The Growth of America

The first book printed in the United States was *The Whole Book of Psalmes*, known as the "Bay Psalm Book". There is no identification of printer, place or date on the book, although it is is known to have been printed in Cambridge, Massachusetts in 1640 by Stephen Daye, and unidentified copies may still be around today. Any book printed prior to 1700 is rare. In terms of European printing, books printed up to 1501 are known as *incunabula*; in America, all books printed up to 1701 fall into this category.

If money were no object, a collection could consist of various areas: the grand colour-plate books of landscapes and the natural history of the country; works relating to the Independence and the early presidents, Abraham Lincoln, George Washington and John Quincy Adams; important books documenting the history of a county such as Thomas Jefferson's *Notes on the State of Virginia* (London,

1787), which first appeared in Paris in 1785; early travel books relating to the discovery of the Americas, such as *An Account of a Voyage for the Discovery of a North-West Passage by Hudson's Streights to the Western and Southern Ocean of America* (London, 1748); books written or printed by Benjamin Franklin, some more easily acquired than others; exotic imprints such as those from the Caribbean, now scarce due to the disintegration caused by the climate. Recent trends have also included Afro-American history, with prices rising rapidly for associated works. For most collectors, money will determine and limit the choice.

While some material relating to the Civil War is expensive, there is still much that is modestly priced, including narratives of commanders involved in the battles – for example, Admiral Raphael Semmes's *Memoirs of Service Afloat* (Baltimore, 1869). Many

◀ **Charles F. Swift**
Cape Cod the Right Arm of Massachusetts an Historical Narrative, Yarmouth, Register Publishing Company, 1897. Local histories such as this can be found quite inexpensively. **£80–120**

▼ **J.Armstrong**
Early Life Among the Indians, illustrations, Wisconsin, 1892.
£40–80

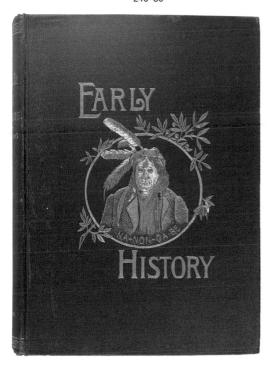

▲ *Arkansas a Guide to the State*
Compiled by Workers of the Writers' Program of the Work Projects Administration in the State of Arkansas, illustrations, New York, Hastings House, 1941. **£30–40**

19th-century books on travels in the interior are quite affordable; Frederick Law Olmsted, best known for designing Central Park, published a series of books on his travels in the South, known collectively as *The Cotton Kingdom*; the individual volumes, such as *A Journey through Texas* (New York, 1857), can be found for a few hundred pounds. Novels on America and travel books written by Europeans can provide an interesting and often amusing aspect to a collection: Charles Dickens' *American Notes for General Circulation* (London, 1843), is an hilarious account of his trip and can be found fairly easily. Some of the most fascinating Americana can be found in self-published works, which are usually very reasonable, such as George Devol's *Forty Years a Gambler on the Mississipi* (1887).

The greatest 20th-century collector of Americana was Thomas Streeter, a New York lawyer and businessman. After his death in 1965, his collection was dispersed by Sotheby Parke Bernet Galleries in New York between 1966 and 1969. The sale catalogue is a major reference tool in its own right (eight volumes including the index issued in 1970), listing 4,421 lots with detailed notes (most written by Streeter while he collected). The Streeter catalogue will introduce the collector to a broad range of material of every geographical region and price range. While many of the books Streeter collected are very rare and expensive, others remain affordable. One can also search out new areas of interest; these could include books issued by the Works Progress Administration, which provide a fascinating insight into 1930s America; local histories and imprints rather than those of national coverage; or the good facsimiles of earlier works issued by the Imprint Society of Barre, Massachusetts or the Grabhorn Press.

Science & Medicine

Understanding man and man's place in the world: Harvey and circulation to Copernicus and the solar system

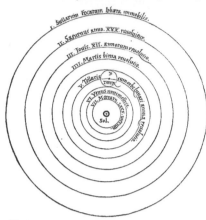

▲ **Nicolaus Copernicus**
De revolutionibus orbium coelestium, diagrams,
Nuremberg, Joannes Petreius, 1543. **£80,000–100,000**
Third edition, Amsterdam, Janson, 1617,
£1,000–2,000; facsimile reprint, Paris, 1927, £100–200

At its grandest, collecting the history of science means collecting some of the world's great ideas, such as Copernicus's *De revolutionibus orbium coelestium* and Darwin's *On the Origin of Species*, both of which sought to establish mankind's place in the universe; or the first announcements of scientific discoveries or inventions that have materially changed the way we live, like James Watt's improvements to the steam engine and the subsequent development of the railway, or James Logie Baird's invention of television. In medicine, Jenner's discovery of vaccination led to the total eradication of smallpox, a disease which

had killed, blinded or disfigured millions (the official eradication of smallpox was not made by the World Health Organization until 8 May 1980). Collecting in this way was first given a focus in the catalogue *Exhibition of First Editions of Epochal Achievements in the History of Science*; the exhibition was held at the University of California at Berkeley in 1934, based on the collection of Herbert McLean Evans. There are a number of more modern guides to this kind of collecting, including Bern Dibner's *Heralds of Science* (New Haven, 1955, second edition, Cambridge, Mass., 1969) and, for medicine, Haskell F. Norman's *One Hundred Books*

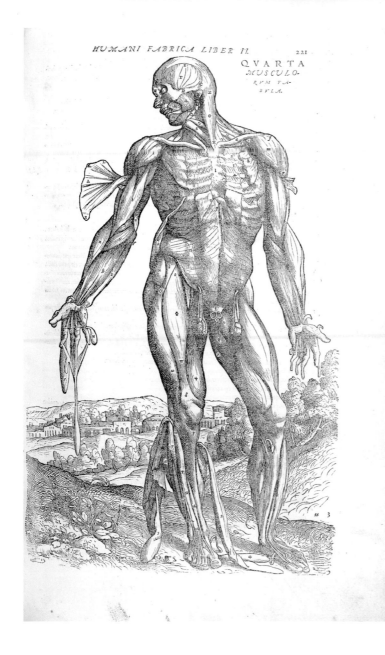

HUMANI FABRICA LIBER II. 221

QVARTA
MVSCVLO-
RVM TA-
BVLA.

◀ **Andreas Vesalius**
*De humani corporis fabrica libri
septem*, woodcut title-page and
illustrations in text, Basle, Joannes
Oporinus, 1555. Second folio
edition. First published in 1543,
this edition of the most important
medical work of the 16th century
was more sumptuous than the first
and contains revisions to the text.
£7,000–10,000
In 1934 the Bremer Press issued
a limited edition facsimile reprint
using the original blocks, which had
been preserved, but which were
destroyed soon afterwards during
the war. £1,500–3,000

Famous in Medicine (New York, The Grolier Club, 1994).

The other approach to collecting in this field is to concentrate on charting the history of a particular science or topic, a medical discipline or an individual disease. Very often this kind of collecting begins with a fascination with the history of one's own professional or amateur interests. Whilst the history of many subjects has been written, the excitement of this kind of collecting lies as much in discovering unknown precursors as in finding the key works known to historians; or in charting the spread of an idea, invention or discovery, geographically or socially. Some

of the best collections, and the most useful for future scholars, have been formed in this way. There is no general guide to this kind of collecting in science, but in medicine the bible is *Morton's Medical Bibliography* (fifth edition, 1991), usually referred to as "Garrison and Morton". This lists nearly 7,000 works arranged by subject, and one can therefore quickly identify the key works in, for example, the history of ophthalmology, or cancer research, or genetics, as the starting point for any collection.

In collecting scientific and medical books, the primary object is to identify the first announcement of a new discovery. If this is in

Q VARTVS. 28
LIBER QVARTVS.
DE VARIETATIBVS NON NATV-
ralis partus, & earundem curis.

G 2 *Quando-*

▲ **Jacobus Rueff**
De conceptu, et generatione hominis, woodcut illustrations, Frankfurt, P. Fabricius for S. Feyerabend, 1587. The first true anatomical pictures in an obstetrics book. (The first edition was published in German in Zurich, 1554.) **£2,000–3,000**

DISCORSI
E
DIMOSTRAZIONI
MATEMATICHE,
intorno à due nuoue scienze
Attenenti alla
MECANICA & i MOVIMENTI LOCALI,
del Signor
GALILEO GALILEI LINCEO,
Filosofo e Matematico primario del Sereniſſimo
Grand Duca di Toſcana.
Con vna Appendice del centro di grauità d'alcuni Solidi.

IN LEIDA,
Appreſſo gli Elſevirii. M. D. C. XXXVIII.

▲ **Galileo Galilei**
Discorsi e dimostrazioni matematiche intorno à due nuove scienze attenenti alla mecanica e i movimenti locali, woodcut illustrations, Leiden, Elzevier, 1638. First edition. **£3,000–5,000**

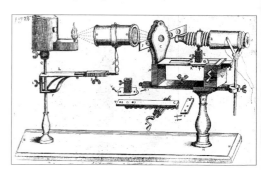

► **Filippo Buonanni**
Observationes circa viventia, quae in rebus non viventibus reperiuntur, engraved titles and 70 plates, Rome, D.A. Herculis, 1691. First edition. Buonanni constructed his own microscopes for scientific investigation. **£300–600**

a book, the same considerations apply as in any other field – issue points, signed and dated copies and so on – but a special feature of scientific publishing (as with natural history) is the scientific journal. This adds a new dimension to collecting and deserves some comment. The first scientific journal, the *Philosophical Transactions of the Royal Society*, began production in 1665 and quickly became the vehicle for fast publication of current research, and from this time on, many first announcements appear in the pages of scientific journals. In the 18th century, the journal publishers began to supply their authors with offprints (in America called reprints): the text of an individual paper, sometimes with a special title-page, and sometimes, but not always, repaginated. These the author would send to friends, potential patrons, and other scientists working in the same field, and so these offprints are often signed. Print runs of offprints vary widely from a handful to 50 or more. Journal articles are offered by dealers in three forms: whole parts or volumes of journals containing the desired article; "extracts", that is the article separated from a bound volume; and offprints. The offprint is by far the most desirable form

◄ **Giambattista Porta**

Natural Magick in twenty books … wherein are set forth all the riches and delights of natural sciences, engraved frontispiece, woodcut illustrations, for Thomas Young and Samuel Speed, 1658. First published in 1558, this popular work comprised chapters on "Beautifying Women", "Strange Glasses", "Pneumatick Experiments" and "Chaos". First edition in English.
£500–1,000

as it is often rarer, often signed, and had probably been distributed before publication of the journal. The journal volume will set the article in context, and the extract is at least still technically the first edition. It is important to bear in mind, however, that journals, even early ones, are not rare and are often discarded by libraries. With patience, most articles can be found for quite a modest sum. If you see an offprint of an article, buy it.

Science collecting is becoming at once more general and more specialized. The price of the high spots is going up rapidly as general collections of great books are put together by wealthy collectors. At the other end of the market, many dealers are actively encouraging collectors in very specialized fields, for example scientific instrument catalogues, or the history of medical electricity. But in the main subject areas such as chemistry, geology and anatomy, fewer collectors have the time or inclination to amass the large numbers of books needed to form comprehensive collections.

ROGER GASKELL

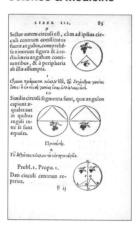

◀ **Euclid**
Euclidis elementorum libri XV, text in Greek and Latin, woodcuts in text, Paris, Hieronymum de Marnef and Gulielmum Cavellat, 1573. **£400–600**

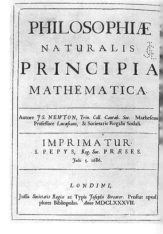

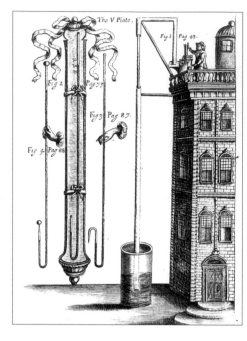

▶ **Robert Boyle**
A Continuation of New Experiments Physico-Mechanical, touching the spring and weight of the air, and their effects, 8 folding engraved plates, Oxford, Henry Hall for Richard Davis, 1669. First edition. A continuation of his earlier work *New Experiments*, 1662, in which he set forth Boyle's Law. This plate shows the experiment in which water is pumped to the top of a building. **£700–1,200**

▲ **Isaac Newton**
Philosophiae naturalis principia mathematica, folding engraved plate and woodcut diagrams, Societatis Regiae ... Josephi Streater, 1687. First edition, first issue with 2-line imprint on title. **£60,000–100,000** Generally seen as the greatest work in the history of science, reprinted on numerous occasions: the last issued in Newton's lifetime, 1726, £400–600; first English edition, 1729, £1,500–2,500

Science

Science is a field in which the major names have often become part of everyday use: hertz, volt, watt. Some, such as Copernicus and Newton, have altered man's outlook on the world, and prices for their first editions are beyond most collectors' reach. The very earliest works (such as Aristotle's) cover a wide range of what later became separate disciplines, and these, printed in the 15th century, are surprisingly affordable.

General works were superseded by specialized studies on astronomy, physics, chemistry, mathematics, electricity or geology, and these make the most interesting collecting. Each field has seminal texts, although several of the early great scientists worked across these divides. One of the earliest names is Archimedes. Through studies in astronomy he became interested in all areas of invention. The first complete edition of his work in Greek was published in 1544, *Opera omnia*. The first modern textbook in physics, *Discorsi e dimostrazioni matematiche* (1638), was published by Galileo Galilei, best known for his works on astronomy. Robert Boyle and his assistant Robert Hooke established the basic physical properties of air; Boyle's most important work, however, was *The Sceptical Chymist* (1661), in which we see the first concept of an element. This first edition is rare, as is the second of 1680.

One of the greatest names of science is Isaac Newton. His first scientific publication, "A Letter of Mr. Isaac Newton ... containing his new theory about light and colours", appeared in the *Transactions of the Royal Society* (1671). Newton expanded upon earlier theories and works for his *Philosophiae naturalis principia mathematica* (1687), often known simply as *Principia*. Great works like this are expensive in first edition and it may be preferable to buy the author's own final edited text, such as the fourth edition of Newton's *Opticks* (1730), or the collected works. Alternatively, related works may be of interest, such as Humphry Ditton's *The General Laws of Nature and Motion* (1709). Ditton was among the first to use *Principia* as a teaching method, and his book is one of the earliest on Newton's theories of mechanics in English, preceding the translation of *Principia* itself by 24 years.

A collection based around mathematics should begin with the father of geometry, Euclid, whose *Elements* was first published in English in 1570. This standard textbook has been reprinted about 1,000 times and is a fascinating piece of printing due to its geometrical diagrams. There are numerous commentaries on Euclid, the first modern edition being by Niccolo Tartaglia in 1543. Alternatively, one could look for a work that simplified the field of

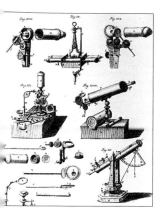

◄ Lorenzo Selva
Sei dialoghi ottici teorico-pratici,
4 folding engraved plates, Venice,
Simone Occhi, 1787. First edition.
£200–400

▼ Antoine Laurent Lavoisier
Traité élémentaire de Chimie,
présenté dans un ordre nouveau et
d'après les découvertes modernes,
13 engraved plates, 2 folding tables,
Paris, Cuchet, 1789. First edition,
second issue. The work that finally
overthrew alchemy. **£2,500–3,500**

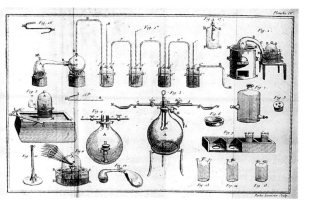

Collecting
Astronomy

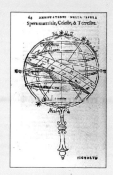

► John Holywood
Annotationi sopra la lettione della
Spera de Sacro Bosco, woodcut
illustrations, Florence, Lorenzo
Torrentino, 1550. First published in
Venice in 1537, this work describes
a new astrolabe. **£300–500**

◄ William Herschel
Descriptions of a Forty-Feet
Reflecting Telescope, 19 folding
engraved plates, 11 June 1795.
Extracted from the *Philosophical*
Transactions of the Royal Society,
1795. **£300–400**

geometry for the modern student, such as Jakob Steiner's *Systematische entwickelung* (1832).

Antoine-Laurent Lavoisier laid the foundations of modern chemistry, but his *Traité élémentaire de Chimie* (1789) is expensive, whereas *Chemistry Applied to Arts and Manufactures* (1807) by his follower Jean Antoine Chaptal, one of the geatest chemical manufacturers of history, is more affordable. William Gilbert gathered together all known opinions on the magnet and put them to the test, the result being *De magnete* (1600), the first important scientific book to be published in England. If it is not possible to obtain this in first edition, you could try looking for the first edition in English, published by the Chiswick Press in 1900.

There is a wealth of 20th-century material, but much is highly specialized and available in journals only. Albert Einstein should be represented; his *Die grundlage der allgemeinen Relativitätstheorie* (1916) is not as prohibitively expensive as one might think. The papers of Nobel prize winners could be collected: John William Strutt, Lord Rayleigh, awarded the prize in 1904, published his *Scientific Papers* between 1899 and 1920. The modern specialist collector may choose to concentrate on the computer, and then Charles Babbage's affordable work *The Ninth Bridgwater Treatise* (1837), would be essential.

Astronomy is one of the oldest sciences and hence many of the earliest names were involved in studies in this field. The father of modern astronomy is regarded as Nicolaus Copernicus, who challenged the beliefs of antiquity and refuted Ptolemy's theories by stating that the sun, not the earth, was the centre of the solar system. His major work, *De revolutionibus orbium coelestium*, was 30 years in the writing, and only published on the eve of his death in 1543. Other major names who continued his studies are Tycho Brahe, Johannes Kepler, Christian Huygens, and Galileo Galilei – whose slim pamphlet *Siderius nuncius* (1610) records the sighting of four satellites of Jupiter and marks the beginning of telescopic astronomy. The works of all these are expensive in first edition, and have to be found as later printings.

More easily affordable writers will be Pierre Simon Laplace, whose *Mécanique celeste* (1798–1825), is one of the greatest cosmological works written, albeit difficult to understand; or John Couch Adams, who discovered Neptune. His *Scientific Papers* (1896–1900), are a good way of acquiring his work. Whilst major texts are often expensive, there have always been more popular works written on astronomy and these can also be more affordable, such as Bernard le Bouvier de Fontenelle's *Entretiens sur la pluralité des mondes* (1686). This was translated into English by Glanville in 1688 as *Conversations on the Plurality of Worlds*, and later editions are fairly easy to find. This popular work on Copernican theories was almost immediately outdated by Newton's *Principia*, but its success was nevertheless enormous and at least 33 editions were published in his lifetime; the Nonesuch Press issued a limited edition in 1929.

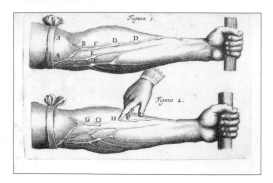

▲ **William Harvey**
De motu cordis & sanguinis in animalibus, anatomica exercitatio,
2 engraved plates, Leyden, Joannis Maire, 1639. Third edition.
One of the most important books in the history of medicine, in
which Harvey propounds his theories on the circulation of the
blood. The first edition was published in 1628 and the second
lacked the plates and part of the text. **£9,000–12,000**

▶ **John Pugh**
A Treatise on the Science of Muscular Action,
engraved title and 15 plates in 2 states, C. Dilly, 1794.
First edition. **£300–600**

Medicine

The ancient Greek physician Hippocrates, gave doctors their oath, and his writings can be found in *Omnia opera* (1525, in Latin). His clinical records were not superseded for over 1,000 years. The first printed medical book was Aurelius Cornelius Celsus's *De medicina* (1478), a standard text for centuries. The first book illustrated with realistic human figures was Johannes de Ketham's *Fasciculus medicine* (1495), which included the first representation of a dissection. In 1543 Andreas Vesalius's *De humani corporis* was published (at the same time as Copernicus's *Revolutionibus* and Leonhard Fuchs's herbal, *De historia stirpium*, two other great scientific works). The superb anatomical illustrations in Vesalius's work were revolutionary. William Harvey was the first to understand the circulation of the blood, as explained in *Exercitatio anatomica de motu cordis et sanguinis in animalibus* (1628; English translation 1635). These early medical books are expensive, often due to the quality of the illustrations, but later editions can be found, and first English editions are worth searching for.

Ancient medical practices were swept away with Philippus Aureolus von Hohenheim, called Paracelsus, who taught the use of specific remedies and treatment and introduced medicines, including opium, arsenic and mercury. His *Opera omnia medica-chemico-chirurgica* were published in 1658.

The 18th century saw a greater specialization, as with other branches of science, and with careful searching and some background knowledge, it is possible to acquire unusual and reasonably priced books. Voyaging and exploration were on the increase, and deaths amongst seamen prompted James Lind's *A Treatise on the Scurvy* (1772), a work of vital importance in which he proposed the addition of citrus juices to a seaman's diet. Early practical methods were often morally dubious; Edward Jenner experimented on a young boy, injecting him first from cowpox sores, and then with the smallpox virus, in order to prove his immunization theories. These experiments were recorded in *An Inquiry into the Causes and Effects of the Variolae Vaccinae* (1798). Once again later editions of these works may have to be sought.

Sir Humphry Davy, inventor of the miner's safety lamp, proved that pure nitrous oxide was respirable, observing in *Researches, Chemical and Philosophical; chiefly concerning Nitrous Oxide* (1800) that it could probably be used in surgical operations as an anaesthetic. (It was more than 40 years before the gas was actually used in this manner, by a Connecticut dentist, Horace Wells, who used it for tooth extraction in 1844.) Other works that could be collected more easily include William Cumberland Cruikshank's *The Anatomy of the Absorbing Vessels of the Human Body*. This work on the lymphatic system is best sought in the second edition of 1790, the first being shorter, with fewer plates. A more unusual work, still reasonably priced, is James Cowles

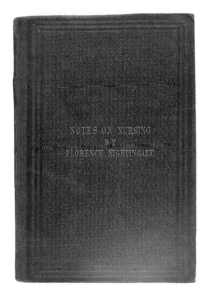

▲ Florence Nightingale
Notes on Nursing, what it is, and what it is not,
Harrison, 1860. First edition, third issue of the most
famous book on nursing, which has advertisements
on the endpapers, distinguishing it from the first issue,
which does not. **£200–400**

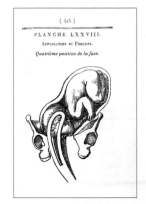

Collecting Obstetrics and Gynaecology

◄ Marie Boivin
Mémorial de l'art des accouchements, 133 woodcut
illustrations, folding table, Paris, Hospice de la
Maternité, 1812. First edition. This book for midwives
was one of a handful of early obstetrical works written
by women. Boivin raised herself beyond the level of
a midwife, increasing her knowledge to become a
gynaecologist in the modern sense. **£1,000–1,500**

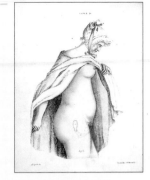

► George Spratt
Obstetric Tables, 2 volumes,
19 lithographed plates, 13 hand-
coloured with movable flaps,
J. Churchill, 1835. Second edition.
£300–500

Prichard's *A Treatise on Insanity and other Disorders Affecting the Mind* (1835), a famous book which became a standard psychiatric manual. Prichard invented the controversial phrase "moral insanity".

Scientific instruments are a fascinating area for exploration. Ambroise Paré's *Opera chirurgica* (1594) would be a book to look for, more affordable in the first English translation of 1634. This French surgeon invented many scientific instruments, as well as artificial limbs and eyes.

One might choose to collect medical books relating to America, in which case Benjamin Franklin's *Experiments and Observations on Electricity* (1751–54) could be of interest, again expensive as a first edition, but affordable in later editions. Benjamin Rush's *An Account of the Bilious remitting Yellow Fever, as it appeared in the City of Philadelphia, in the Year 1793* (1794) would also make a fascinating addition; it has become a classic text in epidemiology, and is surprisingly inexpensive. Rush also wrote the first American psychiatric text, *Medical Inquiries and Observations upon the Diseases of the Mind* (1812).

In dentistry, a first edition of *The Natural History of the Human Teeth* (1771), by founder of modern dentistry John Hunter, will cost £1,000 or more; a third edition from 1803 will be more affordable.

Louis Pasteur, Marie Curie and Robert Koch brought medicine into the modern world as we know it today with their works on bacteriology and radiology, and these works are relatively easy to find.

One of the earliest books on obstetrics is by Jacob Rueff: *The Expert Midwife*, translated into English in 1637, was first published in Latin in 1554. Reprinted on numerous occasions, this classic book was used for well over a century. François Mauriceau published his book *Les maladies des femmes grosses et accouchées* in 1668, just as 17th-century physicians were beginning to take over the practice of obstetrics from untrained midwives. This work contains the best summary of the knowledge of the subject at the time. Its three sections cover all aspects of conception, birth and care, and advocate birth on a bed, not using the traditional birthstool. The third edition was translated into most European languages, revised and reissued for many years, and can consequently be found quite easily. Cosmé Viardel was a highly popular practitioner of midwifery in 17th-century Paris and his *Observations sur la pratique des accouchements naturels...* was first published in 1671. It was reissued many times and revised in 1748 with extensive footnotes and fine plates. A much grander book was that published by William Hunter, 18th-century London's foremost obstetrician, who delivered all six of Queen Charlotte's children. His *Anatomia uteri humani gravidi tabulis illustrata* (1774), contains 34 fine engraved illustrations. Another work of interest for its illustrations it George Spratt's *Obstetric Tables*, where each plate has movable flaps.

Sporting Books

Sporting literature: W.G. Grace and cricket; Bernard Darwin and golf; hunting, shooting and fishing

▲ **W.G. van T. Sutphen**
The Golfer's Alphabet, 28 illustrations by A.B. Frost, New York, Harper & Brothers, 1898. **£300–600**

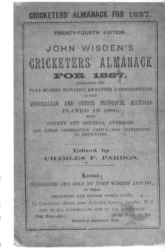

► **John Wisden**
Cricketer's Almanack for 1887, advertisements, 1886. In original wrappers. **£200–300**
A complete run, 1864–1994, £20,000–30,000

The miscellany, describing the sports not just of kings but of the growing ranks of country gentlemen, was one of the earliest and most enduring forms of sporting book.

The first edition of the celebrated *Book of St. Albans* (St. Albans, 1486) dealt simply with hawking, hunting and heraldic arms; the second edition (Wynkyn de Worde, Westminster, 1496) contained a treatise on fishing; by 1596 a section on fowling had been added as well. Nicholas Cox's aptly named *Gentleman's Recreation*, first published 1674, proclaims itself a miscellany on "Hunting,

hawking, fowling, fishing … collected from ancient and modern authors".

In the early 19th century, when a remarkable tradition of sporting illustration reached its heyday, there appeared the magnificent sporting miscellanies of Henry Alken and Samuel Howitt. The most comprehensive survey of all was the "Badminton Library of Sports and Pastimes", edited by the Duke of Beaufort, with contributions by most of the respected authorities of the day. As the foundation for any sporting collection, the relevant volume of the Badminton Library cannot be bettered. Every sport known at the

FHEASANT SHOOTING.

▲ **Henry Alken**

A Collection of Sporting and Humorous Designs,
comprising a Variety of Entertaining Works, solely
executed by Henry Alken, illustrative of the Manners,
Customs, Sports and Pastimes of England, 3 volumes,
314 hand-coloured aquatint and etched plates,
Thomas M'Lean, 1824. A rare collection of Henry
Alken's major works, almost all similar sets having been
broken up and sold as individual plates. **£25,000–40,000**
The National Sports of Great Britain, 50 hand-coloured
engraved plates, 1825, £1,000–2,000; a reprint of
1903, £700–1,000

time is included in this famous series.
However, one has to speak of the relevant
volume rather than the set of 29 volumes,
first published between 1885 and 1896,
since most collectors are interested in one
sport to the exclusion of others. The old
aim of comprehensiveness has given way
to knowledge in depth.

To learn what is available to collect is really
the first and most important step for any
collector. Field sports have the most extensive
literature, being rivalled in antiquity only by
chess. Other leisure pursuits have a literature
which is either far more intermittent or of
much later origin. Fox-hunting, horse-racing,
mountaineering, cricket, golf and boxing are
some of the sports which only began to take
on organized form in the 18th century. Polo,
though played in Persia in 600BC, was
introduced to England only in the later 19th
century. The first lawn tennis sets, complete
with instruction book, appeared in 1874. The
19th and 20th centuries will therefore be the
key period for many collectors. It was in
the 19th century that the range of sporting
literature was expanded to include colonial
game sports and newly popular sports such
as golf and cricket.

▲ Samuel Howitt
The British Sportsman, 72 engraved plates, Edward Orme, 1812.
£600–1,500

► John Scott
The Sportsman's Repository; comprising a series of highly-finished engravings representing the Horse and the Dog, engraved title and 38 plates, wood-engraved frontispiece and illustrations in text, Sherwood, Neely & Jones, 1820. **£400–800**

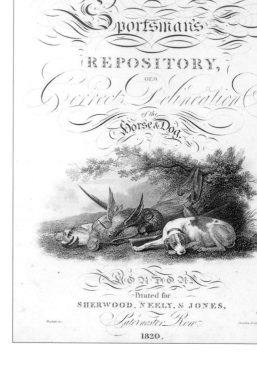

▲ Lt. Col. Peter Hawker
Instructions to Young Sportsmen in all that relates to Guns and Shooting, 10 aquatint or engraved plates, 4 coloured by hand, Longman, Hurst, Rees, 1824. The third edition of this important work. **£150–300**
First edition, 1814, £800–1,500

► Charles James Apperley
The Life of a Sportsman, 35 hand-coloured aquatint plates and engraved title, R. Ackermann, 1842. First edition. **£600–1,500** Later editions vary according to the binding and condition of the plates, £200–800

In common with cricket, the earliest golf literature was in verse. There were three 18th-century editions of Thomas Mathison's *The Goff; An Heroi-Comical Poem*, the first publication entirely devoted to golf. The first golf rules were printed in 1775. But no other poem followed *The Goff* until 1833, and, apart from very rare early issues of the rules, the first prose work entirely on golf, H.B. Farnie's *The Golfer's Manual*, appeared as late as 1857.

Sporting bibliophiles may find themselves specializing even further within the boundaries of a game. With golf, for example, one has a choice of anthologies, general histories, rule books and histories of particular clubs, works on the design and layout of courses, a mass of instructional manuals, biographies and autobiographies, books of humour and even golf fiction. The works of Horace Hutchinson and Bernard Darwin, two outstanding authorities, would provide a sufficient theme for a collection. With cricket, there are collectors whose sole interest is in building a run of Wisden's *Cricketer's*

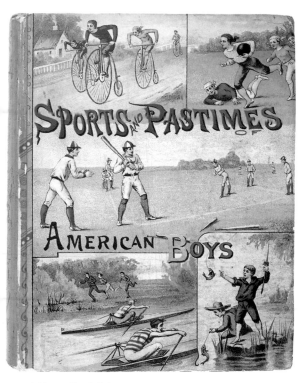

▲ Henry Chadwick

Sports and Pastimes of American Boys, a guide and text-book of Games of the Play-Ground, the Parlor, and the Field, adapted especially for American Youth, 4 chromolithographed plates and wood-engraved illustrations in the text, New York, George Routledge and Sons, 1884. Original pictorial cloth. **£100–250**

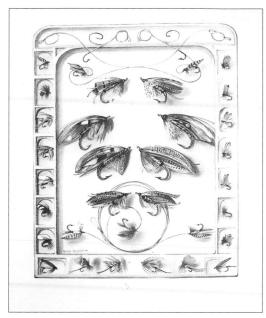

▲ Hugh Sheringham and John C. Moore

The Book of the Fly-Rod, one of 195 copies signed by the artist, 8 hand-coloured plates and 4 printed in colour, Eyre and Spottiswoode, 1931. **£100–200**

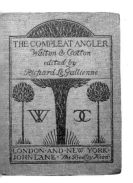

◄ Izaak Walton and Charles Cotton

The Compleat Angler, illustrations by Edmund New, John Lane, The Bodley Head, 1897. **£30–60**
First edition, 1653, £8,000–12,000; second edition, 1655, £1,000–2,000

► The Complete Fisherman, or Universal Angler ... to which is added the Whole Art of Fly-Fishing, engraved frontispiece, Fielding and Walker, c.1780. Second edition. **£200–400**

Almanack, first published in 1864, so unique in its combination of statistical records and very accomplished, if specialized, English prose.

The most successful of all sporting books is Isaak Walton's *The Compleat Angler.* First published anonymously in 1653, this fishing book has enjoyed four centuries of continuous re-publication, attracting the attention of leading illustrators, typographers, and binders, and is in itself the subject for a collection.

Most sports have their own specialist bibliography, the use of which is indispensable for learning about the great classics and intriguing oddities, and for establishing the dates of rare 'first appearances'. However, these bibliographies, targeted at a particular sport rather than an evolutionary period or particular type of book, have perhaps blinkered our view. Other approaches are possible. To form a library of finely illustrated books or of literary classics on a broad range of sports would be as interesting a goal as amassing a collection on only one game.

RUPERT NEELANDS

▲ **Charles Crombie**
The Rules of Golf Illustrated, 24 coloured plates, Perrier,
1905. **£300–600**
Perrier produced a similar promotional book on the car,
Motoritis, or Other Interpretations of the Motor Act, as
well as Crombie's *Laws of Cricket* in 1907, £200–300

◀ **Bernard Darwin**
The Golf Courses of the British Isles,
64 plain and coloured plates by
Harry Rountree, Duckworth & Co.,
1910. **£300–700**

▲ **Burnham Hare**
*The Golfing Swing simplified and its mechanism
correctly explained*, frontispiece, Methuen & Co.,1913.
Second edition. **£60–120**

Golf & Cricket

Golf is one of the most popular sports, around which a thriving industry has arisen: specialist dealers in books and memorabilia; auctions devoted to golfing curios; books on golf memorabilia. The unfortunate result of all this frenetic activity is, of course, high prices. Nonetheless, it is a fascinating area with many good books for the enthusiast, and most can be found in less expensive later editions if the first edition is beyond one's budget.

One of the major names connected with golf is Bernard Darwin, grandson of the great naturalist Charles Darwin. Although trained as a barrister, he decided in 1908 to devote his energy to writing, golf being his favoured subject: he was captain of the British golf team in the first Walker Cup match in the United States in 1922, and of the Royal and Ancient Golf Club in 1934. His books are well written and make fascinating reading even for the non-golfing enthusiast, leading inevitably to great demand for the first editions. Horace Hutchinson captained the first four Oxford golf teams, between 1878 and 1882, was an amateur champion, and played for England against Scotland from 1902 to 1904 and 1906 to 1907. His most famous book is *Hints on the Game of Golf* (1886), and his many other books include *The Book of Golf and Golfers* (1899), as well as works on shooting – *Big Game Shooting* (1905) – fishing and other sports. Other sought-after books are R. Clark's *The Royal and Ancient Game of Golf* (1875) and Harold Hilton's and Garden Smith's *The Royal and Ancient Game of Golf* (1912), a limited edition of 900 copies only and consequently

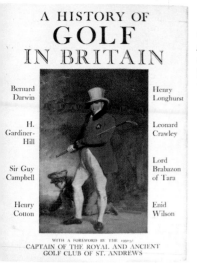

◀ Bernard Darwin and others
A History of Golf in Britain,
4 coloured plates and other
illustrations, Cassell and Company,
1952. **£100–200**

▶ The Duke of Beaufort
The Badminton Library of Sports
and Pastimes, edited by His Grace
the Duke of Beaufort, *Cricket*, by
A.G. Steel and Hon. R.H. Lyttelton,
10 plates and illustrations in the text,
Longmans, Green & Co., 1889.
£20–40

▼ C.B. Fry
*The Book of Cricket, a Gallery
of Famous Players*, illustrations,
George Newnes, c.1899.
£80–150

▼ Rev. James Pycroft
*The Cricket-Field or the History and
Science of the Game of Cricket*,
engraved frontispiece and one plate,
Longmans, Green & Co., 1862.
Fourth edition. **£50–100**

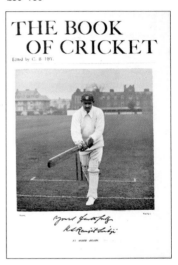

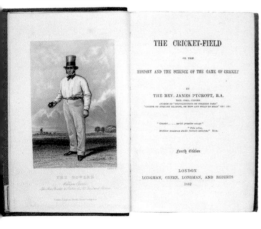

▲ W.G. Grace
Cricket, one of 662 copies signed
by the author, 46 plates, Bristol,
J.W. Arrowsmith, 1891. **£200–400**

expensive. Whilst these books from the late 19th century and early part of the 20th century will cost rather more than the average sports collector may wish to spend, there are numerous other books from later this century that can be acquired for far less.

Books on cricket are generally more easily found, and there is of course the greatest sporting annual ever: John Wisden's *Cricketer's Almanack*. This enormously popular almanac, still in existence today, was first published in 1864. The early volumes from the mid-1860s are extremely hard to find in their original wrappers, and even rebound copies may cost more than £1,000. It was not, however, until 1870 with the inclusion of W.H. Knight's accounts of matches that the *Almanack* acquired its special blend of concise fact and reportage. Some collectors choose

to acquire ready-made runs of several years whilst for others the enjoyment is in gradually finding individual copies themselves.

The first prose work on the game is John Nyren's *The Cricketer's Tutor* (1833), which was reprinted 11 times, each edition with slight variations, and is also available in one of seven modern reprints. The second edition, published in Edinburgh, is the most scarce. According to many, this is the "classic" cricket book and it has even occasioned its own bibliography, of which only 20 copies were published: G. Neville Weston's *"Nyren" a Short Bibliography* (1933). There are books on individual clubs, matches, tours, players, grounds, rules, all aspects of the game, making a large and varied field from which the collector can choose.

▶ **James Forbes**
Travels through the Alps of Savoy and other parts of the Pennine Chain with Observations on the Phenomena of Glaciers, 9 lithographed plates, tinted frontispiece, other illustrations, 2 maps, Edinburgh, Adam & Charles Black, 1843. **£150–300**

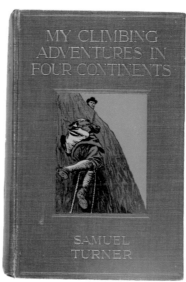

ON THE UNTER GRINDELWALD GLACIER.

◀ **E. Elliot Stock**
Scrambles in Storm and Sunshine among the Swiss and English Alps, 32 plates, John Ouseley, 1910. **£60–120**

▲ **H.B. George**
The Oberland and its Glaciers Explored and Illustrated with Ice-axe and Camera, 28 photographs, map, Alfred Bennett, 1866. **£200–400**

◀ **Samuel Turner**
My Climbing Adventures in Four Continents, 74 illustrations, T. Fisher Unwin, 1911. **£60–120**

Mountaineering & Field Sports

Another popular sport for which there exists a large selection of books is that of mountaineering. The majority of mountaineering books are from the 19th century, and many are not expensive; they can be illustrated with maps, early photographs, aquatint and lithographed plates, as well as often being in particularly attractive pictorial cloth bindings. These are the books of heroes and adventure, danger and challenge, and much of their appeal lies in this element.

One could choose to concentrate on a particular mountain, for example Mont Blanc. An early account is Sir Charles Fellows's *A Narrative of an Ascent to the Summit of Mont Blanc* (1828), of which the most desirable, but therefore the most expensive, edition would be one of 50 large-paper copies. John Auldjo's *Narrative of an Ascent to the Summit of Mont Blanc* (1828), has also been issued as a large-

paper copy, and has been reprinted, providing a range of choices according to budget. Martin Barry's *Ascent to the Summit of Mont Blanc in 1834* (1835) can be found in the edition privately printed for the author, and the later edition published in Edinburgh in 1836. Charles Hudson's and Edward Shirley Kennedy's *Where there's a Will there's a Way: an ascent of Mont Blanc by a new route and without a guide* (1856) is the account of the first ascent of Mont Blanc without a guide and the first to reach the highest point of Monte Rosa. John Ball's *Peaks, Passes and Glaciers, A Series of excursions by members of the Alpine Club* (1859–62), would provide a fascinating way of learning about many of the early climbs and can be found as the complete four volume set as well as in individual volumes, the first having been reprinted several times. Douglas Freshfield wrote a fairly common book, *Italian Alps*

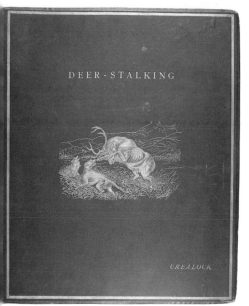

◄ Henry Hope Crealock
Deer-Stalking in the Highlands of Scotland, one of
255 copies, 40 plates, illustrations in the text,
Longmans, Green & Co., 1892. **£300–600**

▲ Martin Ross and E.O.E. Somerville
A Patrick's Day Hunt, coloured plates and illustrations
in the text,1902. **£30–60**

► Lionel Edwards
The Passing Seasons, one of 250 copies,
18 coloured plates, each signed in the mount by the
artist, Country Life, 1938. **£800–1,500**
Ordinary edition, £100–150

◄ Earl of Lonsdale
The Lonsdale Library of Sports, Games and Pastimes,
edited by the Earl of Lonsdale and Eric Parker. *Shooting
by Moor, Field and Shore, a practical guide to modern
methods*, by Eric Parker and others, 150 illustrations,
Seeley, Service & Co., 1929. **£20–40**

(1875), which can be found for a few pounds; he also wrote one of the most rare of Victorian mountaineering books, *Across Country from Thonon to Trent, Rambles and Scrambles in Switzerland*: privately printed in 1865, it was later withdrawn by the author. Although rare, it is not as expensive as, for example, certain golf books of the same era. The works of Edward Whymper are not uncommon and even his account of the first ever, disastrous ascent of the Matterhorn, *The Ascent of the Matterhorn* (1880), is not expensive.

For those whose interests lie with the more traditional field sports, one of the most useful reference works is C.F.G.R. Schwerdt's *Hunting, Hawking, Shooting Illustrated in a Catalogue of Books, Manuscripts, Prints and Drawings* (four volumes, 1928–37), itself a collected work, but also available in a 1985 reprint. If one chooses to narrow this interest

down further, and perhaps concentrate on an artist such as Henry Alken, then R.V. Tooley's *English Books with Coloured Plates, 1790–1860* (1954), will be invaluable, and Walter Sparrow's *British Sporting Artists* (1965) could also be of interest. Henry Alken's early work appeared under the pseudonym of "Ben Tallyho". His images of the hunt are far more exciting than those of his predecessors in which the riders and horses appeared composed and restrained. The first book published under his own name was *The Beauties and Defects in the Figure of the Horse* (1816), and this is an inexpensive book when compared with his great general sporting works. Alken's first series of sporting plates was issued in 1817 in six monthly parts called *Sporting Sketches*, each with six plates. The new collector will probably have to be content with later editions of his work and not be too fussy about the binding.

THE FAMOVS GAME
of Chesse-play.

Being a Princely exercise; wherin the
Learner may profit more by reading of
this small Book, then by playing
of a thousand Mates.

Now augmented of many materiall things
formerly wanting, and beautified with a three-
fold Methode, viz. of the Chesse-men,
of the Chesse-play, of the
Chesse-lawes.

By Jo. BARBIER. P.

If on your man you light,
The first draught shall you play:
If not, 'tis mine by right,
At first to leade the way.

Printed at London

► **Athletic Sports,
The Out of Door Library,**
illustrations, Kegan Paul, 1898.
£50–100

◄ **Arthur Saul**
The Famous Game of Chesse-Play,
woodcut illustration of a chess-game
repeated 3 times, and of a
chessboard, T. Paine for John
Jackson, 1640. Third edition.
£300–500

► **Arthur Barker**
Squash Rackets, 13 plates and
illustrations in text, Eyre and
Spottiswoode, 1936. **£10–25**

◄ *Boxiana or Sketches of
Ancient & Modern Pugilism,*
frontispiece, title-page and 62
engraved plates, c.1840. This classic
work on the prize-ring by Pierce
Egan and John Bee, was issued in
parts and in volumes between 1812
and 1829. This volume comprises
the plates only bound as 1 volume,
with an additional 5 plates not found
in the bound volumes. **£300–500**
Complete five volumes, £300–600

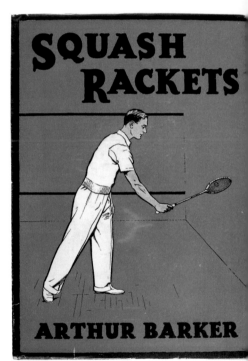

Angling & Other Sporting Books

Angling is a hugely popular sport with many participants throughout the world, and there are numerous books on the subject, whether your interest is fishing at sea or in fresh water. Some of the most interesting books are those devoted to the tying of flies. Many of these have examples of the actual flies themselves, inserted in sunken mounts. Others are illustrated with fine lithographed plates, or with the illustrations of the flies coloured by hand to capture the fine colours of the originals. Frederic Halford was a prolific author of books on dry-fly fishing at the beginning of this century, and whilst several of his books were issued in limited de-luxe editions and will cost a few hundred pounds, such as *Dry Fly Fishing in Theory and Practice*, 1889; others will be more affordable. Salmon fishing and trout fishing are two more subjects that have spawned a vast quantity of specialist literature. Whilst angling books can be found from the 18th century, the majority are from the 19th and 20th century. They are often finely illustrated, and make a fascinating addition to a keen angler's knowledge.

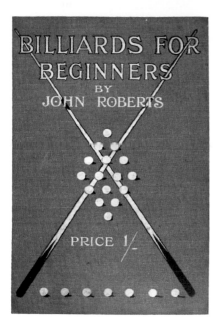

▲ John Roberts
Billiards for Beginners, diagrams, Sands & Co., 1901.
Third edition. **£10–25**

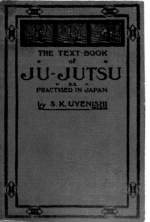

◄ S.K. Uyenishi
The Text Book of Ju-Jutsu as practised in Japan, 41 plates, Athletic Publications Ltd., 1921. **£15–35**

► Charles Hierons
How to Learn Lawn Tennis, 31 plates, Ward, Lock & Co., c.1922. Revised and enlarged edition. **£20–50**

Whatever one's sporting interest, whether it be chess or backgammon, squash or tennis, billiards or snooker, football or rugby, judo or boxing, pheasant-keeping or dogs, angling or shooting, athletics or gymnastics, there will always be books written by other enthusiasts for you to collect, with many at very reasonable prices. Some will be in the form of simple pamphlets, others will be grand, illustrated pieces, technical books of rules, or items of ephemera, but they will all add to your knowledge and appreciation of the sport.

Collecting
Football Books

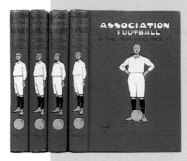

◄ Alfred Gibson and William Pickford
Association Football & The Men Who Made It, a complete set of 4 volumes, 97 plates, **£200–300**

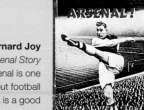

► Bernard Joy
Forward Arsenal! The Arsenal Story 1888–1952, 1952. Arsenal is one of the most written-about football clubs in England, and this is a good example of the popular works of the period. **£30–40**

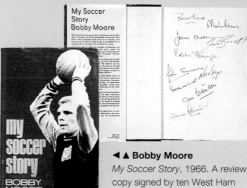

◄ ▲ Bobby Moore
My Soccer Story, 1966. A review copy signed by ten West Ham United players. **£80–120**

Unlike cricket and golf, the game of football did not spawn much good literature in its early days. The Duke of Beaufort first devoted one of his Badminton Library volumes to the game (together with athletics) in 1887, and *The Badminton Library: Football* was issued separately in 1899. *Association Football & The Men Who Made It* (1907) in four volumes, by Alfred Gibson and William Pickford, can be regarded as one of the first 20th century literary works on the game, and should represent the corner-stone of any collection. However, many of the collectable football books available today, were published during the 1940s and 1950s, the "golden age" of football. This wide range includes players' autobiographies and biographies, team histories, and instructive books on techniques and tactics. For the football enthusiast there is a huge choice, and although football books are a relatively recent collecting area, much of the material is very reasonably priced.

Architecture
& Design

▲ **Colen Campbell**
Vitruvius Britannicus, or the British Architect, 5 volumes,
391 engraved plates, some double-page, 1715–71.
£6,000–8,000
Volumes 1–2 only, £1,500–2,500

Palladian, Gothic and Modernist: books on the design of buildings and ornament

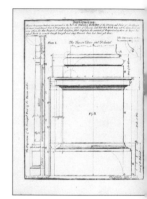

▶ **Batty Langley**
The City and Country Builder's and Workman's Treasury of Designs on the Art of Drawing and Working the Ornamental Parts of Architecture, 200 engraved plates, John and Francis Rivington, 1770. **£200–400**
Langley produced several similar works all within this price range.

Some of the finest colour-plate books of the early 19th century were architectural, due to the fashion for the picturesque. Buildings came to be regarded as an integral part both of the landscape and of the social environment: Rudolph Ackerman's fine books on the buildings of Oxford, Cambridge, and London are good examples. Quite separate from these desirable studies is a wide range of more practical architectural works, including pattern books, books of designs, builders' manuals and textbooks; price books; and books on building materials, on surveying and measuring and the requisite instruments. There are also works of architectural criticism to be collected, and often very attractive monographs of country houses displaying perspective views, architectural and graphic ornament.

From the mid-16th to the 20th century the basis of architecture was the classical orders – the ways in which a column related to its surrounding support and decoration – and books on these orders were intended for architects, free-masons, carpenters, carvers and other craftsmen. The earliest texts in use in England were translations of Italian, French or Dutch works. Three authors in particular were copied, adapted and translated into English: Roland Fréart's *Parallel of the Antient Architecture with the Modern* (1664), Claude Perrault's *Treatise of the Five Orders* (1708), and Sebastien Le Clerc's *Treatise of Architecture* (1723–24). The writer and diarist John Evelyn had discovered Fréart's work and brought the original text back from France, and his desire for a renaissance in the arts, together with his concern for the improvement of building, led him to prepare a translation.

The first architectural treatise of the Renaissance was Leon Battista Alberti's *De re aedificatoria* (Florence, 1485). Its influence on Renaissance and later architecture was immense, yet only a few editions had appeared before its translation into English. With increased interest in architecture in the early 18th century, its translation and the addition of engravings – which occurred between 1726 and 1730 – were inevitable. The late Renaissance architect Andrea Palladio's *I Quattro libri dell'architettura* (1570) revived interest in classical Roman antiquity; although it first appeared in English in 1663, Giacomo Leoni's translation of 1715 to 1719 really established Palladio's fame and influence in

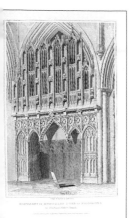

◀ **Edward Blore**
Monumental Remains of ... Eminent Persons, 30 plates, Harding, Lepard and Co., 1826. **£150–300**

▼ **Thomas Talbot Bury**
Coloured Views on the Liverpool and Manchester Railway, facsimile reprint, Hugh Broadbent, 1977. **£100–150**

▶ **Francis Orpen Morris**
A Series of Picturesque Views of Seats ... of Great Britain, 6 volumes, W. Mackenzie, 1880. **£150–300**

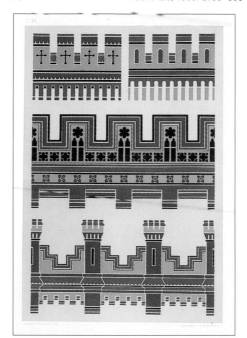

▲ **George Ashdown Audsley.**
The Practical Decorator and Ornamentist, 102 chromolithographed plates, Glasgow, 1892. **£400–800**

▲ **John Gloag**
The English Tradition in Design, illustrations, Penguin, 1956. **£20–30**

18th-century England and led to the revival of Palladio's classical theories, in the movement that became known as Palladianism. Other influential and popular works were the compilation *Vitruvius Britannicus, or the British Architect* (1715–25) with plates engraved by Colen Campbell, William Kent's *Designs of Inigo Jones with some Additional Designs* (1727), and Isaac Ware's *Designs of Inigo Jones and others* (1731) – all of which were important works that became standard pattern books.

These publications were not available to every builder or architect and there was a huge market in compilations produced specifically for the mass market. One of the earliest such works was *The Mirror of Architecture*, edited by William Fisher in 1669, reprinted many times in the 18th century. The purpose of these handbooks was to make the rules of the orders available and comprehensive to all involved in building. Books such as James Smith's *Carpenter's Companion* (1733), Edward Hoppus's *The Gentleman's and Builder's Repository* (1737) and Batty Langley's *Builder's Compleat Assistant* (1738) were enthusiastically received and can be acquired quite easily today.

In the late 18th and early 19th centuries, books on farms, cow byres, cottages, gates and gatehouses, chimneys and other detailed features, began to appear to satisfy the demand for romanticized designs for these smaller buildings, such as John Plaw's *Rural Architecture* (1785) and John Papworth's *Rural Residences, consisting of a Series of Designs for Cottages, Decorated Cottages, Small Villas, and other Ornamental Buildings* (1818).

The 1820s brought a revival of interest in the Gothic, which was enormously influential amongst architects and designers. Augustus Welby Pugin was the main force behind the Gothic revival, and his works, including *Floriated Ornament, a Series of Thirty-One Designs* (1849) and *The Present State of Ecclesiastical Architecture in England* (1843), are probably the most important to look out for.

The 20th century brings books celebrating and recording the work of fine architects such as Sir Edwin Lutyens and those of the modernist movement, Le Corbusier and Frank Lloyd Wright. Architecture was popularized once again by the series of guides to buildings in the counties of England by Nikolaus Pevsner and John Betjeman's *Shell Guides*.

Aeronautical & Maritime

Flying ships and sailing ships: collecting books on transport in the air and at sea

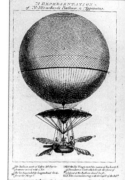

There are a few early books that explore the possibility of flight – including the earliest illustrations of flying machines, effectively showing boats with wings – but the history of aeronautical books really begins in the year 1783, with the first successful ascent of the balloon designed by the brothers Joseph Michel and Jacques Etienne Montgolfier on 27 August. The first human being to ascend in a balloon was François Pilatre de Rozier; he was the first to undertake an unrestrained flight, on 21 November 1783, and in 1785 he became the first casualty of the new sport. On 1 December 1783 M. Charles ascended from the Jardin des Tuileries in Paris. The first flight in England was that of Francesco Zambecarri in November, although the most famous balloonists in England at the time were Jean-Pierre Blanchard and Vincent Lunardi. All aeronautical books from the first few years (1783–95) are uncommon and yet can often still be found for a few hundred pounds. Most of the early pieces written by these pioneering balloonists are fragile, consisting of only a few pages, usually with one or more engraved plates depicting one of the early flights.

Apart from the works of the early balloonists themselves, there are pieces such as Barthélemy Faujas de Saint-Fond's *Description des expériences de la machine aérostatique de Mm. de Montgolfier* (1783), the first authoritative historical and technical treatise on aerostation, as flying was called in its infancy. A second volume was published in 1784. There are numerous works from the late 18th century describing various types of airships and balloons, some purely imaginary, others actually realized.

The 19th century brought a wealth of aeronautical books; Gaston Tissandier and his brother Albert were two of the most prolific writers of this period, as well as being practical balloonists themselves. Works such as *Histoire des ballons et des aéronautes célèbres 1783–1800, 1801–1890* (two volumes, 1887–90) are immensely valuable reference sources, as well as making fascinating reading. These late 19th-century French books are often inexpensive and bound in attractive decorative or pictorial cloth. Hatton Turner's *Astra Castra. Experiments and Adventures in the Atmosphere* (1865) is also a useful reference book, listing the first 500 aeronauts with

◄ Philip Brannon
The Air Boat for Arcustatic Air-travel, dispensing with the use of gas, hydrogen, hot or vapor air balloons, illustrations, By the Author, 1879. Brannon was a civil and sanitary engineer who designed a "Levitation Air Ship". **£200–400**

► J. Lecornu
La navigation aérienne, illustrations, Paris, Vuibert and Nony, 1912. Fifth edition. **£40–60**

▲ Romuoldo Bianchi
Il cochio volante o sia viaggia per l'aria di Mr. de Gas, engraved folding frontispiece, Milan, G. Batista Bianchi, 1784. This illustration is a fine example of how close early flying machines were in the minds of the inventors to sailing ships. **£300–500**

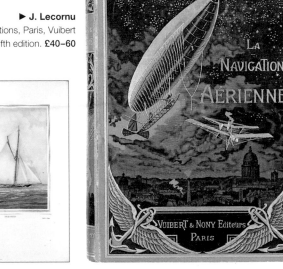

► Sir John Shelley-Rolls
Yachts of the Royal Yacht Squadron, 1815–1932, 143 plates, one coloured, Zaehnsdorf Ltd., 1933. This frontispiece depicts the *Britannia*. **£200–400**

the date and place of their ascent and a bibliography of books on the subject to that date.

Maritime books, by comparison, exist in far greater numbers, and – apart from the early books with engraved plates, often detailed works on marine architecture with informative text – most can be picked up for very little. There is a wide variety available to collectors, encompassing naval books, books on whaling, those about the early traders or navigators, or works on the history of the East India Company; books on motor boats, model boats, steamships or sailing boats; alternatively you may be interested in the history of the ports or docks such as Bristol, Liverpool or London.

One of the best-known pictorial records of shipping is by E.W. Cooke, *Sixty Five Plates of Shipping and Craft* (1829). The early part of the 20th century witnessed a wealth of similar books containing illustrations of old sailing ships, such as the prolific Edward Keble Chatterton's *The Old East Indiamen* (1914), Basil Lubbock's *The Colonial Clippers* (1920) and Carl C. Cutler's *The Story of the American Clipper Ships* (1930). The practical side of shipbuild-

ing has been the subject of many titles, including general works such as William John Rankine's *Shipbuilding, Theoretical and Practical* (1866), or more specific books on rigging, masts or sails, like George Riddlecombe's *The Art of Rigging* (1848).

A work aimed at the popular market, without engraved plates, will cost a fraction of the price of a similarly dated work with plates: for example, the unillustrated *The Shipbuilder's Repository, or a Treatise on Marine Architecture* (1788) will be much less expensive than Marmaduke Stalkart's *Naval Architecture or the Rudiments and Rules of Ship-Building exemplified in a Series of Draughts and Plans* (1781), which has 14 double-page or folding engraved plates.

The 20th century provides the collector with a wealth of material for both aeronautica and maritime collectors. Much of it is printed ephemera, such as on the great ocean-going liners and the early aeroplanes. In many instances this 20th-century material, especially that relating to the famous early flyers such as Wilbur Wright, is more expensive than the earlier pieces.

Performing Arts

Collecting books on the theatre and the ballet; conjuring and circus; film and music

The performing arts – ballet, theatre, cinema, conjuring, the circus, mime, music hall, and all kinds of music – is a wide collecting field, and one with an enormous variety of intriguing and visually appealing material across all price bands.

The most expensive of theatrical and ballet books will be the 18th- and early 19th-century architectural books that display the interiors and exteriors of the theatres, such as Charles Garnier's *Le Nouvel Opéra de Paris* (1878–81), or Alexis Donnet's and Jacques-Auguste Kaufmann's *Architectonographie des Théâtres ou parallèle historique et critique de ces édifices* (1837–40), each with views, plans and elevations; and the hand-coloured costume and set design books of the 18th through to the 20th century. George Barbier, Léon Bakst and Georges Lepape are particularly desirable names from the early part of this century, their illustrations being coloured by

hand by *pochoir*. Periodicals such as *Costumes et annales des grands théâtres de Paris*, published in weekly parts from 1786, contained many fine engraved plates. Whilst these will be expensive, there are other volumes of costume designs that are more affordable, such as Rupert Mason's *Robes of Thespis, Costume Designs by Modern Artists* (1928), with designs by, amongst others, Albert Rutherston, Edward Gordon Craig and Charles Ricketts.

A great deal has been published over the years on the plays of William Shakespeare, including books of costumes and set designs such as the series produced by J.R. Planché in the 1830s. In the early part of the 20th century the Shakespeare Head Press in Oxford issued a fine series of the individual plays each with costume and set designs by Rutherston and other artists, and these can be acquired for a relatively small outlay.

▲ Will Goldston
Modern Card Tricks without Apparatus, illustrations,
For the Author, 1915. **£30–60**

▲ *The Art of Conjuring made Easy*
Devonport, Samuel and John Keays,
c.1840. **£60–100**

▼ Gioacchino Rossini
Le barbier de Séville, 393 pages,
engraved throughout, words in
Italian and French, Paris, *A la lyre
Moderne*, before 19 September
1821. The first edition of the full
score. **£800–1,500**

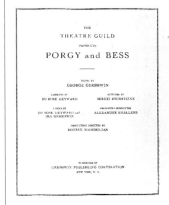

► George Gershwin
Porgy and Bess, vocal score, 559
pages, portrait of Gershwin, New
York, Gershwin Publishing Corp.
1935. This is the rare first edition of
the vocal score of one of the
greatest American stage musicals of
the 20th century. **£600–1,200**

Although the visual side is often more immediately appealing, some collectors concentrate on the dramatic texts themselves, or on the history of the theatre. The 19th century is a fertile period for memoirs and biographies of actors, playwrights and managers, and names such as Sarah Bernhardt, John Philip Kemble, Sarah Siddon, Charles Macklin, David Garrick, Henry Irving and Ellen Terry crop up again and again. The celebrated clown and pantomimist Joseph Grimaldi was immensely popular, and all material connected with him is of interest, from prints to his memoirs edited by Charles Dickens, *Memoirs of Joseph Grimaldi* (1838).

Books on conjuring and the circus attract avid collectors. Whilst some of the early and fragile pieces from the 18th and early 19th century can be quite rare and command a few hundred pounds, any early edition of *Hocus Pocus or The Whole Art of Legerdemain* will command several thousands of pounds; the first edition of 1634 is the earliest separate book on sleight of hand. By far the majority of books in this area can still be found under £100. Will Goldston, Harry Houdini and Maskelyne and Cooke are names worth looking out for. Useful reference books are Raymond Toole Stott's *A Bibliography of English Conjuring* (1976–78) and Trevor Hall's *Old Conjuring Books* (1972), as well as the auction catalogue of J.B. Findlay's enormous collection of conjuring books sold at Sotheby's from 1979 to 1980. Periodicals and programmes can be one of the least expensive ways of beginning a collection in this field, programmes from the 20th century costing at the maximum a few pounds, and those from the 18th century, printed on a single sheet of paper (known as a broadside) and often having decorative type and illustrations, rarely costing over £100.

Cookery

Mrs. Beeton to Elizabeth David; books on confectionery and cuts of meat; menus and suppliers' lists

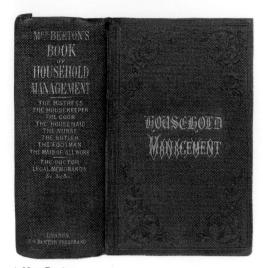

▲ **Mrs. Beeton**
Book of Household Management, S.O. Beeton, 1861.
Originally issued in parts. First edition. **£250–500**

▼ **Susannah Carter**
The Frugal Housewife, 12 engraved plates, E. Newbery,
c.1800. First published in 1790. **£200–400**

Books for cooks or for those simply interested in the history of food and wine? Many people come to collect cookery books as an extension of their interest in or love of food; collectors are often professional cooks. Frequently such a collection begins with the great stalwarts of the 20th century, Elizabeth David and Jane Grigson. For many, these two names radically changed the whole nature of cooking, and their books therefore form a logical starting point. Elizabeth David's cookery books often come in attractive dust-jackets by John Minton and can still be found priced under £100. Jane Grigson's works are more recent but still classics in their own right.

It does not matter whether one is interested in general recipe books, in books on recipes for fish or vegetables, on cuts of meat, on the art of running a household, on confectionery or cake, or on foreign foods, there will be numerous titles over the years to pursue. Suppliers' lists and menus can also be an unusual and informative addition to any collection.

As with all areas of collecting, there will be a premium for a fine copy as opposed to a worn one; nonetheless, many collectors still prefer the addition of contemporary notes: the remains of a personal touch from a former owner.

Cookery is a vast field, with more specialist dealers entering the market every year, and all but the earliest rarities are usually reasonably priced: even a first edition of Mrs. Beeton's *Book of Household Management* (1861) will only be around £500 – quite reasonable when one considers how influential this book was.

Collections of recipes date back to Roman times, and while it is not uncommon to find quite early manuscript recipe books, it was not until the 18th century that such collections were produced commercially. The majority of cookbooks from the 18th century, although not common, will not generally command more than a few hundred pounds. These early works were often small books with simply an engraved frontispiece or woodcut illustrations in the

▲ **Joseph Bell**
A Treatise on Confectionery in all its Branches, 4 engraved plates, Newcastle, For the Author, 1817. This book contains a whole section on making different types of ice cream. **£200–350**

► **Sandringham Royal Dinner Menu**
5 December, c.1881. **£200–400**

▼ **Frederick Strange**
Restaurateur, Crystal Palace, Sydenham. *Special List of Wines*, Truscott, Son and Simmons, c.1870. **£80–150**

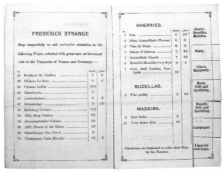

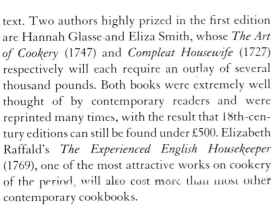

◄ **Mrs. F.L. Gillette and Hugo Ziemann**
The White House Cook Book, Chicago, The Werner Company, 1894. It is unusual to find this book, written by the steward of the White House and a previous caterer for Prince Napoleon, in such good condition. **£30–50**

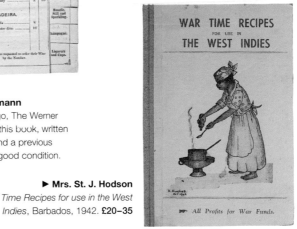

► **Mrs. St. J. Hodson**
War Time Recipes for use in the West Indies, Barbados, 1942. **£20–35**

text. Two authors highly prized in the first edition are Hannah Glasse and Eliza Smith, whose *The Art of Cookery* (1747) and *Compleat Housewife* (1727) respectively will each require an outlay of several thousand pounds. Both books were extremely well thought of by contemporary readers and were reprinted many times, with the result that 18th-century editions can still be found under £500. Elizabeth Raffald's *The Experienced English Housekeeper* (1769), one of the most attractive works on cookery of the period, will also cost more than most other contemporary cookbooks.

It was the Victorians, however, who were responsible for the great rise in the number of cookbooks and books on household management. Mrs. Beeton's famous work, and *Modern Cookery for Private Families* (1845) by Eliza Acton, are the most expensive in first edition, as they were highly regarded at the time and also by subsequent generations. Numerous reprints of both authors are available at a fraction of the cost of the first edition.

Other 19th-century works include general recipe books for the ordinary household, recipes for the Court and for entertaining on special occasions, and also books on health and diet such as *The Art of Invigorating and Prolonging Life* (1820) by William Kitchiner, whose views were rather colourful and controversial. James Robinson and his father were curers of meat in Cheshire, and their work *The Art and Mystery of Curing, Preserving, and Potting all Kinds of Meats, Game and Fish* (1864), was highly regarded in its time and, although it is scarce now, it can still be found for less than £200. One of the most popular of Victorian cookery books, which was reprinted within six weeks of publication, was Alexis Soyer's *The Modern Housewife or Menagère* (1849), although it is uncommon to find copies in good condition. By far the majority of cookbooks can be found under £100, and one can form a really varied collection with ease: one that can be read with enjoyment and that can also be, if one wishes, actually put to practical use.

Glossary

Any specialized area of knowledge will have its own words and phrases which can mean little or nothing until explained. For the book-collector such words quickly pass into everyday terminology. Useful guides are John Carter's *ABC for Book Collectors* (5th edition, 1972), a personal view from one of the great book-trade names, still invaluable and widely used, even by those in the trade. A more recent guide is Jean Peters's *The Bookman's Glossary* (6th edition, 1983).

SIZES

The size or format of a book is expressed by the number of times a single sheet of paper is folded into the sections which, when gathered and sewn, make up the finished volume. The sizes of a sheet will vary but never the number of folds (generally the size of the sheets has increased over the years), and once you have mastered this terminology, it will be easier to understand the physical description of a book in a catalogue. There are other sizes in use, but these are becoming increasingly uncommon, and usually indicate a variation within one size (royal 8vo, crown 8vo). Occasionally, unusually large or small books will be measured in inches or millimetres to provide a more accurate description.

Folio
1 fold 2 leaves   Fo. or 2o

Quarto
2 folds 4 leaves   4to

Octavo
3 folds 8 leaves   8vo

Duodecimo *"twelvemo"*
4 folds 12 leaves   12mo

Sextodecimo *"sixteenmo"*
5 folds 16 leaves   16mo

Vicesimo-quarto *"twentyfourmo"*
6 folds 24 leaves   24mo

Tricesimo-secundo *"thirtytwomo"*
7 folds 32 leaves   32mo

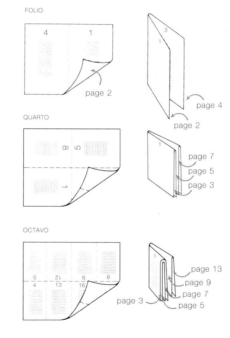

FOLIO

page 2

page 4

page 2

QUARTO

page 7

page 5

page 3

OCTAVO

page 13

page 9

page 7

page 3

page 5

DATES

The printed date on a book is often present only in Roman numerals.

M	1000	1655 *is* **MDCLV**
D	500	1890 *is* **MDCCCXC**
C	100	1899 *is* **MDCCCXCIX**
L	50	
X	10	*Where a numeral is placed* BEFORE *one of greater value it is* SUBTRACTED
		90 *is* **XC** 9 *is* **IX**
V	5	
I	1	*Where a numeral is placed* AFTER *one of greater value it is* ADDED
		110 *is* **CX** 11 *is* **XI**

Cross references to other entries in the glossary are printed in SMALL CAPITAL LETTERS.

antique Of bindings: a modern imitation of an old style, usually in CALF.

aquatint A process of engraving (see Illustration Processes pp.20–5).

armorial Being stamped with the arms of a previous owner, usually a binding.

association copy Early ownership is associated with the author.

autograph Anything written in the hand of the author (see HOLOGRAPH).

bibliography 1. The history and scientific description of a book; 2. a list of books on a particular subject or by an author for further reading, arranged alphabetically, chronologically or by other means.

black letter An early group of types, often called Gothic, designed in Germany.

blank An unprinted LEAF forming part of the original book.

blind-tooled Decorative impression on book covers made without gold or colour.

browning Brown patches caused by damp reacting with acid in paper (see FOXING AND SPOTTING).

calf A type of smooth, polished leather, made from the hide of a calf.

called for An indication of the completeness of a book according to a particular bibliographer, and not necessarily accepted alsewhere.

cancel Any part of a book substituted for what was originally printed, often the result of a printing error or, in the case of a "cancel title", a later edition with a new TITLE-PAGE inserted.

case, cased 1. A ready-made box for the protection of a book, a slipcase, or SOLANDER case; 2. a form of machined cloth binding made in quantity.

catchword A word printed in the bottom right-hand corner of a PAGE below the last line of text, which duplicates the first word over the page, used as a binder's aid.

chain lines Widely spaced lines, normally vertical, faintly visible in the texture of hand-made paper, resulting from the wire mesh in the papermaker's tray.

chromolithograph A form of colour printing (see Illustration Processes pp.20–5).

cloth Of binding: usually linen (buckram), silk or cotton, used from the 1820s.

collate 1. To check the physical completeness of a book; 2. to gather the SHEETS for binding.

collotype A photographic process of illustration, in use from the 1870s.

colophon A note at the end of the book giving details of printing, place, date etc.

commission A bookseller who buys at auction, or privately, on behalf of a customer, is "buying on commission" and will usually charge a fee of 10 per cent.

contemporary Of date: in terms of binding or colouring, this will mean within a decade, or more loosely a quarter of a century, from the date of publication.

corrigenda Corrections to the text noted after publication and inserted on slips of paper (see ERRATA).

cropped Of margins: heavily trimmed, often with loss of text or illustration.

crushed Of MOROCCO: heavily pressed or rolled so there is no evidence of GRAIN.

deckle Of edges: rough and untrimmed edges of hand-made paper.

dentelles Decoration on bindings, a gilt border with a lacy pattern, usually on the inside edges of the leather where it is turned over the board.

device Trademark used by a printer or publisher on the TITLE-PAGE or COLOPHON.

diced Of leather: stamped or ruled into a pattern of diamond squares.

disbound Books or pamphlets removed from a composite volume.

doublure Inside lining of a book made of leather or silk rather than paper.

drop title/dropped-head title Indicates no TITLE-PAGE, the title being placed at the head of the first PAGE of text.

dry-point Form of ENGRAVING, with a more blurred outline than a normal engraving.

dust-jacket/wrapper Protective cover on modern books, used from the 1830s.

edition The total number of copies of a book printed from one setting of type.

endpaper The double LEAVES attached to the inside of the binding at the beginning and end. That pasted inside the cover is known as the paste-down and the other the free endpaper.

engraving A process of illustration (see Illustration Processes pp.20–5).

errata Errors in the printing of a book noted on a separate slip of paper (see CORRIGENDA).

etching A process of illustration (see Illustration Processes pp.20–5).

extra-illustrated having additional illustrations inserted, often portraits or views.

facsimile An exact reproduction of an original LEAF or entire book.

fleuron A printer's ornament, originally flower-shaped.

footnote A descriptive note in a catalogue after the main BIBLIOGRAPHICAL[1] entry.

fore-edge The front or outer edge of the PAGES of a book. Occasionally this will have a fore-edge painting: that is, a painting seen by fanning the pages, the edges of which are gilded after being painted.

format Size and shape of a book (see SIZES above)

fount, font A set of type created to one design.

foxing Brown spots or stains in paper

caused by metallic or chemical impurities (see BROWNING AND SPOTTING).

frontispiece Illustration facing the TITLE-PAGE.

gathering A single group of LEAVES formed by folding one SHEET of paper to the required size (see QUIRE).

gauffered GILT EDGES decorated by heated tools.

gilt edges (g.e.) The edges of a book decorated with gold leaf before binding (see TOP EDGE GILT).

Gothic 1. Of type (see BLACK LETTER); 2. of binding: decoration in the style of Gothic architecture.

grain Pattern on leather.

guard Strip of paper, or stub, which is pasted to the edge of a PLATE[1], or other LEAF printed separately to ensure its secure insertion in the book.

gutta-percha A type of binding in which the LEAVES are held together by a form of rubber solution, rather than being sewn.

half-title The LEAF before the TITLE-PAGE, usually printed only with the book's title.

half-tone A form of illustration printed from an image photographed through a screen composed of small dots.

hand-coloured Watercolour added by hand to a printed illustration.

headband Silk band at the head and foot of the SPINE.

head-piece Decoration at the beginning of a chapter.

hinge The inside junction of the board with the back of the book (the SPINE).

historiated Of initials, capitals or borders: decoration of figures of men and animals added to manuscripts or early books.

holograph Entirely in the hand of the author; similar to AUTOGRAPH.

illuminated Decoration by hand in gold, silver and colours, usually of flowers and similar designs; also printed books imitating the style.

impression The number of copies of a book printed at one time from one setting of type; a further impression could be printed from the same setting at a later date, and these would then be the first and second impressions of the first EDITION.

imprint The details of printing/publishing (name, place and date) usually at the foot of the TITLE-PAGE. Where the printer is not the publisher the printer's details may appear elsewhere.

incunabula Books printed with MOVABLE TYPE before 1501. American incunabula are books printed before 1701 in the United States of America.

inlay Insertion of coloured leather into the main skin of the binding.

inscribed Added to hand, usually indicating ownership or PRESENTATION. "Inscribed by the author" indicates the

author has autographed the book.

issue Part of an EDITION, corrections or rearrangements to the text having been made.

italic A sloping type initially designed for printer Aldus Manutius in Venice c.1500.

Japanese vellum A type of glossy cream paper also known as japon, often used in the printing of de luxe EDITIONS.

joint The outside junction of the board with the back of the book (the SPINE).

laid down Mounted on a stronger sheet of paper, usually an illustration or a damaged LEAF which has been removed.

laid paper Paper, made by machine or hand, exhibiting a pattern of crossed lines (see CHAIN LINES and WIRE LINES).

large-paper copy One of a small number of special copies of an EDITION printed on larger SHEETS of paper, generally producing wider margins.

leaf (leaves) The single piece of paper comprising two PAGES, one the front and one the back.

Levant Of MOROCCO: high-grade, loose-grained and usually highly polished.

limited edition An EDITION limited to a stated number of copies.

limp A binding of VELLUM, leather or cloth not backed by boards.

line-block A process of photographically reproducing a drawing.

lithograph A form of illustration (see Illustration Processes pp.20–5).

loose LEAVES or PLATES that are wholly or partly detached from the binding.

make-up The practice, now frowned upon, of making up or completing a book found to be lacking LEAVES or PLATES[1].

marbled Of paper: decorated by inserting the paper into a bath of water, on the surface of which are colours combed into a pattern.

mezzotint A form of illustration (see Illustration Processes pp.20–5).

misbound Having some LEAVES or PLATES[1] bound in the wrong order.

morocco Tanned goatskin used for binding.

mottled An effect given to CALF by staining the leather with flecks of acid.

movable type Printing type invented by Gutenberg in the 15th century, where each letter is on a separate piece of metal.

no date (n.d.) After further enquiry no date of publication can be found.

Niger Of MOROCCO: a soft skin with a variable GRAIN, naturally a buff colour.

not subject to return Used by auctioneers after a catalogue description to indicate that the book has not been COLLATED and could possibly be incomplete (see WITH ALL FAULTS).

offset Transfer of ink or discolouration from an illustration or text opposite.

Glossary

original As published; for example, "original cloth".

out of series An unnumbered book in an EDITION which is otherwise limited and numbered.

page One side of a LEAF.

pagination Consecutive numbering of PAGES.

papier mâché Of binding: paper, pulp and liquid adhesive, shaped and moulded or carved, used especially in the mid-19th century.

parchment The inner piece of the split skin of a sheep, prepared for use for writing, printing and binding, an inferior VELLUM.

part One instalment of a book issued in instalments, popular in the 19th century.

perfect Complete as originally published.

photogravure A form of reproducing an illustration photographically from a relief-printed metal PLATE[2].

pigskin A type of leather: a rugged skin with a distinctive GRAIN not usually decorated.

pirated An EDITION published without permission of or payment to the author.

plate 1. A full-page illustration printed separately from the body of the text; 2. a metal or plastic cast of a typeset PAGE from which SHEETS are printed; 3. an engraved piece of metal for printing from.

plate mark The indented mark at the edge of an ENGRAVING left by the metal PLATE[3].

pochoir Colour added by hand to illustrations through STENCILS, used especially in France and England in the 1920s and 1930s.

point Any distinguishing feature noted in a BIBLIOGRAPHY[1] used in the identification of one ISSUE from another.

preliminaries All the LEAVES, blank or printed, before the main body of the text begins, including the TITLE-PAGE and FRONTISPIECE.

presentation copy A book inscribed and presented, usually by the author, to someone else.

provenance The previous history and ownership of a particular book.

proof Advance or trial IMPRESSION of text or illustrations.

quarter-bound The SPINE is covered with leather of some kind; also described as "CALF-backed boards".

quire A group of LEAVES folded together before binding (see SIGNATURE, GATHERING).

rag paper Paper made from a pulp of rags.

rebacked The SPINE of a book has been replaced due to wear and tear, usually with a material similar to the original.

recto The front of a LEAF, that is, the right-hand page of an open book (see VERSO).

roan A thin, soft sheepskin used as a cheap substitute for MOROCCO.

roll Of binding: 1. a tool in the form of a wheel with a continuous or repeated design engraved on the edge; 2. the impression of this rolled design on the cover.

roman The familiar rounded type-face as distinct from GOTHIC or ITALIC.

rubbed Indicating some wear to a binding, in particular the SPINE, JOINTS, corners or edges (collectively called the extremities).

rubricated Having headings to chapters or initial capital letters to paragraphs and elsewhere added in red, either printed or by hand.

runner One who sells books but has no stock, acting as a middleman between one dealer and another.

running head/title The title of a book or chapter printed at the top of each PAGE.

Russia A durable type of leather, with a rich, smooth finish, originally scented and often decorated (see DICED).

sheet The large piece of paper which when folded gives a GATHERING of folio and so on.

signature The numbers and letters at the bottom of a PAGE indicating the correct sequence of binding. Sometimes each GATHERING is referred to as the signature.

solander case A type of protective box which will open up with at least one side falling flat.

sophisticated A polite way of indicating that a book has been doctored or MADE UP in some manner, such as with the insertion of a LEAF in FACSIMILE.

spine the back of the book joining the upper and lower covers.

spotting (See FOXING AND BROWNING.)

sprinkled Of CALF and the edges of LEAVES: coloured with small specks.

sprung A book that has a weak SPINE and PAGES that are beginning to come loose.

state Of text and illustrations: indicating one IMPRESSION or another.

stencil Usually a thin sheet of metal or card from which a design has been cut out. The stencil is laid on the paper and colour applied, a different stencil being used for each colour.

stereotype A mould is taken of the original type-setting of a PAGE of text, cast in metal as one solid PLATE[2] and used to print subsequent EDITIONS.

stipple-engraving A process of illustration that is a mix of ENGRAVING and ETCHING, in which tone is rendered through dots and flicks; most fashionable in England in the late 18th century.

tall A book that has had the head and tail margins only lightly trimmed.

three-decker A book issued in three parts, particularly 19th-century fiction.

tipped-in Lightly attached at the inside or top edge, usually of a PLATE[1], or referring to the addition of associated material such as an AUTOGRAPH letter.

title-page The preliminary PAGE supplying details of title, author, date and publisher.

top edge gilt (t.e.g.) The top edge alone of a book has been gilded, the remaining edges usually left UNCUT.

tree Of CALF: a decorative pattern, reminiscent of the trunk of a tree, caused by a chemical reaction, and usually highly polished.

typography The art and skill of designing printed matter, especially words.

unbound Never having had covers.

uncut Of paper: the rough edges have not been trimmed by the binder.

uniform Of books in sets: bound in the same style.

unopened The folded LEAVES of a book are still joined along the upper or outer edges.

unsophisticated Genuine and unrestored (see SOPHISTICATED).

variant A copy of a book which appears to differ from other copies in some manner.

vellum The degreased skin of a calf used for writing, printing and binding.

verso The back of a LEAF, in other words, the left-hand PAGE of an open book (see RECTO).

vignette Small picture or design used as decoration on the TITLE-PAGE or at the head or foot of a chapter or section.

volume The physical object; one book can comprise several volumes.

watermark Papermaker's trademark or date incorporated in the wire mesh of the tray, which becomes visible in the paper when held up to the light. Often used to determine the date of books with no printed date.

wire lines Of paper: the close-set lines that run at right-angles to the CHAIN LINES.

with all faults (w.a.f.) A warning sign signifying that even if a book is incomplete the seller has no legal obligation to take it back once purchased (see NOT SUBJECT TO RETURN).

woodcut A form of illustration (see Illustration Processes pp.20–5).

wood-engraving A form of illustration (see Illustration Processes pp.20–5).

wove paper A form of paper used from about 1757 showing no lines, being made on a woven mesh of wires.

wrappers Paper covers of a book, plain, printed or marbled.

yapp edges the turn-in to the edges found on some leather bindings, often limp, named after a London bookseller called Yapp who invented the style in about 1860.

Further Reading

Many of the following books have been used as references for this guide. For each subject there will be many more specific bibliographies than it is possible to list here, and a useful guide will be T. Besterman's *A World Bibliography of Bibliographies* (Lausanne, 1965–66). Some of the books listed are in print, others have been reprinted and the reprint date only is given here, but the majority will have to be acquired second-hand.

Price guides

Annual price guides compiled from auction catalogues:
American Book Prices Current, Washington
Book Auction Records, Folkestone
Annual price guides compiled from booksellers' catalogues:
International Rare Book Prices, edited by Michael Cole, York: volumes on Voyages, Travel and Exploration; The Arts and Architecture; Modern First Editions; Science and Medicine; 19th Century Literature

Journals

Antiquarian Book Monthly Review, monthly, Ruislip
Antiques Trade Gazette, weekly, with a section reporting on books sold at auction, London
The Book Collector, quarterly, London
A.B. Bookman's Weekly, weekly, New Jersey
The American Book Collector, every two months, New York

General Introduction

Nicholas Barker, ed. *Treasures of the British Library*, London, 1988
Philippa Bernard, ed. *Antiquarian Books, a companion for booksellers, librarians and collectors*, Aldershot, 1994
John Carter. *Taste and Technique in Book Collecting*, 3rd impression, Pinner, 1970
John Carter and Percy Muir, ed. *Printing and the Mind of Man*, 2nd revised edition, Munich, 1983. Influential book based on the exhibition held at the International Printing Machinery and Allied Trades Exhibition (IPEX) in 1963
A.N.L. Munby. *Portrait of an Obsession*, ed. Nicholas Barker, London, 1967. An abridged version of the original 5-part study of the collector Thomas Phillipps.
Michael Olmert, ed. *The Smithsonian Book of Books*, Washington, 1992
Jean Peters, ed. *Collectible Books: Some New Paths*, New York, 1979
Alan Thomas. *Great Books and Book Collectors*, London, 1975
Grant Uden. *Understanding Book Collecting*, Woodbridge, 1995 2nd edition

Bibliographical Aids and Glossaries

John Carter. *ABC for Book Collectors*, 5th edition, London and New York, 1972
Philip Gaskell. *An Introduction to Bibliography*, Oxford, 1972
Jean Peters. *The Bookman's Glossary*, 6th edition, London and New York, 1983
Fredson Bowers. *Principles of Bibliographical Description*, London, 1994

General Bibliographies

C.J. Brunet. *Manuel du libraire et de l'amateur de livres*, Paris 1860–64
H. Cohen. *Guide de l'amateur de livres à gravures de XVIIIe siècle*, 6th edition, revised by Seymour de Ricci, Paris, 1912
F. Madan. *Oxford Books*, 3 volumes, Oxford, 1985
A.W. Pollard and G.W. Redgrave. *A Short-Title Catalogue of … English Books … 1641–1700*, 2nd edition, London, 1986–1976
D. Wing. *Short-Title Catalogue … of English Books … 1641–1700*, 3 volumes, New York, 1972, 1982, 1951

Early Printed Books

Colin Clair. *A History of European Printing*, London, 1976
Elizabeth Armstrong. *Robert Estienne, Royal Printer*, Cambridge, 1954
Colin Clair. *Christopher Plantin*, London, 1960
Martin Lowry. *The World of Aldus Manutius*, Oxford 1979
H.C. Adams. *Catalogue of Books Printed on the Continent of Europe, 1501 1600, in Cambridge Libraries*, Cambridge, 1967
Catalogue of Books Printed in the XVth Century now in the British Museum, London, 1963–71
H.W. Davies. *Catalogue of a Collection of Early French [German] Books in the Library of C. Fairfax Murray*, London, 1961–62
Italian Book Illustrations and Early Printing. A Catalogue of Early Italian Books in the Library of C.W. Dyson Perrins, Oxford, 1914
F.R. Goff. *Incunabula in American Libraries*, New York, 1973

English Literature

Jacob Blank. *A Bibliography of American Literature*, New Haven, 1955–. Still in progress, this will eventually cover the works of all significant American authors up to 1930
D.F. Foxon. *English Verse 1701–50*, Cambridge, 1975
A.S. Herbert. *Historical Catalogue of the Printed Editions of the English Bible 1525–1961*, London 1968
John Hayward. *English Poetry, an Illustrated Catalogue of First and Early Editions*, Cambridge, 1950
T.H. Howard-Hill. *A Bibliography of British Literary Bibliographies*, Oxford, 1969
Morris Parrish. *Victorian Lady Novelists, George Eliot, Mrs. Gaskell, The Brontë Sisters*, London 1933
The Carl Pforzheimer Library: English Literature, 1475–1799, New York, 1940
Michael Sadleir. *XIX Century Fiction: A Bibliographical Record*, Cambridge, 1951
Robert Lee Wolff. *Nineteenth-Century Fiction: A Bibliographical Catalogue based on the Collection formed by Robert Lee Wolff*, Folkestone, 1993
Colin Franklin. *Shakespeare Domesticated, the eighteenth-century editions*, Aldershot, 1991
W.P. Courtney and David Nichol Smith. *A Bibliography of Samuel Johnson*, London, 1925
D. Gibson. *A Bibliography of Jane Austen*, Oxford, 1982
John C. Eckel. *The First Editions of the Writings of Charles Dickens*, Folkestone, 1993
E. Walter Smith. *Dickens in the Original Cloth*, Los Angeles, 1982–83
Donald Gallup. *T.S. Eliot. A Bibliography*, New York, 1969
Richard Lancelyn Green and John Michael Gibson. *A Bibliography of A. Conan Doyle*, Oxford, 1983
B.J. Kirkpatrick. *A Bibliography of Virginia Woolf*, 3rd edition, Oxford, 1989
H. Teerinck. *A Bibliography of the Writings of Jonathan Swift*, Philadelphia, 1963
John Collins. *The Two Forgers. A Biography of Harry Buxton Foreman and Thomas James Wise*, Aldershot, 1992
John Carter and Graham Pollard. *An Enquiry into the Nature of Certain Nineteenth-Century Pamphlets*, Aldershot, 1983

Fine Printing & Typography

Colin Franklin. *The Private Presses*, Aldershot, 1990
Ruari McLean. *Typography*, London, 1980
Will Ransom. *Private Presses and their Books*, New York, 1929
Philip Gaskell. *John Baskerville*, Cambridge, 1973
Philip Gaskell. *The Foulis Press*, London, 1964
Geoffrey Keynes. *William Pickering*, London, 1924
William Peterson. *A Bibliography of the Kelmscott Press*, London, 1984
Dorothy Harrop. *A History of the Gregynog Press*, London, 1980
Giovanni Mardersteig. *The Officina Bodoni*, 1923–77, Verona, 1980

Bindings

Mirjam Foot. *The History of Decorated Bookbindings in England*, 1992
Ruari McLean. *Victorian Publisher's Bookbindings in Cloth and Leather*, London, 1974; *Victorian Publishers' Book-bindings in Paper*, London, 1983
Bernard Middleton. *A History of English Craft Bookbinding Techniques*, London, 1988
Howard Nixon and Mirjam Foot. *The History of Decorative Bookbinding in England*, Oxford, 1992
Howard M. Nixon. *Five Centuries of English Bookbinding, London, 1978. And many other works.
Maurice Paker. *Bookbinders of Victorian London 1837–1901*, London, 1991
Michael Sadleir. *The Evolution of Publishers' Binding Styles 1770–1900*, London, 1936
Marian Tidcombe. *The Doves Bindery*, London, 1991; *The Bookbindings of T.J. Cobden-Sanderson*, London, 1984

Illustrated Books

David Bland. *A History of Book Illustration*, London, 1969
Rodney Engen. *Dictionary of Victorian Wood Engravers*, Aldershot, 1985
Edward Hodnett. *Five Centuries of English Book Illustration*, Aldershot, 1988
Simon Houfe. *The Dictionary of British Book Illustrators and Caricaturists, 1800–1914*, Woodbridge, 1978
Ruari McLean. *Victorian Book Design*, 2nd edition, London, 1972
Brigid Peppin and Lucy Micklethwaite. *Dictionary of British Book Illustrators in the Twentieth Century*, London, 1983
Geoffrey Wakeman. *Victorian Book Illustration*, Newton Abbot, 1973
Iain Bain. *The Watercolours and Drawings of Thomas Bewick and his Workshop Apprentices*, 2 volumes, London, 1990
Richard Riall. *Arthur Rackham*, London, 1994
The Engravings of Eric Gill, Wellingborough, 1983

Americana

Milton Waldman. *Americana, the Literature of American History*, New York, 1925
Bibliotheca Americana. Catalogue of the John Carter Brown Library, 2nd edition, New York, 1961–65
Charles Evans. *American Bibliography*, 12 volumes, Chicago, 1903–34
Wright Howes. *U.S.iana*, New York, 1962
C. William Miller. *Benjamin Franklin's Philadelphia Printing*, Philadelphia, 1974
J. Sabin, W. Eames and R.W.G Vail. *A Dictionary of Books Relating to America*, 29 volumes, New York, 1868–1936
The Celebrated Collection of Americana formed by Thomas Winthrop Streeter, 7 volumes, New York, 1966–69

Children's Books

Brian Alderson and Marjorie Moon. *Childhood Re-Collected. Early Children's Books from the Library of Marjorie Moon*, Royston, 1994
Jacob Blanck. *Peter Parley to Penrod*, 2nd edition, New York, 1956. A selection of classic American children's books
Tessa Chester and J. Irene Whalley. *A History of Children's Book Illustration*, London, 1988
F.J. Harvey Darton. *Children's Books in England; five centuries of social life*, 3rd edition, Cambridge, 1982
Gerald Gottlieb. *Early Children's Books and their Illustration*, New York, 1975. Catalogue of an exhibition at the Pierpoint Morgan Library
Percy Muir. *English Children's Books 1600–1900*, London, 1954
Iona and Peter Opie. *The Classic Fairy Tales*, London, 1974
Judith St. John. *The Osborne Collection of Early Children's Books, 1566–1910*, Toronto, 1966
d'Alté A. Welch. *A Bibliography of American Children's Books Printed Prior to 1821*, New York, 1972
Leslie Linder. *A History of the Writings of Beatrix Potter*, London, 1971
Marjorie Moon. *John Harris's Books for Youth, 1801–1843*, Cambridge, 1976–83. Her other

books include studies of Benjamin Tabart and Mary Elliott

Sidney Roscoe. *John Newbery and his Successors*, 1744–1814, Cambridge, 1973

Thomas Schuster and Rodney Engen. *Printed Kate Greenaway. A Catalogue Raisonné*, London, 1986

Sidney Herbert Williams and Falconer Madan. *Lewis Carroll Handbook*, revised by R. Lancelyn Green, Oxford, 1962

Natural History

Wilfred Blunt. *The History of Botanical Book Illustration*, London, 1993

Alan Jenkins. *The Naturalists. Pioneers of Natural History*, London, 1978

Sacheverell Sitwell and Wilfred Blunt. *Great Flower Books*, London, 1956

Sacheverell Sitwell, H. Buchanan and J. Fisher. *Fine Bird Books*, London, 1953

A Magnificent Collection of Botanical Books … from the Celebrated Library formed by Robert de Belder, London, 1987

R.B. Freeman. *British Natural History Books, 1495–1900*, Folkestone, 1980

R.B. Freeman. *The Works of Charles Darwin*, London, 1977

W.H. Mullens and H.K. Swann. *A Bibliography of British Ornithology from the Earliest Times to the End of 1912*, London, 1917

C. Nissen. *Die botanische Buchillustration*, Stuttgart, 1951–55. Others by the same author on bird and zoological books.

A.H. Perrault. *Nature Classics: A Catalogue of the E.A. McIlhenny Natural History Collection at Louisiana State University*, Baton Rouge, 1987

J. Quinby and A. Stevenson. *Catalogue of Botanical Books in the Collection of Rachel McMasters Miller Hunt*, Pittsburgh, 1958–61

Travel & Topography

T. Chubb. *The Printed Maps in the Atlases of Great Britain and Ireland. A Bibliography, 1579–1870*, London, 1927

John Goss. *The Map Maker's Art. A History of Cartography*, London, 1993

Carl Moreland and David Bannister. *Antique Maps. Christie's Collectors Guides*, 2nd edition, Oxford, 1986

R.V. Tooley. *Maps and Map-Makers*, 5th edition, London, 1972

J.R. Abbey. *Scenery of Great Britain and Ireland in Aquatint and Lithography; Travel in Aquatint and Lithography*, 2 volumes; *Life in England*, London, 1952, 1957,1953

M.K. Beddie, ed. *Bibliography of Captain James Cook*, Sydney, 1970

E.G. Cox. *A Reference Guide to the Literature of Travel*, 3 volumes, Folkestone, 1992

National Maritime Museum Catalogue of Library, vol. I: *Voyages and Travels*, London, 1968; II and III: *Atlases and Cartography*, London, 1971

J.A. Ferguson. *Bibliography of Australia*, Sydney, 1941–1969

Kenneth E. Hill. *The Hill Collection of Pacific Voyages*, San Francisco, 1974–83

L. Navari. *Greece and the Levant: the Catalogue of the Henry Myron Blackmer Collection of Books and Manuscripts*, London, 1989

Norman Penzer. *An Annotated Bibliography of Sir Richard Francis Burton*, Folkestone, 1993

R.V. Tooley. *English Books with Coloured Plates*, Folkestone, 1978

Science & Medicine

One Hundred Books Famous in Medicine, New York, Grolier Club, 1994

Bern Dibner. *Heralds of Science*, Norwalk and Washington, 1980

R. Durling. *A Catalogue of Sixteenth Century Printed Books in the National Library of Medicine*, Maryland, 1967

R. Eimas. *Heirs of Hippocrates … a Catalogue of Historic Books in the Hardin Library for the Health Sciences, the University of Iowa*, Iowa, 1990

F.H. Garrison and Leslie T. Morton. *Medical Bibliography*, edited by Jeremy Norman, Aldershot, 1991

Robert Honeyman. *The Honeyman Collection*, 7 volumes, London, 1978–81

Diana H. Hook and Jeremy M. Norman. *The Haskell F. Norman Library of Science and Medicine*, San Francisco, 1991

Harrison D. Horblit. *One Hundred Books Famous in Science, based on an exhibition held at The Grolier Club*, New York, 1964

R. Sparrow. *Milestones of Science. Epochal Books in the History of Science as represented in the Library of the Buffalo Society*, New York,1972

A Catalogue of Printed Books in the Wellcome Historical Medical Library, 3 volumes, London, 1962–76

Sport

C.F.G.R. Schwerdt. *Hunting, Hawking, Shooting Illustrated in a Catalogue of Books, Manuscripts, Prints and Drawings*, 4 volumes, London, 1928–37

Walter Shaw Sparrow *British Sporting Artists*, London, 1965

David Rayvern Allen. *Early Books on Cricket*, London, 1987

R.A. Hartley. *History and Bibliography of Boxing Books*, Alton, 1989

Joseph Murdoch. *The Library of Golf 1743–1966*, Detroit, 1968

E.W. Padwick *A Bibliography of Cricket*, 2 volumes, London,1984–91

Ray Riling. *Guns and Shooting, a selected chronological bibliography*, New York, Greenberg, 1951

T. Westwood and T. Satchell. *Bibliotheca Piscatoria. A Catalogue of Books on Angling*, facsimile, Folkestone, 1966

Architecture & Design

L.H. Fowler and E. Baer. *The Fowler Architectural Collection of the John Hopkins University*, Baltimore, 1961

E. Harris. *British Architectural Books and Writers, 1556–1785*, Cambridge, 1990

Aeronautical & Maritime

Paul Brockett. *Bibliography of Aeronautics (Smithsonian Miscellaneous Collections vol. 55)*, facsimile, Detroit, 1966

J.E. Hodgson. *The History of Aeronautics in Great Britain from the Earliest Times to the Latter half of the Nineteenth Century*, Oxford, 1924

R.G. Albion. *Naval and Maritime History, an annotated bibliography*, Connecticut, 1963

The Performing Arts

Raymond Toole Stott. *Circus and the Allied Arts. A World Bibliography*, 3 volumes, Derby, 1958

Trevor Hall. *Old Conjuring Books*, London, 1972

Cookery

Eric Quayle. *Old Cook Books, an Illustrated History*, London, 1978

Mary Margaret Barile. *Just Cookbooks! The Only Directory for Cookbook Collectors*, New York, 1990

William P. Cagle. *A Matter of Taste: a Bibliographical Catalogue of the Gernon Collection of Books on Food and Drink*, Indiana, 1990

Virginia Maclean. *A Short-Title Catalogue of Household and Cookery Books published in the English Tongue, 1701–1800*, London, 1981

Gail Unzelman. *Wine and Gastronomy. A New Short-Title Bibliographical Guide based on the André L. Simon Bibliotheca, Viniana, Gastronomica and Bacchia*, Santa Rosa, 1990

Useful Addresses

Most reputable booksellers will be a member of one of their national associations: the main ones are listed below. For other countries contact ILAB, who will provide details of the relevant association. Each association will have a code of rules to determine the conduct of its members.

The Antiquarian Booksellers' Association (ABA), Suite 2, 26 Charing Cross Road, London, WC2H ODG

Provincial Booksellers' Fairs Association (PBFA), The Old Coach House, 16 Melbourn Street, Royston, Herts. SG8 7BZ

Antiquarian Booksellers' Association of America (ABAA), 50 Rockefeller Plaza, New York, NY, 10020, USA

International League of Antiquarian Booksellers (ILAB), Secretary: Helen R. Kahn, P.O. Box 323, Victoria Station, Montreal, Quebec, H3Z 2VB, Canada

Private Libraries Association, Ravelston, South View Road, Pinner, Middlesex, HA5 3YD. International society of book-collectors which publishes a quarterly journal.

AUCTION HOUSES

Great Britain

James Bellman Auctioneers, New Pound, Wisborough Green, Billingshurst, West Sussex RH14 0AY

Bloomsbury Book Auctions, 3 & 4 Hardwicke Street, London EC1R 4RY

Bonhams, Montpelier Street, London SW7 1HH; and 65 Lots Road, London SW10 0RN

Christie's, 8 King Street, London SW1Y 6QT

Christie's South Kensington, 85 Old Brompton Road, London SW7 3LD

Lawrence Fine Art of Crewkerne, South Street, Crewkerne, Somerset, TA18 8AB

Phillips, 7 Blenheim Street, London W1Y 0AS; sales are also held in Bath, Edinburgh, Leeds, Oxford and elsewhere

Sotheby's, 34–35 New Bond Street, London, W1A 2AA; also sales at Glasgow and Pulborough

Dominic Winter Book Auction, The Old School, Maxwell Street, Swindon, Wiltshire SN1 5DR

Y Gelli Book Auctions, Broad Street, Hay on Wye, Hereford, HR3 5DB

Wooley and Wallis, 51 Castle Street, Salisbury, Wiltshire, SP1 3SU

North America

California Book Auction Galleries, c/o Butterfield & Butterfield, 220 San Bruno Avenue, San Francisco, CA04103

Christie's International, 502 Park Avenue, New York, NY 10022

Christie's East, 219 East 67th Street, New York, NY 10021

Richard E Oinonen, Box 470, Sunderland, MA 01375

Phillips, 406 East 79th Street, New York, NY 10021

Sotheby's, 1334 York Avenue (at 72nd Street), New York, NY 10021

Swann Galleries, 104 East 25th Street, New York, NY 10010

Europe and the Rest of the World

Christie's, Sotheby's and Phillips all have offices throughout Europe, with salerooms in some countries; also in Australia, Hong Kong and Japan; details available from their London offices. *American Book Prices Current* lists the auction houses it reports from in Germany and elsewhere, and in *Book Auction Records* can be found auctioneers in France and other countries.

DEALERS

These are a few of the many thousands of dealers; others can be found in *Sheppard's Book Dealers in the British Isles*, published annually by Richard Joseph, who also issue guides to dealers in North America, Europe, Australia and New Zealand, and India and the Orient.

Great Britain

Bankes Books, 6 Margaret's Buildings, Bath, Avon, BA12 1LP. *Illustrated and children's books, literature and modern first editions.*
George Bayntun, Manvers Street, Bath, Avon, BA1 1JW. *General stock, especially bindings.*
D.M. Beach, 52 High Street, Salisbury, Wiltshire. *General stock, travel and children's books.*
Blackwell's Rare Books, 38 Holywell Street, Oxford, Oxfordshire OX1 3SW. *General stock, literature, illustrated and children's books.*
Canterbury Bookshop (David Miles), 37 Northgate, Canterbury, Kent CT1 1BL. *Children's books, local topography.*
Janet Clarke, 3 Woodside Cottages, Freshford, Bath, BA3 6EJ. *Cookery and wine.* Private premises.
Cooper Hay, 203 Bath Street, Glasgow G2 4HZ. *General stock, Scottish, fine bindings.*
Claude Cox, College Gateway Bookshop, 3/5 Silent Street, Ipswich, Suffolk, IP1 1TF. *General stock, printing, topography.*
Dawson UK Ltd., Cannon House, Folkestone, Kent. *Bibliography and reference books.*
Deighton Bell & Co., 13 Trinity Street, Cambridge, Cambridgeshire, CB2 1TD. *General stock, bibliography, fine printing.*
Dylans Bookstore, Salubrious Passage, Swansea, W. Glamorgan, SA1 3RT. *General stock, Welsh history and literature.*
Peter Eaton Ltd., Lilies, Weedon, Aylesbury, Buckinghamshire. *General antiquarian stock.*
Christopher Edwards, 63 Jermyn Street, London SW1Y 6LX. *English literature and history.* By appointment.
Toby English, Lamb Arcade, Wallingford, Oxfordshire OX10 0BS. *General stock, Thames topography, fine printing, wood-engraving, science fiction.*
Ferret Fantasy, 27 Beechcroft Road, Upper Tooting, London SW17 7BX. *Literature, science fiction, detective fiction.* Private premises.
Simon Finch, Clifford Chambers, 10 New Bond Street, London W1Y 9PF. *English literature, history and bindings.*
Roger Gaskell, 17 Ramsey Road, Warboys, Cambridgeshire PE17 2RW. *Science and medicine.* Private premises.
Gekoski, Pied Bull Yard, 15a Bloomsbury Square, London WC1A 2LP. *20th-century literature in first editions.*
Grant and Shaw Ltd., 62 West Port, Edinburgh, Lothian EH1 2LD. *General stock, travel and topography.*
Robin Greer, 29 Oxberry Road, London SW6. *Children's and illustrated books.* Private premises.
Harrington Bros., The Chelsea Antique Market, 253 Kings Road, London SW3 5EL
Thomas Heneage, 42 Duke Street, St. James's, London SW1Y 6DJ. *Art reference, fine ar.*
G. Heywood Hill Ltd., 10 Curzon Street, London W1Y 7FJ. *General stock, architecture, literature, natural history.*
Holleyman and Treacher Ltd., 21a & 22 Duke Street, Brighton, East Sussex, BN2 1EE. *General stock.*
Howes Bookshop, Trinity Hall, Braybrooke Terrace, Hastings, East Sussex TN34 1HQ. *General stock, bibliography.*
Marjorie James, The Old School, Oving, Chichester, West Sussex PO20 6DG. *Children's and illustrated books.* Private premises.
Jarndyce, 46 Great Russell Street, London WC1B 3PA. *19th-century literature and history, London.*

Eric Korn, 47 Tetherdown, Muswell Hill, London, N10 1NH. *Natural history, children's books, literature.* Private premises.
Lloyds Bookshop, 27 High Street, Wingham, Kent CT3 1AW. *General stock, children's books and music.*
McNaughtons, 3a & 4a Haddington Place, Leith Walk, Edinburgh, Lothian, EH7 4AE. *General stock, architecture, travel, Scottish books.*
Maggs Brothers Ltd., 50 Berkeley Square, London W1X 6EL. *General antiquarian books, bindings, travel.*
Map House, 54 Beauchamp Place, London SW3 1NY. *Maps and atlases.*
Barrie Marks, 11 Laurier Road, Dartmouth Park, London NW5 1SD. *Illustrated books.* Private premises.
Marlborough Rare Books Ltd., 144/6 New Bond Street, London W1Y 9FD. *General antiquarian books, architecture.*
D. Mellor & A.L. Baxter Ltd., 121 Kensington Church Street, London W8 7LP
Colin Page, 36 Duke Street, Brighton, East Sussex BN1 1AG. *Travel, topography, natural history, illustrated books.*
Pickering & Chatto Ltd., 17 Pall Mall, London SW1Y 5NB. *General stock, literature and history, science and medicine, economics.*
Jonathan Potter, 125 New Bond Street, London W1Y 9AF. *Maps and atlases, associated reference books.*
Bernard Quaritch Ltd., 5–8 Lower John Street, Golden Square, London W1R 4AU. *General antiquarian books, literature, incunabula, travel, science.*
Reg & Philip Remington, 18 Cecil Court, London WC2N 4HE. *Travel.*
Bertram Rota Ltd., 31 Long Acre, London, WC2 9LT. *Modern first editions.* Appointment only.
Bernard Shapero, 80 Holland Park Avenue, London W11 3RE. *Natural history, travel, architecture.*
Sims Reed, 43a Duke Street, St James's, London SW1Y 6DD. *Illustrated, art reference.*
David Slade, 85 Park Street, Bristol, Avon BS1 5PJ. *Literature, history, bibliography.*
Henry Sotheran Ltd., 2–5 Sackville Street, London W1X 2DR. *General stock, travel, children's and illustrated books.*
Ken Spelman, 70 Micklegate, York, North Yorkshire, YO1 1LF. *General stock, art books, literature.*
Robert Steedman, 9 Grey Street, Newcastle upon Tyne NE1 6EE. *General antiquarian books, literature, travel.*
Barbara Stone, Antiquarius, 135 Kings Road, London SW3 4PW. *Children's and illustrated books.*
Thomas Thorp, 9 George Street, St. Albans, Hertfordshire, AL3 4ER. *General stock, literature, private press.*
Tombland Bookshop, 8 Tombland, Norwich, Norfolk, NR3 1HF. *General stock, art, architecture.*
Tooley Adams & Co., 13 Cecil Court, Charing Cross Road, London WC2N 4EZ. *Maps and atlases.*
Ulysses Bookshop, 31 & 40 Museum Street, London WC1A 1LH. *Modern first editions, illustrated and travel books.*
R.E. and G.B. Way, Brettons, Burrough Green, Newmarket, Suffolk, CB8 9NA. *Hunting, shooting, fishing, big game, racing.* Private premises.
Wheldon & Wesley Ltd., Lytton Lodge, Codicote, Hitchin, Hertfordshire SG4 8TE. *Natural history and science.* Private premises.

North America

Thomas Boss, 355 Boylston St., 2nd Flr., Boston, MA02116. *Literature, private press, illustrated.*
Brattle Bookshop, 9 West St., Boston, MA 02111. *General stock.*
Gotham Book Mart, 41, W. 47th St., New York, NY 10036. *Literature, modern first editions.*

Joshua Heller, P.O. Box 39114, Washington, DC 20016-9114. *Fine printing, illustrated, bindings.* Private premises.
Heritage Bookshop and Bindery, 8540 Melrose Avenue, Los Angeles, CA 90069. *Literature, illustrated books, bindings.*
Daniel Hirsch, P.O. Box 5096, Chapel Hill, NC 27514. *Children's and illustrated books. Original drawings.* Private premises.
H.P. Kraus, 16 E. 46th St., New York, NY 10017. *Incunabula, early science, early Americana, bibliography.*
D. and E. Lake, 239 King Street East, Toronto, Canada M5A 1J9. *Travels, incunabula, Canadiana and Americana.*
Leaves of Grass, 2433 Whitmore Lake Rd., Ann Arbor, MI 48105. *General stock, Americana, literature.* Private premises.
Jeremy Norman, 720 Market Street, San Francisco, CA 94102. *Science, medicine, natural history, economics.*
Oak Knoll, 414 Delaware St., New Castle, DE 19720. *Bibliography, printing, binding, all books about books.*
Philip J. Pirages, 2205 Nut Tree Lane, P.O. Box 504, McMinnville, OR 97128. *Early printed, illustrated, private press, literature.* Private premises.
William Reese, 409 Temple Street, New Haven, CT 06511. *Americana, literature, natural history, travel.* Private premises.
Jo Ann Reiser, 360 Glyndon St. N.E., Vienna, VA 22180. *Illustrated and children's books. Original drawings.* Private premises.
Justin Schiller, 135 East 57th Str., 12th Fl., New York, NY 10022. *Children's and illustrated books.* Original drawings.
Serendipity, 1201 University Ave., Berkeley, CA 94702. *Modern first edition, literature, fine printing.*

We have listed only a few of the many dealers in Europe and the rest of the world; further details can be found in Sheppard's directory. Each country has a national association of booksellers similar to the ABA and ABAA, and these addresses can be obtained from ILAB.

Europe

Librairie Pierre Berès, 14 Avenue de Friedland, 75008 Paris, France. *Literature, fine printing, binding.*
Herbert Blank, Melonenstrasse 54, 7000 Stuttgart 75, Germany. *General stock, modern first editions, illustrated and private press.*
Bjorck & Borjesson, Odengatan 23, S-11424, Stockholm, Sweden. *Travel, Scandinavia, early science.*
Boghallens Antikvariat, Radhuspladsen 37, DK 1785, Copenhagen, Denmark. *General stock, art.*
Eos Buchantiquariat Benz, Kirchgasse 22, CH-8024, Zurich 1, Switzerland. *Medicine, literature, children's books, natural history.*
Nico Israel, Keizersgracht 526, 1017EK Amsterdam, Netherlands. *Travel, natural history, science.*
Antiquariat Junk, Van Eeghenstraat 129, 1071 GA Amsterdam, Netherlands. *Natural history, travel.*
Librairie Louis Moorthamers, 124 rue Lesbroussart, 1050 Brussels, Belgium. *General stock, science, history.*
Libreria Antiqua Pregliasco, via Accademia Albertina 3 bis, 10123 Turin, Italy. *Fine arts, topography.*
Librairie Thomas-Scheler, 19 rue de Tournon, 75006, Paris, France. *Incunabula, illustrated books.*

Australia

Peter Arnold, 463 High Street, Prahran, Victoria, 3183, Australia. *General stock, Australiana.*
Hordern House, 77 Victoria Street, Potts Point, Sydney, New South Wales 2011, Australia. *Australiana.*

Index

Acknowledgements

The publishers would like to thank the following sources for supplying pictures for use in this book or for allowing their pieces to be photographed.

The author and the publisher have been unable to make contact with the copyright holders of the images marked with an asterisk. If you have any information concerning the copyright of these images please contact us.

KEY

BQ Bernard Quaritch Ltd.
CL Christie's London
RB Special photography by Ken Adlard for Reed Books
S Sotheby's London, Sotheby's New York

10RB; 11RB; 12RB; 13RB; 14RB; 15RB; 16 all RB; 17 all RB; 18 all RB; 19 all RB; 20 RB; 21 tRB, brRB; 22 blRB, trRB, crRB, brRB; 23 tlRB, blRB, tcRB, brRB; 24 clRB, blRB, cRB; 25 tRB, cRB, brRB; 26 S; 27 S; 28 tlS, blS, cS, trS, brCL; 29 lS, tcS, bcS, brRB; 30 lRB, cRB, rS; 31 lS, tcS, bcRB, rS; 32 S; 33 S; 34 lS, cRB, rRB; 35 lRB, rS; 36 lS, rS; 37 lRB, cRB, rRB; 38 lRB, cS, rS; 39 lS, clS, crRB, rS; 40 lRB, rS; 41 lRB, cRB, rS; 42 lS, rRB; 43 lRB, cRB, rRB; 44 lRB, cS, rS; 45 lRB, cbRB, trRB, brRB; 46 lRB, cS, rS; 47 lS, rRB; 48 lRB, rRB; 49 lRB, cS, rS; 50 S; 51 l reproduced by permission of Hamish Hamilton Ltd., cRB, rRB; 52 tlRB, blS, trRB; 53 tlRB, blS, tcRB, bcRB, brRB; 54 lRB, rRB*; 55 lRB, rS; 56 tlRB, bcRB, trS; 57 blRB*, tcRB, brRB; 58 tlRB, bcRB, rRB; 59 tlRB, blRB, cRB, trRB; 60 tlRB, blRB, cRB, trRB*; 61 lRB, cRB, rRB; 62 tlRB, tcRB, bcRB, blS; 63 lRB, tcRB, bcRB*, trRB, brRB; 64 blRB, bcRB*, trRB, crRB, brRB*; 65 lRB, clRB*, crRB*, r reproduced by permission of Victor Gollancz Limited; 66 RB*; 67 lRB, rRB*; 68 RB; 69 lRB, rRB; 70 lRB, trRB, brRB; 71 blRB, tcRB, rRB; 72 lRB, cRB, rRB*; 73 lRB, clRB, crRB, rRB; 74 lRB, bcRB, rRB; 75 lRB*, bcRB, rRB; 76CL; 77 RB; 78 tlRB, bcS, rRB; 79 tlRB, cRB, brS; 80 blS, tcCL, rRB; 81 lS, bcS, trCL; 82 S*; 83 S*; 84 lS*, rS*; 85 l reproduced with the permission of Tom Philips, trS*, brS*; 86 lS, rRB; 87 S; 88 lRB; 89 tS, bS; 90 tlRB, blS, rS; 91 S; 92 lS, rS; 93 tS, bS; 94 l reproduced with permission of Chambers Harrup Publishers Ltd., rS; 95 lS*, trS*, brRB; 96 lRB, r reproduced with permission of Elizabeth Banks; 97 lS*, rRB; 98 lRB*, rRB*; 99 l reproduced by permission of Penguin Books Ltd., cRB*, rRB*; 100 S; 101 tlS, brS; 102 lS, r reproduced by kind permission of Frederick Warne & Co.; 103 tlRB, bcS, tr reproduced by kind permission of Frederick Warne & Co.; 104 lS, rS; 105 lS, cS, brS; 106 tlS, blS, rS; 107 tlS, blS, cS, trRB; 108 lS, rS; 109 lRB, cS, brS; 110 blRB, tcRB, r reproduced by kind permission of Frederick Warne & Co.; 111 tl ©Disney, bl TM & © Express Newspapers plc., bcS*, trRB; 112 lRB*, cRB*, trRB; 113 lS, rRB*; 114 RB; 115 S; 116 lS, rS; 117 lS, rS; 118 lRB, rS; 119 lS, rS; 120 lS, cRB, rRB; 121 lRB, r reproduced by permission of the Tryon Gallery Ltd.; 122 lS, cS, rRB; 123 lRB, cRB, rRB; 124 lRB, cS, rS; 125 lRB*, cRB, rRB; 126 lRB, cRB, rRB; 127 lS, trS, brRB; 128 lS, cS, trRB, brRB; 129 lRB, cS, brS; 130 lRB, rRB; 131 lRB, cRB, r reproduced by permission of David Leighton; 132 S; 133 S; 134 lS, rS; 135 tlS, blS, trS; 136 lS, bcRB, trRB; 137 lS, trS, brRB; 138 lS, cRB, rS; 139 lRb, cRB, rRB; 140 tlS, blS, rRB; 141 tlS, blRB, bcRB, trS; 142 tlRB, blRB, trRB, brRB; 143 lRB, trS, brS; 144 lRB*, rRB; 145 lS, cRB, rRB; 146 lS, rRB; 147 lS, cS, rS; 148 lRB, rRB; 149 lRB, cRB, rRB; 150 S; 151 lS, rS; 152 lS, tcRB, trS, brS; 153 blS, trS; 154 lS, cS, trRB, brS; 155 tlS, blRB, rS; 156 BQ; 157 S; 158 lS, trS, brS; 159 S; 160 lRB, cS, rS; 161 tlS, blS, cRB, trS; 162 lRB, rRB; 163 lRB, rRB, cS; 164 tlRB, bRB; 165 S; 166 tlRB, blRB, trRB, brS; 167 tlRB, blRB, trRB, brRB; 168 tlRB, blRB, rRB; 169 tlRB, blRB, cRB, trRB, brRB; 170 lRB, tcRB, bcRB, trRB; 171 tlRB, bcRB, trS, brRB; 172 tlRB, blRB, trRB, brRB; 173 tlRB, blRB, tcRB, bcRB, trRB, brRB; 174 tlRB, brRB; 175 tlRB, blRB, cRB, trS, brRB; 176 tlS, crS, blRB; 177 tlS, tcS, bcRB, brS; 178 tRB, cRB*, bRB; 179 lRB, cS, trS, brS; 180 tlS, brRB; 181 tlRB, blRB, cRB, trRB, brRB

With many thanks to all the contributing writers, in particular Roger Gaskell.

The book would not have been possible without the help of Sotheby's who gave us permission to use photographs from their archives, and in particular many thanks to my colleagues in the Book Department in London and to Katherine Reed in New York.

The following kindly lent books from their stock for photography or allowed us to use photographs from their archives.

Christie's (Auctioneers)
Henry Sotheran Limited
Bertram Rota
Robin Greer
Barbara Stone
E. Joseph Ltd.
Ulysses Bookshop
Simon Finch Rare Books
Pickering and Chatto Limited
Bernard Quaritch Limited
Maggs Brothers Limited
Marlborough Rare Books Limited
William Reese
David Chambers
Bernard Shapiro and The Travellers' Bookshop
Janet Clarke

To Hylton Bayntun-Coward who allowed us to spend a day photographing his binders at work at George Bayntun, Manvers Street, Bath, Avon BA1 1JW

Finally thank you to Amanda Lockyer for reading the manuscript, to Ellen Roberts and Kim Ridge.